AFTER THE DESPOTS

AFTER THE DESPOTS

Latin American Views and Interviews

ANDREW GRAHAM-YOOLL

Edited by Norman Thomas di Giovanni

BLOOMSBURY

First published in Great Britain 1991

Copyright © 1991 by Andrew Graham-Yooll and Norman Thomas di Giovanni

The moral right of the author has been asserted

Bloomsbury Publishing Ltd, 2 Soho Square, London W1V 5DE
A CIP catalogue record for this book is available from the British Library

ISBN 0 7475 1 0075

Typeset by Hewer Text Composition Services, Edinburgh
Printed by Richard Clay, Bungay, Suffolk

For
Micaela, Inés, Luis, and Isabel,
Lisa, Joanne, Nicolás, and Lydia,
Vanesa and Solange

CONTENTS

AFTER THE DESPOTS

ACKNOWLEDGEMENTS

One or two of the pieces in this volume have been previously published in their entirety while most of the others have appeared only in part. Some of this material, then, has been published in other forms in Great Britain in *London Magazine*, the *Guardian*, the *New Edinburgh Review*, the *Independent*, and *Index on Censorship*. Sections of the interviews with Mario Vargas Llosa, Jorge Amado, Augusto Roa Bastos, Graham Greene, Harold Pinter, Carlos Fuentes, and Gabriel García Márquez were printed in *South*. 'River Plate School-Days' also appeared in the *Bedside Guardian* for 1982. 'Breakfasting with Borges' has appeared in the United States in *The Antioch Review* and the piece by Ernestto Sábato quoted in the Epilogue appeared originally in *Translation* under the title 'On Morals and State Terrorism'.

The author wishes to thank Micaela Graham-Yooll, who travelled with him and helped with recordings and photography, and Inés Graham-Yooll, who made a number of transcriptions and draft translations. He is also indebted to Juan Antonio Masoliver Ródenas, Celia Szusterman, Lita Vogelius, Musa Moris Farhi, Marcela Mora y Araujo, Cristina Guzmán, Juan Cristóbal Rautenstrauch, Judith Vidal Hall, Nissa Torrents, and Biba McLellan for assistance in a variety of ways. His thanks also go out to many writers, among them: Luisa Valenzuela, the late Luisa Mercedes Levinson, Mempo Giardinelli, Mario Paoletti, Héctor Tizón, Marta Mercader, Pedro Orgambide, Juan Gelman, William Shand, and the late Humberto Costantini, of Argentina; Eduardo Galeano, of Uruguay; Ted Córdoba-Claure, of Bolivia; Carmen Naranjo and Samuel Rovinsky, of Costa Rica; León David and José Bobadilla, of the Dominican Republic; Luis Suardiaz, of Cuba; Antônio Torres and Antônio Olinto, of Brazil; the Guatemalans Victor Perera, Augusto Monterroso, and Arturo Arias; Manlio Argueta, of El Salvador; and Fernando Alegría, Poli Délano, and Antonio Skármeta, of Chile.

AFTER THE DESPOTS

The editor thanks Susan Ashe for her assistance in editorial matters and for her collaboration in much of the translation. His gratitude as well to Elena Uribe de Wood and, for a number of bibliographic points, to Jason Wilson.

Author and editor are grateful to Gabriel García Márquez for his permission to print here 'William Golding Glimpsed by his Neighbours'. The original article was published in *El Espectador, Bogotà, 1983*.

INTRODUCTION

On the eve of the 500th anniversary of Columbus's first voyage to the New World and two or three decades after the eruption in Latin American literature known as the boom, our perception – the European and North American perception – of that continent and a half which is the Latin New World strains to become clearer as Latin America is forced more and more into our consciousness. Smug Europe, however, until only a generation or so ago itself ridden with vile dictators and repressive regimes and the perpetrator of the most destructive war in history, still looks on Latin America with incomprehension, seeing it mainly in terms of economic chaos, political instability, and irrational bloodshed. The record of the United States is more complex and hypocritical. North American governments hold Central America in virtual enslavement and, via the chequebook and other less subtle forms of intervention, manipulate the rest of the Latin New World. At the same time, Mexicans, Puerto Ricans, Salvadoreans, and Cubans provide large parts of the United States with cheap labour. Yet the general tenor of the United States' isolationism, the evangelical spell it casts over itself with the incantation of the words 'the American way of life' (or, in its Mk. II version after Grenada, Panama, and the Gulf, 'kick ass'), keeps the average American in a cocoon of ignorance about life south of the border.

Where in this state of affairs does the intelligentsia of Europe and North America stand? The best often fall into well-meaning but myopic partisanship, embracing just causes at the expense of deeper truths. Mistaking one part of Latin America for all the rest, they apply the same judgements to all cases. 'Why can we not write about the human heart?' Argentine writers complain. 'Why do Europe and North America pay attention to us only when we write about torture, political murder, and military repression?' Or take the academic critics, again well-intentioned but whose outlook is hopelessly narrow. Priests of literature, they delve for secret and hidden meanings, offering us jargon and mystification instead of clear explanation. The term 'magic realism' is a case in point. Adopted by the academic community to deal with something it did not understand (which was Latin America) and discredited by every Latin American writer I have ever spoken to, the pernicious phrase has become a byword when even its users are in disagreement about what it means.

Latin America is vast and diverse, and its twenty republics are so rife with local custom and usage that the differences among them may very well outnumber those things they have in common. This should not be surprising. The territory itself stretches from Tijuana to Cape Horn, roughly the distance from the Orkneys to Java. At the heart of the continent, in huge tracts of Paraguay, Bolivia, Peru, and Brazil, the Spanish and Portuguese languages barely function. A novel, like one of Ernesto Sábato's, written in the Spanish of Buenos Aires, must carry a glossary when it is published in Barcelona. Even an institution like the Catholic Church is, on opposite banks of the River Plate, significantly unalike. 'I don't think of myself as Latin American,' Jorge Luis Borges claimed. 'I think of myself as Argentine or Uruguayan, perhaps, but certainly not a Peruvian or a Colombian or a Mexican.' Usually, as George Pendle points out in his admirable essay on Latin American civilization, it is only when Latin Americans meet outside Latin America that they feel in themselves 'some common quality which distinguishes them from the rest of mankind'.

The pieces and interviews by Andrew Graham-Yooll that are collected here offer, in a refreshingly readable form, a coherent view of contemporary Latin America and its writers and make this book a perfect introduction to the subject. Graham-Yooll has travelled everywhere and not only knows scores of novelists, poets, and storytellers but as the author of the classic *A State of Fear*, an extraordinary account of the civil war in Argentina that preceded the military takeover in 1976, is himself widely known and respected by them both as a writer and a champion of human rights. As a Latin American himself and able to speak to his subjects in their own language as one of them, there is an uncomplicated naturalness to Graham-Yooll's approach. At the same time, as an Anglo-Argentine who has now lived in Great Britain for fifteen years and as a journalist and magazine editor whose work has brought him to the four corners of the globe, he has a remarkable objectivity and fair-mindedness that keep him from falling into either easy or fashionable viewpoints.

Refreshing also is the variety of writers Graham-Yooll has chosen to speak to. In addition to the obvious big names like Borges, Gabriel García Márquez, Jorge Amado, Mario Vargas Llosa, and Carlos Fuentes, he has sought out others like Daniel Moyano and Margo Glantz, who have only recently made débuts in English, as well as two outspoken English writers, Graham Greene and Harold Pinter. At the same time, a number of Graham-Yooll's own pieces complement the interviews. His leisurely essay on Paraguay, followed by a long conversation with Augusto Roa Bastos, that country's most famous literary figure (recorded in his home in the south of France), does more. Not only are the two pieces mutually illuminating but together they present an indelible record of the human condition in much of the heartland of the South American continent.

Time and again, as revealed by the experiences of so many of those who appear in these pages – the author himself included – we are reminded that exile and wandering are constants among Latin American writers. Few of the men and women in this book, in fact, were interviewed on their own home ground. But Graham-Yooll has been to their countries, sometimes as a gadfly at PEN conferences, and his numerous insights and candid 'snapshots' – a moving glimpse of Salvador Allende's secret tomb in Chile, a rare understanding of Borges's politics, and any number of curiosities, such as a Venezuelan literary party, when a bottle of rum is poured on the book being launched and the guests are asked to sign the dripping pages – are always straight to the mark.

This book – the book, not the separate pieces in it – had its origins in an accident. Graham-Yooll and I first met in Buenos Aires some twenty years ago when he worked at the *Buenos Aires Herald*, which had begun to publish a number of the Borges stories that I was in Argentina to translate. Much later, both of us living in England, Graham-Yooll asked me to make English versions of a few of his interviews for *South* magazine, which he then edited. They were impressive. I liked the broad historical and political perspectives that writers like Carlos Fuentes and Augusto Roa Bastos so easily fell into with a fellow Latin American like Graham-Yooll and I mentioned that he ought to consider conducting more of these conversations and getting out a book of them. 'I've a drawerful now,' he told me, 'mostly unpublished. I'll send them to you and you make the book.' Happily he also sent a dozen or more pieces of his own, inviting me to cannibalize them for whatever purpose I saw fit. In effect, we treated the big bundle of papers as draft material, as a quarry, and, as the work was revised, rewritten, added to and subtracted from, the pieces simply fell into place to set the conversations in wider and more vivid contexts. Midway, a satisfying shape began to emerge, a coherent view of Latin America, which made the enterprise more than a random collection of individual pieces.

Of the interviews, a number were translated from the Spanish, while certain others were conducted directly in English. Guillermo Cabrera Infante, as is his custom, wrote his out, partly in English, partly in Spanish. For my part, I am no longer sure which originated in what language, a sign not of fading memory I hope but proof of the kind of seamlessness we sought when making the book.

To illustrate the nature of Latin American culture, George Pendle quoted 'a North American long acquainted with the people':

> The world will hardly look to the Latin American for leadership in democracy, in organization, in business, in science, in rigid moral values. On the other hand, Latin America has something to contribute to an industrialized and mechanistic world concerning the value of the individual, the place of friendship, the use of leisure, the art of conversation, the attractions of the intellectual [life], the equality of races, the juridical basis of international life, the place of suffering and contemplation, the value of the impractical, the importance of people over things and rules.

The condescension expressed in the opening line is just the sort of sneer that Graham-Yooll's book sets out to combat. This remark apart (it may, after all, be accounted for by the date of the statement – pre-1959), there is great truth here to those of us who have lived and worked in that world, who love it and hold high hopes for its future.

Norman Thomas di Giovanni
June 1991

Prologue
FOLLOWING THE DESPOTS

From time to time Europe looks at Latin America and sticks convenient European labels on Latin American reality. Left, Right, Fascist, Marxist, Socialist – these terms of reference are often meaningless and inapplicable. Military dictatorships are dismissed as native fascism. Economic disorder is branded bad housekeeping. The labels become a substitute for real understanding. As a consequence, the fact that European democracies may have helped to keep the despots in power is overlooked; so too is the contribution of greedy international banks to the financial chaos. In Latin America the European labels are simply inadequate to deal with the complexity of life presented by the multitude of races and nationalities which makes up the bottom half of the New World.

At the same time, Latin Americans, who see themselves as expatriated Europeans, readily adopt Europe's labels in the desperate hope of achieving acceptability and understanding in the eyes of the Old World. The result of this is the Latin American's confusion about who he is and where his roots lie.

The European who reads any account of Latin America thinks of a good yarn about a remote place. No matter what the subject, it will be a yarn in which unrestrained human cruelty combines day-to-day reality with fantastic projects, deep wretchedness, and rich eroticism. In Europe, the Latin American writer is expected to deliver denunciation, radical proposals, recipes for violent change, and the bloody overthrow of unjust regimes in a prose that the French, German, Italian, or English writer can no longer create. But, paradoxically, Europeans expect their standards of economic and political development, acquired through half a millenium, to be achieved overnight by their post-colonial heirs, who have still to reach two centuries of political independence. Regarding themselves as the rejected children of the old empires, Latin Americans ask that they be seen as they are rather than as surrogate actors in the fantasies of older cultures.

The demands of Old Europe are impossible to meet. Europe is a ferment of cultures and political and social factions that fought one another, expelling those it could not conquer, driving into exile its undesirable poor, assimilating the defeated, splitting up friendships and alliances, finally to impose the result on other lands by colonization and emigration. This is how Latin America came to be.

Latin America's true history, the tale of its people, has still to be written. Colombia's Gabriel García Márquez, with his meandering chronicles *One Hundred Years of Solitude* and *The Autumn of the Patriarch*, has perhaps come closer than any other of the continent's authors in telling the Latin American story. He certainly comes closer than Argentina's celebrated Jorge Luis Borges – inspired by England and lionized by Europe – whose achievement is so much on European terms that it obscures his Argentineness. García Márquez and Borges must be used as the yardstick because their work is the best known and most widely translated.

In a vast land where fiction and fact readily mix and become inseparable, the writer of fiction is the historian, while the historian, trained to distance himself from fantasy – which in the context of Latin America can often mean everyday reality – is reduced to being a dry recorder of fact. A good point, then, from which to start telling the story of a continent first ravaged in the name of the Christian faith and in the quest for lucre, later exploited by the commercially-oriented evangelism of the nineteenth century, then wooed, won, or lost by pragmatic political and economic religions of the twentieth century, is the moment when the novelist has been acknowledged the principal historian.

In March 1990, for the first time in its history, Latin America is a continent ruled by elected governments. This date marked the end of the overlong season of the despots. Will the continent have a new beginning, a better life at the close of the twentieth century?

Looking down the Pacific coast at Ecuador, Peru, Bolivia, and Chile, or up the Atlantic at Argentina, Uruguay, Paraguay, and Brazil, all were ruled by military regimes – some of them right through the 1980s. That left out Venezuela and Colombia, under constitutional rule but subject to the whim of commercial or industrial despots. Oh yes, and there was Guyana, Surinam, and French Guiana; but those jungle-locked territories on the sea have always been regarded less as South American than as an extension of European colonialism in the Caribbean.

Venezuela is rich and, by European standards, one of the continent's few democratic societies, second only to Costa Rica in its freedoms and institutions. Yet three so-called 'Maoist' groups – National Liberation Armed Forces, Punto Cero, and Red Flag – operated guerrilla forces in the back lands of the country throughout the decade. Colombia had a constitutional machinery which functioned in conjunction with corruption, censorship, and brutality in a government-sharing system agreed by the principal parties as the only way to overcome the age of *La Violencia*, a ten-year civil war which ended by exhaustion in 1958.

Under the old military regimes, liberals reasoned as conservatives, while revolutionaries clamoured for democracy, embraced tyrants, and became their victims. Ostensibly right-wing thinkers led socialist parties, industrialists clamoured for human rights, priests championed guerrillas, bankers acted as capitalists for violent groups bent on the overthrow of capitalism, the ordinary man held down three jobs to keep up with inflation, governments accused rational individuals of being terrorists, and terrorism, i.e., indiscriminate violence to demonstrate that the individual citizen is orphaned of protection, has been a practice mostly of security forces employed by those very governments.

Brazil's military rulers, custodians of law and order, used death squads of off-duty policemen to clean the streets of petty crime, and few bothered to ask why – not even the civilian opposition, which stopped politicking to profit from the economic boom of the early 1970s. Chile, controlled by the armed forces between September 1973 and March 1990, felt under no pressure to explain the disappearance of over 2,000 people detained in prisons. Neither were Argentina's military rulers in any hurry to report on 15,000 people missing since the seizure of power of March 1976, which, effectively, was defeated in the South Atlantic conflict of 1982, to be followed by constitutional government in December 1983. The *coup d'état* of 1976 had been preceded by a civilian administration riddled with corruption, of which the commanders who made the coup partook without scruple, thereafter to appropriate government and impose law and order. Their armed opponents, the guerillas, had been exiled, imprisoned, or exterminated, yet under the guise of continuing with these anti-subversion operations, military officers abducted obviously non-terrorist individuals and held them to ransom.

Peru's military president, who seized power in 1968, was five years later hailed as a defender of freedom of the press and a true democrat after he expropriated newspapers (at the same time imposing a censorship law) in order to ensure for the people the opportunity to express themselves. This is the reality that cannot be defined by labels.

It has, therefore, been easier for Latin Americans to interpret this reality by tilting at British and North American imperialism or Soviet encroachment and attributing the predicament of the southern continent to foreign conspiracies designed to keep it enslaved and deprived. This is certainly a simpler way to deal with a land whose past is unaccounted for and whose present is unexplained. But such an interpretation is imaginary and self-patronizing. Now, after the despots have gone, it is time for the writers to step in and winkle the truth out of the fiction.

Andrew Graham-Yooll
April 1990

BREAKFASTING WITH BORGES

Jorge Luis Borges entered the Pedemonte Restaurant, on the Avenida de Mayo, with the stiff steps of the unseeing, his face jutting forward to sense what his eyes were unable to take in. It was the twenty-third of August 1982. In anticipation of his eighty-third birthday the next day, Borges was eating out. The restaurant, an old gathering place for Buenos Aires politicians and intelligentsia, was packed. A few faces looked up to note the entrance of the master of Latin American letters, on the arm of his secretary.

A few weeks earlier, Nicanor Costa Méndez, the Argentine Foreign Minister who had conducted diplomacy throughout the recent Falkland Islands crisis, had entered the Pedemonte, swinging his game leg and cane in a slow hopscotch on the chessboard-patterned tiled floor, to the standing ovation of the restaurant's patrons.

Not so with Borges on this particular evening – except for a single fat man, the journalist and broadcaster Chango Mendieta, one of those personalities who seem to know everybody in Buenos Aires. He moved his gigantic form, draped in a poncho, away from the bar and, with the joyful laughter of fat men – so loud it cracked wine bottles – he embraced Borges and his secretary with one vast fat swing of the arms. After they had disengaged and were greeting common acquaintances, one or two people approached Borges to pay their respects.

But not many. Borges was in the doghouse – something he should have been accustomed to by then. Was it that he took pleasure in his abrasive remarks? Certainly his friends were concerned that his unpopular statements and contrary views had lost him the Nobel Prize. To win that award a writer needs the support of a government or of a noticeable sympathetic group. At the very least, he needs to have myths and variegated anecdotes circulating about him, which Pablo Neruda, Miguel Angel Asturias, and Gabriel García Márquez all had. Borges never received any official support, and as for myths, they are there not in his curriculum but in his writing.

1

Still, he went on making his silly remarks. In 1972, in *La Nación*, he expressed his anti-Peronism in ultramontane terms, provoking the left to call him an unreadable reactionary – or was it a reactionary and unreadable? The order doesn't matter; they called him both. In March 1976, Borges said that the generals who led the coup against the Peronist government were gentlemen. In 1978, as Argentina was bursting with euphoria and the military administration warmed to the idea of war with Chile over three frozen islands in the southern Beagle Channel, he caused a big ripple of nationalist indignation when he said that 'a war between Argentina and Chile would be madness, a crime'.

Then, in 1980, he turned on the military and said, in *La Prensa*, that he could 'not remain silent in the face of so many deaths, so many disappearances. I do not approve of this form of struggle by which the end justifies the means.' Here, two years later, he was in trouble again. In March, he said that he saw no sanity in a battle for the Falklands. A short piece that coincided with his birthday, a prose poem published in the newspaper *Clarín*, had become Borges's epitaph for the Falklands and for two soldiers, Juan López and John Ward:

> The two might have become friends, but they met face to face only once, on some too notorious islands, and each of them was Cain, and each Abel.
>
> They were buried in the same grave. Frozen ground and corruption know them.
>
> The events I relate took place in a time it is given none of us to understand.

Such soldiers suited Borges's sense of the timelessness of human stupidity and political insensitivity. Later, in the casual manner in which he usually made his loaded political statements, Borges was to remark, 'Not all of us Argentines are demented; we are not accomplices.' But his most cutting comment – a butcher's cleaver into patriotism – was still to come. The war, he said, was 'like two bald men fighting over a comb.'

Borges was often recorded in casual, private conversation, when he came out with opinions that the writer would surely have revised or let fall into oblivion. Expressing his distaste at being sought out for political statements, he once described himself as without politics, an enlightened conservative or philosophical anarchist without loyalty to any group. He may even have been a member of the Argentine Conservative Party for a short time. One got the impression that Borges knew that the public awaited his views and offhand remarks, his wisdom and wisecracks, with mischievous anticipation even when it found it hard to admit that it enjoyed his debunking. As with any other repressed community, Buenos Aires found it preferable to enjoy Borges's folly – like his writing – in private.

On that evening, Borges sat down to supper with six Spanish journalists.

The story I tell took place during a breakfast with Borges. At ten o'clock on the morning of Friday, 11 June 1982, three days before the Argentine surrender at Port Stanley, from the landing outside his door I heard the bell ringing somewhere in Borges's flat.

The Pope had just arrived, and I had to file a story on his visit, the first ever of a pontiff to Buenos Aires. But popes are many, and they come and go. The Falkland Islands dispute was two and a half months old – this chapter of it, at least – and it was dragging on. But there was only one Borges, and opportunities to sit with him in quiet were not many. I apologized for taking his time, which he might have devoted to listening to the radio reports of the papal tour.

'My time is largely empty. I am an old man. Most of my friends have died, and I know few people. Buenos Aires is a big city and tends to divide people.

'What I would like to say is that all my people were military. My grandfather Borges was a colonel who married an Englishwoman. War to him was something natural. Our winning of the West was called the Conquest of the Desert. Before that, a great-grandfather fought in the War of Independence. Another took his troops across the Andes with the advance of General San Martín. They were all military men. But I am a pacifist.

'A very fine translator of Anglo-Saxon elegies, Gavin Bone, wrote that kings looked best in the past. And I say now that wars also look best in the past.

'What I would also like to say is that being decidedly pacifist I think that war is essentially wrong. If you admit or explain war, all wars will find justification. I think of war as an evil, which reminds me of that book by Juan Bautista Alberdi, *El crimen de la guerra* (The Crime of War). All wars are a crime. What are they but the organization of manslaughter? Especially now. In the past, wars were fought by small armies. Nowadays, whole nations take part, all the people, and that is really awful. All people stand in danger not only of being killed but of killing, which is worse.

'Perhaps I should not say that I would like to go to England. People will say that I am a turncoat. I have quite a few enemies – well, perhaps one or two.'

Borges has given so many interviews that his remarks tend to be repetitive. His preferences are always the same and his views do not basically alter. His politics are conservative. His recollections are of military forebears; of his mother, who died aged ninety-nine; of his father's library of English writers; of school in Switzerland; of the arrest of his sister and mother by Perón; of his own demotion under Peronism from a librarian to an inspector of poultry in the public markets; of Buenos Aires and the tango; of his predicted death; of his passion for Old English, which began in 1955 when he was appointed Director of the Argentine National Library; and of his Saturday morning studies of the ancient language. Perhaps because he has been shut in by darkness, his experiences are mainly of the imagination. Events which are physical and common to ordinary people in him become memories; they are never updated but are repeated in the course of conversation, and those memories he cherishes attain a spacial embellishment of fantasy.

The photographer accompanying me introduced himself. 'I am John Fernandes.'

Borges picked him up on it. 'That sounds like Robinson Crusoe's island, Juan Fernández. A boyhood friend, Robinson Crusoe – a very good friend. A man living in loneliness and with nothing to wish for, just working and not feeling sorry for himself.' Borges's hand patted the tablecloth until he located a spoon that he aimed at a soup plate. 'Hm, the morning cornflakes. That's almost a good metaphor: corn flakes.'

Borges asked if I were a Roman Catholic and I said no.

'I'm not either. I am not even sure of being a Christian. If I were, I would probably choose the Catholic sect. My great-great-grandfather was a Methodist preacher. So you can imagine that they had no use for the Pope.'

It was raining quite hard. A remark about the weather was in order, so I said that I did not know if the heavens were crying for Argentina or for the Pope.

'I suppose the Pope will have been provided with an umbrella,'

Borges said, munching noisily on a spoonful of cornflakes. 'I don't suppose that an umbrella would be of much use to God.

'The Pope is a shrewd politician, but I am sure he means well. In Buenos Aires there will be thousands of people wanting to see him.'

It would be more like millions, I said.

'Do you mean millions or many?' Borges asked.

I confirmed my belief that it would be millions.

'Really?' he asked with mischief. 'I thought that was just a mistake. As when you say forty winks you do not mean forty, you mean many. My grandmother used to say, "I'll have forty winks." She meant a nap.

'I have studied Old English – Anglo-Saxon. And therein I found a verb that took me back. In Old English the word for nap was *hnappian*. So the Saxons had naps.'

He spoke slowly, he always speaks slowly – haltingly is perhaps the right word – yet he never stalls. His speech does not have a stutter, but his statements come in bursts, as might those of a severe asthmatic, who searches for air to live through another phrase.

'It is a very difficult time for all of us. For the world. The world is very involved. Maybe we are beginning the third and last war.

'Let us hope that you and I will survive – at least you. I am old. I have lived my span. I am over eighty. And as I have said, sometimes I am rather impatient with death. My death might come at any moment. But let us hope that it will let me finish my cornflakes and coffee, and then have a fine chat. And after that I'll die and things will be over – at least for me.

'My grandmother was English,' Borges said, reminded by some memory. 'A great-great-grand-relative – or something – of mine was a friend of Keats. I found that out by chance in a recent book on Keats. His name was William Haslam. My grandmother was a Haslam. Haslam, I have been told, was really Hazel Hamlet, and then it was shrunk to Hazel Ham and then Haslam. It should have had a Z for the hazels, but perhaps it was thought to be more fancy without. I never found out how it came about. But I always remember my grandmother saying that her name was Haslam. Another name in my family was Davis. That was Welsh. And Buckley, which could be English or Irish. It must be the same as Berkeley, which sounds English – or Irish. Oh, well, Irish – why not? You can change the past so easily. It must be changed all the time by our memories.'

He is absorbed by the making of history. He also holds in contempt

Argentina's short pedagogical account of its past, which is studied in all its oppressive and meaningless detail and spans little more than the lifetimes of two men. Hence, perhaps, Borges's fascination with an older past, with Nordic myths, legends without source, and kings without origin, which he transposes into the fantasies of his fiction. In Borges, memory is enriched as well as plagued by history.

Borges said that he had once asked his grandmother if there was any Scots or Irish or Welsh ancestry in the family. He was anxious to know whether he could find a link of his own with the legends that he was so attracted to. 'No,' she had told him, 'I am just plain English – thank goodness.'

'There was nothing fancy about her,' he comments. 'I suppose that in English the equivalent of my name is Burgess, or Burgher, which is rather limiting.'

He tried to chase the last reluctant cornflakes about the soup plate, then pushed the plate away. Fanny, his robust maid, came in, and he asked her for a cup of coffee. She ordered him to finish those last cornflakes. He argued that he had finished, but she said that he had not. When she left the room to fetch the coffee, he said, 'She's bossy, eh? She looks after me. She has been in this house for thirty years and now she bosses me about. She was here when my mother died.

'My mother died when she was ninety-nine. She lived in fear of being one hundred. It loomed over her. One hundred sounds awful – or it sounds like history, a whole century. It must have something to do with the pressures of the decimal system.'

His mother had once said that she only stayed alive to be able to read to her blind son. Georgie, she called him. That was her purpose in life.

'When I was eighty, I thought it was awful. It must have been because there is a certain prestige to being eighty. But now that I am beyond that it seems less impressive. Being eighty-one or eighty-two is like being seventy-eight or sixty-eight. There is nothing to it.'

Beppo, Borges's large old white cat, had followed the photographer through all his movements and had watched us throughout our conversation. Now, apparently exhausted by the aimless voices, he dropped on to his side and closed his eyes.

'I am fond of cats,' Borges said as the cat touched his foot. 'I like black dogs – well, large dogs. Small dogs I hate. Pekingese and that kind of thing I think of as small monsters. But a cat is as beautiful as a tiger in a small way. This cat is beautiful. He eats very little. And still he is a fat cat.'

Borges laughed a muffled laughter, his lips pursed. The blare of a bus's horn, used as an alternative to brakes in the suicidal Buenos Aires traffic, came up from the street and through the closed window. It was a reminder of where we were. Buenos Aires had temporarily dissolved about us, even if it is part of Borges and he has given the city a special significance, which sometimes means that he is sure that it has ceased to exist. Sun followed the rain. It shone on to the room's bare floor, a blind man's room, spare of furniture and devoid of scatter rugs. The dining table was pushed close to the bookcases, a standing lamp, the other chairs, a sofa, and the small desk and glass-fronted cabinet were all pushed close to the walls. The room looked as if it were about to be swept by a housewife obsessed with cleaning.

Borges had once been a feature of Buenos Aires as he walked, on the arm of a friend or a secretary or even a journalist who had been granted an interview, under the trees along the paved paths of the Plaza San Martín, just a few steps from his flat, or progressed slowly along Calle Florida, the ten-block-long pedestrian shopping street, where all Buenos Aires goes to be seen. In Borges's conversation, Buenos Aires is less a place than a state of mind, and on that state of mind Borges has an influence as strong and as indefinable as those urban cooking smells that are part of the making of a place.

Buenos Aires, squatting on the flat edge of the River Plate on terrain that is unchanging all the way to the Andean foothills, is a capital without a distinctive physical feature. For many, artists and writers in particular, the city's charm resides in its people, and it is they who make up the capital's chief characteristic.

But Borges was only recently back from New Orleans and wanted to talk about that. 'It's a city of jazz. Jazz is with you all the time, wonderful jazz. Blues, spirituals, hot jazz, and so on. Tango is the music of Buenos Aires, but you do not hear tango here – not the way you hear jazz in New Orleans.

'Tango interested me at one time. It evolved in the brothels. That was around 1880. Its instruments were the piano, the flute, and the violin. This proves that the tango was not widely popular at the time, because no guitar was included. The tango belonged to the world of young men about town, pimps, whores, and so on.'

Borges celebrated some of the scenes of the tango in his first book, *Fervor de Buenos Aires*, published in 1923.

'Nobody knows where the tango came from. People from Montevideo claim the Uruguayans evolved it, and people from

Rosario say Rosario. There is agreement on the date – about 1880 – but here in Buenos Aires it is supposed to have begun at the corner of Lavalle and Junín, where the main brothels were. This is the Jewish quarter now.

'In Rosario they say the tango came from Rosario Norte, Sunchales, and in Montevideo from Yerbal Street. All these are streets which had brothels or were linked with pimps – or whore-masters, as they used to be called in English. That is a finer word than pimp – whoremaster.'

He spat the word, enjoying the impact.

'Pimp sounds weak, derogatory, and insignificant. But whoremaster – there's a fine word. I think whoremonger was also used.

'People in Buenos Aires are always running about. If you read the papers you get the impression of living in a frenzy. But if you talk to people, I think they stand still. In fact, we all stand in need of money here. We are all very poor. We all seem to be millionaires because we are talking of prices in millions, but all of us are poverty-stricken.'

The economic slump was bringing the tramps back to park benches, and perhaps the rapists too. Once, they had been shot out of the trees by trigger-happy police who, when they had finished molesting adolescents in the cafés under the pretext of anti-guerrilla security, took the place of child molesters and teenage abusers. The molesters would find their prey in the parks again now that girls could not afford to wait for friends in cafés.

'What is important is that Buenos Aires is essentially a friendly city. I hope it will remain so. The city is rather drab and grey. There is no local colour of any kind. Well, we have some sham local colour.'

There are colours which Borges cannot see and which are special to Buenos Aires. One is the strange pink light of dawn that gives each morning an impression of being ahead of the hour. It is part of the city's frenzy to live as if in another time of day.

'When I was a boy I thought of Buenos Aires as being a tiny Paris.'

That is how every artist has described the jewel on the River Plate. But Buenos Aires is also a mixture of many things and it cannot decide which it wants to be. Buenos Aires always wants to be somewhere else.

'People are born in hospitals now. In my time they were born at home. I was born in the same house in which my mother was born. People were born and died in the same house then.

It gave people and places a sense of permanence. Nobody seems to need that nowadays. The whole city was made of single-storey houses then.'

It was not a city. The historian Lucio Vicente López called Buenos Aires *La Gran Aldea*, the big village, in a fictional account of the capital that few Argentines will have read since leaving school but whose title has entered South American Spanish as a cliché for the village life of the quarters and sections of any big city.

'These low houses had flat roofs and several patios. There were no tall houses. The first apartment building went up near the Plaza de Mayo; it was four or five storeys high. But most people lived in small houses with water cisterns in the patio. Turtles were put in the cistern to purify the water. In Montevideo, they used frogs.

'These animals would live in the cistern where they would eat all the vermin. Most of us children were brought up drinking what our parents referred to as turtle water. It might have been polluted by the turtle but it did us no harm. It was rain water. Whole generations had that kind of water.'

He made his way across the room from the table to the sofa, refusing my offer of assistance. He wanted no arm to guide him, just words. 'Right a little and then straight.' He dropped into one end of the sofa and briefly judged his breakfast as satisfactory.

'Food is still very good in this city. You can get good Italian food at any restaurant. That began in 1910. When I was a child, Italian food was unknown; now it is everywhere, especially on Sundays. People always have ravioli, *ñoquis*, and so on.

'Buenos Aires is a very Italian city. I think that half the population comes of Italian stock. We called them 'gringos' in the old days. The gauchos called an Englishman a 'mister'. A Frenchman was a *musiú*. Every Spaniard was a *gallego*, not just one from Galicia. All Italians were 'gringos' or, when they came from Naples, *tanos*, as in *napoli*-tano.'

The concept of a 'gringo' classifies people into generations. In Buenos Aires, up to World War II, it had referred to Italians. North American travellers, diplomats, self-conscious about being outsiders, assumed that the word referred to all foreigners and particularly them. And throughout the continent the North American became the 'gringo'.

'They say that the origin of the word 'gringo' is *griego*, Greek.'

I said that some of us were taught that it came from Robert Burns's 'Green grow the rashes o'.

'I don't think so,' Borges said. 'But it might have been somebody who spoke Italian in the old days and, as it would have been incomprehensible, they called this foreign tongue Greek.'

There was a long pause. He had wearied of the subject and lost interest in the conversation. Then suddenly he raised his head.

'In wartime, people go crazy. Madness is encouraged. If you are not mad you become a traitor.

'I don't think Anglo-Argentines like you have suffered any personal indignity. The people have tried to keep their wits. I think the newspapers are crazier than the people. That always happens.

'But people are torn. I keep thinking that this war is impossible. I have a nightmare feeling about it, a sense that this is part of the past which has caught up with us and is preserved for prolongation into the future. I don't know when I will wake up. This cannot possibly be happening.

'And yet it is, and it will go on. Everybody seems so ready to fight over something so insignificant. It is a sad time for all of us. Let us hope that the fighting will be over soon. It is not worth fighting for this, especially as our territory is already so extensive – far too extensive. Most of it is desert in the south. Of course, there are such things as honour and loyalty, which are very dangerous words. Honour, loyalty . . . ' Borges chuckled. 'Such words impress people. It is like witchcraft. Two months ago, in New York, I was so worried about the war that I forgot the name of the person I was walking with.'

Borges's apprehension is contagious. His own fears, his talent for making events timeless, his well-known capacity for warning of the permanence of disturbing issues, are immediately felt. Gabriel García Márquez gives us that same sense of the past having a foot in the future, and he admits to being inspired by Borges.

Borges said he thought that all Americans, North and South, were Europeans in exile. 'I think of myself as a European in exile, because I am not an Indian – though I may have a drop of Indian blood. But I have little in common with the local Indians, or the Incas or the Aztecs. In fact, I have nothing in common with them – except perhaps that I have perhaps more in common with them than I have with the Japanese or the Chinese.

'I think we are expatriated, low-lying Europeans. In the end, that may be all to the good. The European is apt to forget that he is European; he thinks in terms of being a Scot or a German or Double-Dutch. But here we try to inherit the whole of Western tradition, embracing all nations.

'I have more Spanish blood than any other running in me. But that puts me no closer to Spain. For all I know, maybe I am closer to England. Many people feel that way. We Argentines have always thought of South America as something foreign to us. In the last few weeks we have been told that we are South American, that the continent is close to us. But I have never thought of myself as Latin American. I do not think that such a thing exists. People in Peru think of themselves as Peruvians; and people in Uruguay are Uruguayans. I think that Latin America is a concoction created for practical purposes. I have no such internationalist sense; I wonder if anybody has.

'I know that I am Argentine, because I know what I am not: not a Spaniard, not a Bolivian. Yet I can hardly define the word Argentine. In terms of etymology, there is no doubt: River Plate, Argentina, *argentum*. But that does not run very deep. For instance, I feel closer to a man from Montevideo than I do to someone from Jujuy or Mendoza in my own country. An Uruguayan's blood is the same as that of somebody in Buenos Aires.

'Even if I cannot define what the word Argentina means, I can feel it. That may be more important. I suppose the words "English" and "Scottish" are more elementary than the word "British". British has a political sense, not a feeling of belonging.'

His thoughts moved on again. 'To me English literature is *the* literature, especially English poetry. Poetry came to me through the English language. It was all in my father's library. He taught me to love English poetry. I did not understand it too well, but I felt it, and that too is important.

'When I lost my sight I thought that I would try something new, so I began to study Old English.'

As evidence of his studies, he recited the Lord's Prayer in Anglo-Saxon, discovered years before in his Saturday meetings with fellow enthusiasts.

'I think of Robert Louis Stevenson as one of the world's greatest writers. I have read his works many times over since I first read *Treasure Island* as a boy. He was a wonderful writer and a good poet too.'

All of a sudden Borges was entranced. He spoke without stopping of style, of the way Stevenson had written *Treasure Island*. He recited Stevenson's 'Requiem', which seemed close to Borges's own idea of

11

what death should be and explained his impatience with death:

> Under the wide and starry sky,
> Dig the grave and let me lie.
> Glad did I live and gladly die,
> And I laid me down with a will.

'A fine verse, written with elementary words, simple words.' He repeated them. 'Stevenson is one of my heroes.'

He moved on to Scottish writers, largely as a mark of respect for my own Scottish ancestry.

'I have read an essay by Thomas Carlyle on the Paraguayan dictator Francia – *El Supremo*. Of course, Carlyle was fond of dictators. He said that democracy is chaos provided with ballot boxes. I think Carlyle must have been the inventor of the Nazis. I was told that Hitler was a reader of Carlyle. I cannot think of Hitler as a reader. But maybe he had read Carlyle. I have also read Carlyle's *Frederick the Great*, which I suppose nobody else has read.'

Borges's own line about democracy is also peculiar. It is, he holds, for the enlightened, perhaps, but certainly not for everybody. In May 1976, after lunch with the Argentine President General Videla, Borges had said that he thought the military should stay in government for years. It was not the job of civilians to elect a government. 'There were elections three years ago, and what happened? Seven million imbeciles voted for Perón, bringing the country disorder, robbery, and sycophancy.' The remark was more Borges's repugnance to Peronism than an antipathy to democracy. Perón's previous government had mistreated Borges. 'Why should people take part in choosing a government?' he had asked in 1976. 'Would you expect them to participate in chemical analysis, which is an exact science – as government should be?'

But a military regime that had lasted six years and had murdered thousands was too much for Borges. 'I think the only hope now is democracy – to hold elections. Democracy is a superstition based on statistics. But it is the only way to be rid of the dictatorship. The government we have has made me change my opinion. The government fought terrorism with terror, they kidnapped people. An investigation is needed. That is why we may not have elections.'

He did not read any modern writers. He re-read much: Boswell's *Life of Johnson*, Gibbon's *Decline and Fall of the Roman Empire*, and so forth. 'Or contemporary writers like Bernard Shaw, G. K.

Chesterton, and Bertrand Russell, whom I like because he was a pacifist. People come and read to me in French. I am going over Voltaire. I learned French and Latin when I lived in Geneva between 1914 and 1921. I taught myself German to read Schopenhauer.

'I would like to go to England again, but I wonder if I can get a passport. I do not know what my travels will be.'

One of his publisher's agents came in. It was time for work, for correspondence with his translator into English, Norman Thomas di Giovanni, and for discussion of new editions. For me, it was time to write a story about the Pope's visit.

*

In a biographical entry on Borges in the *Enciclopedia Sudamericana*, to be published in Santiago, Chile, in the year 2074, the following is recorded:

He liked being classed a member of the middle class, which is attested to by his name. To him, the lower class and the aristocracy – devoted as they were to money, gambling, sports, nationalism, success, and celebrity – seemed much of a muchness. Borges's years coincided with his country's decline. He came of military stock and felt a nostalgia for the epic destiny of his forebears. His secret and possibly unintentional ambition was to weave a mythology, which never existed, of his native Buenos Aires. Over the years, all unwitting and unaware, he contributed to the glorification of barbarism whose culmination was the worship of the gaucho.

1982

RIVER PLATE SCHOOL-DAYS

The Islas Malvinas are Argentine. This is something I have known since I was six, when General Juan Perón, sometime dictator of Argentina by popular acclamation, ordered it so taught in all the country's schools. Argentina's military confirmation of the assertion in April 1982, I must admit, left me somewhat rattled. After all, *I* was already convinced.

Anglo-Argentines, that grey component of British nationality that constitutes a community in the Argentine, have never doubted that the Malvinas belong to Argentina. But at the same time there was always a certain inner comfort to be derived from the knowledge that the British way of life – or the colonial version of it – had not disappeared completely from the continent but endured in a smidgen some three hundred miles off the Patagonia coast.

There was a time when Scots residents in Argentina, fortune seekers who had built ranching empires by taming inhospitable land, visited the islands regularly from their farms in Patagonia. Many owned small coasters and had trading stores on the mainland, as well as friends and relatives on the islands. The Welsh in northern Patagonia traded on the mainland with the native Indians and the settlers and on the islands with the native Scots.

That was in my father's day, in the 1930s, when he had started farming in Patagonia. It was also a time when the British still controlled Argentina's economy and Britons talked about the 'Battle of the Falklands' – which had taken place in the early months of World War I – as if it had happened the week before. It was the closest that that war had come to them. World War II changed customs, the private coastal trade declined, and so did the visits to the Falklands.

After the war, at the outset of my school-days, there was the S S *Darwin*, which ran between Montevideo and Port Stanley. It must have been a new ship at one time, but that part of the *Darwin*'s past was kept well hidden. The fact that it had been named after a

14

naturalist who had called Patagonia one of the most barren places on earth I found strange and slightly offensive. This was obviously irrelevant to everyone but me – if, indeed, anyone else had ever dwelled on the association. All its steaming life, the *Darwin*, a very ordinary tramp owned by the Falkland Islands Company, remained Port Stanley's only way of catching up with a world that had raced away out of reach.

The *Darwin* took Gilbey's gin and newspapers and Cadbury's chocolates to the Kelpers and brought Montevideo some of their wool clip for trans-shipment to British ports by freighters that called every three months. The *Darwin* also meant school holidays, their beginning and end – a great novelty for those of us who lived in Buenos Aires and sometimes made the voyage from Uruguay to the islands for the summer, but I myself never got there. For Falklanders going to Britain, the *Darwin* was the compulsory first stage of the approximation to Nirvana, which for the British colonial was the slow boat 'Home'.

The *Darwin* must have called at other places at some time or other, but in my memory of those days there seemed only the ports of Montevideo and Stanley. It was a strange and fascinating voyage. Argentina's South Atlantic coast was never out of sight, a bewildering view of endless beaches and rock cliffs off which sand curls twirled, blown by the endless Patagonian wind. But that coast might not have existed, for, politically, it was not there to the *Darwin* and the Falkland Islands Company. Since the *Darwin* did not call at any Argentine port, 'Anglos' from Argentina took the nightboat from Buenos Aires to Montevideo and boarded the Falklands vessel there.

In those days, when I went to school first in Buenos Aires and then in Montevideo, apart from the *Darwin*, there was also – twice a year – H M S *Protector*. It was a converted World War II minesweeper, with a helicopter deck, and we called it a destroyer. It carried dozens of sailors, who, on arrival in Montevideo, would spoil the fun for us boys at the British School because they wooed – though they never had quite enough time to win – all our girlfriends at the mixed school. The sailors got very drunk at the Montevideo Cricket Club, and the petty officers got too sunburned to complete the two-day cricket tests against the community sportsmen or the top form of the British School.

The sailors had the advantage of uniforms, which attracted the girls. But in the end, not just when the *Protector* sailed away, we

15

won. The British community may have been true Brits but that did not mean that mothers trusted fellow Brits in naval uniform. So we had to chaperone the girls on tours and teas aboard H M S *Protector*. I liked it better than H M S *Endurance*, a supply ship that plied between Britain and Port Stanley, via Montevideo, for, without the sleeker lines of *Protector*, *Endurance* always seemed little more than a floating wool shed.

After H M S *Protector* sailed, the girls, and sometimes their brothers, would receive postcards of the jetty at Port Stanley. That is, if the cards were not stolen in the Montevideo post office. In Buenos Aires, on mail from the Falklands, the stamps bearing the silhouette of the British monarch's head were deliberately damaged, which was distressing to schoolboy collectors.

At both Saint Albans College, in the southern Buenos Aires suburb of Lomas de Zamora, and at St George's College, in another suburb that owed its life to the British-built Argentine railways, were boys from the Falklands who boarded. Their parents, perhaps not wealthy enough to send them to a school at 'Home', settled for the British community's imitation of a public school in Argentina.

The custom of sending boys from the islands to school in Buenos Aires, where the British had built the best of these establishments in South America, remained from before World War II. But after the war came Perón, who imposed on all schools the dictum that 'the Malvinas are Argentine by right of inheritance from Spain and they were usurped by Britain in 1833'. God, how we Anglo-Argentines were sick of that line!

The boys from the Falklands, though British subjects, had to recite that along with the rest of us at ceremonies to mark the Day of the Islas Malvinas. Whenever that was I have forgotten, because there was a day for almost everything in Argentina and some days took in a couple of days, otherwise the year was not long enough.

On the Day of the Islas Malvinas, school inspectors would descend on all English-speaking educational institutions to hear the little Brits and Anglos recite the required line. Then the Falkland boys would be asked to repeat it several times, and the visiting inspectors would mimic them, mocking their funny English accents when they spoke Spanish. The boys went to bed exhausted and in tears.

Among Argentines, the islands grew and grew as a political curiosity. Buenos Aires bookshops became populated with an increasing variety of treatises, brief as well as bulky, setting forth the grounds for Argentina's claim. With the multiplication of such texts, school-boy memories of cricket matches and of an island community which sought to be preserved in a colonial past became papered over with political pontificating. The books, to the last one, were boring – terribly boring – and those strange islands and their beautiful people really deserved better.

I no longer remember how many books of such repetitive contents I have read, each of them recalling that the British ship *Endeavour* removed all British colonists from the islands in May 1774 under pressure from Spain. Argentina considers that that was an acknowledgement of Spanish authority, which reverted to Buenos Aires after independence in 1816. The argument began in January 1833, when Britain objected to the Argentine claim. Britain's seizure came on the heels of a dispute between the United States and Buenos Aires after the Falklands governor – a delegate named by Buenos Aires – had captured three North American sealing ships for not paying him a tax on their catch.

In 1982, it seemed a relief that this boring story was about to come to a conclusion. It was a pity that outside politics talk about the Falklands should be confined to nostalgia. They are beautiful islands, but irrelevant. The Argentine people are beautiful too, and as for Anglo-Argentines – well, we are all a family. I never thought it would end in tears.

I have been assured that the dispute goes on at another level. Somewhere in Buenos Aires province, on a ranch owned by a Briton, two large Amazonian parrots, taught by their owner, start each morning with the same exchange.

'Keep the Falklands British,' says one.

'Rubbish,' replies the other.

1982

DANIEL MOYANO: THE WHITE WALL AND THE SPIDERS

I ncarceration and terror affect different people in different ways. When I interviewed Daniel Moyano in Madrid in August 1987, he spoke only casually of what had happened to him at the hands of the military governors of La Rioja eleven years earlier. Maybe because I had known Moyano for years, it did not seem necessary to press him for his story. Maybe because I too had known the terror of the Argentine military, and poured my mind out in my book A State of Fear, *I did not need to ask him. After Norman Thomas di Giovanni had translated my earlier interview with Moyano and learned that I was to visit him again, he pressed me to get Moyano to talk about his twelve days before the white wall. I did. When I returned to London and presented di Giovanni with a transcription of the new conversation, he and I both felt that we should suppress all my own words and allow Moyano to tell his story uninterrupted. As on the earlier occasion, our talk took place in Moyano's flat in Madrid; the date was 8 November 1988.*

A. G-Y.

In Buenos Aires once, asked by someone on the paper *La Opinión*, I tried writing about my detention but never got beyond the second page. Perhaps this is my chance to tell the story in full.

Before the military takeover of 24 March 1976, I had received threats from the Triple-A, a paramilitary death squad. At the time, our local radio station was reading over the air a chapter a day of my novel *The Devil's Trill*, which had been published the year before. The station itself received threats to the effect that if they kept reading my book their building would be blown up. When I was threatened as well, I went to the Governor of the Province of La Rioja, Carlos Menem, who is standing as the Perónist candidate in the forthcoming presidential elections, and he gave my home police protection.

On the day of the coup, I was 260 miles away in Córdoba, trying to enrol in the philosophy department of the university. There was gunfire, which I had to go out of my way to avoid as I headed for the bus terminal. I returned home to the city of La Rioja that night. As we entered town, I saw that control posts had been set up as if the place was under occupation. A girl getting off the bus was fondled by a soldier, giving us a foretaste of the abuse that was to come. We were all made to lie down on the ground and we were threatened. But the girl was being touched up while the soldier cooed sweet words to her.

When I got home, I learned that the military forces had picked up almost all of La Rioja's intellectuals. Many of them worked on the newspaper, *El Independiente*; one, the poet Ramón Eloy López, was a well-known Christian Democrat. Of the three members of the Rioja Communist Party, who were a father and two sons named Leonardi, one was taken into custody. A few members of the Peronist Youth were arrested too, as well as the architect who'd built the local jail and who was placed in one of its four isolation cells.

I told my family not to be surprised if I too were arrested. I got up the next morning to begin studying for my university entrance; I was in my pyjamas, sitting at my desk, which faced the street, reading Charles Bally's *Language and Life*, published by Losada in 1944.

I had just opened the book (which I have kept as a sort of relic), when I saw a car stop outside. It wasn't an army car, but three soldiers got out of it dressed in fatigues and carrying sub-machine-guns. A fourth soldier stayed in the car. The three began slowly to make their way towards my house. My daughter, María Inés, who was three at the time, was fast asleep, and my fourteen-year-old son Ricardo was up playing with two friends. My wife Irma was off in some other part of the house. I hurried to open the door before the soldiers kicked it in or even before they knocked. When I did, they asked, 'Daniel Moyano? You are to come with us.' And they barged in. That was on 25 March, the day after the coup. Obviously my name was on some list.

I asked if I could get dressed. They said I could but must hurry and they accompanied me to the bedroom. I put on a pair of trousers, shoes, a shirt, and, since I didn't know how long I'd be, a light jacket. That's the time of year autumn begins in Argentina. I wanted to take my house key but they told me not to. I asked if I should take my identity papers and they said that wouldn't be necessary. This gave me a moment of fright. In Argentina, even to go out to the corner, it is advisable to carry your identity card.

At the time, in addition to my work as a novelist and musician, I was a correspondent for the Buenos Aires daily, *Clarín*. In that capacity, I had always exposed any failings on the part of the government of La Rioja – within the limits of what a right-wing newspaper like *Clarín* allowed. But my concern was not so much with the government as it was with calling attention to the problems that beset the province, one of the poorest in the country.

I was driven in silence to the army barracks, which was quite near my home in Corrientes Street. There, pushing and shoving me, they marched me to an enormous room where half the intellectuals of La Rioja were standing up against the wall with mattresses beside them. But they were not allowed to sit down. I saw Carlos Mamonde, my assistant on *Clarín*, and any number of friends and acquaintances.

We were there from eight o'clock in the morning until around six in the afternoon. At midday we were brought a revolting gruel of the kind served up in police stations. No one even attempted to eat it.

They made us fill in a card on which we had to give our names, professions, and ideologies. I didn't know what to say for ideology, because I had never established exactly what my ideology was. My upbringing was not Catholic but Protestant. I could have put down Christian, but I was not sure a religion implied an ideology. I suppose what they wanted me to put down was Communist. Leonardi, one of the three Communists in La Rioja, later told us that, as a good party member, he had written the word Communist in capital letters. But I was not a Communist; nor could I write down capitalist. I was a writer. I don't know what piece of nonsense I put down in the end.

At six that afternoon we were herded together and made to board a huge bus. We were about fifty. We had been held in silence all day except for the guards' words of command. Nor had we been allowed to sit. I have no idea what the mattresses were there for.

The bus's windows were covered with newspaper, either so we couldn't see out or so nobody could see us. But through the windscreen I could see where we were headed. Behind us, as the back windows were also uncovered, we could make out a lorry with thirty soldiers in it pointing sub-machine-guns at the bus.

20

The man beside me, who came from the town of Chilecito some way off over the mountains, asked me where we were being taken. 'From here to the city arch is three blocks,' I told him, 'and it's two blocks to the turnoff towards the Rioja jail. If in two streets we turn left, that's where we're going; if we pass it, then we are leaving the province.' The latter, we later learned, would have proved even more dangerous.

That moment, when it seemed that the bus ought to be turning left but wasn't, felt like an eternity. But finally it did. We arrived at the jail in the dark. I was familiar with it because whenever something at home needed mending we took it to the inmates there so they could earn some money. Half of La Rioja did the same.

We were shoved against a wall, and then the guards began to shout at us. There were quite a few soldiers in addition to provincial police and the border patrol from Chilecito. Facing the white wall, we were made to stand a pace apart. 'Stare at the little spider on the wall and at nothing else,' we were ordered. 'If there is no spider, find one. Don't look at anyone else and don't speak. Our guns are very jealous and they might let out a shot or two.' The part about the little spiders I put into my novel *The Flight of the Tiger*.

There was a sound of safety catches being released and then a terrible silence. Carlitos Mamonde, who was beside me, said, 'I think they're going to kill us.' My mind was in a daze. I had no way of understanding what was going on. I was in a state of stupor. I was wondering how they were going to clean the wall afterwards, it was so white.

As we waited to be shot in a silence that lasted for who knew how long, we suddenly heard our thirty guards break out into a forced laugh. It had all been a sham. Then one of them put a spoon behind our backs under each of our belts. I shall never figure out why. When he finished this, another man came along and took them away. Again the guards all burst into laughter. They probably knew we were hungry and would think that the spoon meant they were going to feed us. But they didn't. Was it some form of torture? I don't know.

Next, one by one, they asked our names and professions. I said journalist. 'What paper?' I was asked by a fat man with three chins. I told him *Clarín*. 'So you're the slave of Noble's widow, then.' I didn't answer, but it was obvious that they were out to be offensive. They took away my shoelaces and belt, and, holding up my trousers, I was shoved along with the butt of a rifle. We climbed a staircase, a door was opened, and with a kick in the behind I was forced inside. They locked the door, and no light filtered in from anywhere. I never knew whether it was day or night. I was in that cell for eight days, fed through a little opening six inches square. I found a nail on the floor and, once I got used to the dark, I scratched on the wall the lines of the musical staff. I wrote notes and sang them. I also recalled these verses from the *Romancero*:

> I did not know the night from day
> but for a bird that sang each dawn:
> an archer slew it; God make him pay!

After eight days a man came and led me to another cell, this time not an isolation cell. It had a small window, from which I could look down into both the front and rear courtyards. From time to time I could see other prisoners standing in front of the glass doors of their cells. All day we could not sit or lie down but had to stand up against the glass doors so the guards could see us. I would take advantage and do some exercises whenever the guard turned his back. When they brought our meal – the revolting prison meal – it was so bad we used it as an excuse for not eating. Nor did I want to ask for water, because that would mean having to urinate, and sometimes they wouldn't let you go.

The prisoners kept leaving their cells to be interrogated. They interrogated Ramón Eloy López, the Riojan poet and teacher, a close friend of mine, who was in the next cell. When we went to wash our plates, we would pass each other. We couldn't speak but we managed to mime words and make signs. I asked how he'd been treated. 'They didn't torture me,' he told me that night. 'They asked about my friends, and I said you were one.' At that point the guard shouted for silence. I asked him for the time and he said, 'You are incommunicado.'

I began to measure time by the shadows and sunlight and by a little bird which appeared, as in the *Romancero*, every day at the same time, landing on the same roof tile (this I also recorded in *The Flight of the Tiger*), and flying off in the same direction. In that cell at least I saw daylight. Father Pelanda, the army chaplain, came and told me I should have faith in God and resign myself. Then an officer came in and asked how I was. Not at all well, I told him. Another officer appeared. He was not, like all the other jailers and

22

soldiers, from Buenos Aires. He was from La Rioja, which surprised me. I saw he had the face of a Riojan, and so I wasn't afraid; I did not associate this crime with Riojans. He began shoving me backwards, prodding me in the chest into a corner of the cell, where I fell down. Looking towards the door, since evidently he was not supposed to talk to me, he said, 'Listen, Professor, I want to tell you that your family is well. Is there anything you need?' It turned out that he was a relative of one of my students at the Conservatory. I asked for a toothbrush and a book or two.

Books were impossible, but he said he'd try. What book? Something acceptable, say the *Arabian Nights*, he suggested. Much later, the writer and poet Mario Paoletti, who remained in that jail until 1980, told me that he had seen one of the common jailbirds in the courtyard downstairs reading my novel *El oscuro*, which had won the Primera Plana Prize in 1966. It seemed very odd to me that they had let such a book in. My novel had been taken from La Rioja bookshops and burnt. They had burnt the copies at the army barracks, together with books by Julio Cortázar and Pablo Neruda, by which they did me an honour.

The next day an officer of the border patrol from Chilecito came to see me. 'Are you Moyano? I want to tell you something. You don't know me but I know you. I don't know what's going to happen to you. But whatever does, I want you to know that I am not a criminal. I am a soldier, but not a criminal.' I thanked him. In one way what he said scared me – his uncertainty. On the other hand, it was a human gesture.

The *Arabian Nights* reached me, and a toothbrush and a towel. It was April and the cold began. We had inflatable mattresses but mine had a puncture. I'd spend half the night blowing it up and the other half watching it deflate. The bed was a hard metal grill; all I had to sleep on was that deflated length of canvas. Whenever I could I did exercises. I lost over fifteen pounds in eleven days.

I kept thinking that a helicopter was going to come and rescue us. Another prisoner later told me that he thought of making himself a great pair of wings out of glued matchsticks and cloth from shirts and flying away. But I thought about a celestial helicopter.

One day I spied out of my little window that Carlos Mamonde was being taken away, with his hands tied behind his back, by a subaltern with a sub-machine-gun. They were taking him to some sheds to be interrogated. I had seen a number of men pass that same way. When Carlos went by I saw that he tried to escape and that they fired a shot and that his hands were cut. I began to shake all over. At meal time I told someone, 'They've cut Carlos Mamonde's hands.' The next day I met Carlos and I stared at his hands. They were both fine. I asked if he had been tortured. 'No,' he said, 'they asked me about you.'

I had never before had hallucinations nor have I ever had them since. It appalled me. I have never been able to write about this, nor can I account for it.

Two days later, on my twelfth day of incarceration, the border guard from Chilecito reappeared at about eight o'clock in the morning. 'Please, don't say anything to anyone in your secret language. You're leaving tonight – free. I'm telling you so you won't be scared.' No one was ever told when he was moved if he was going free or going to be shot. That night, when they called, 'Moyano, outside with all your belongings,' the other prisoners looked at each other in fear. I managed to say to Cacho Paoletti, 'I'm getting out. Is there anything you want?'

'The second volume of Dostoyevsky's works,' Cacho said.

Once outside, we were put in a car. The wife of the poet Ariel Ferraro was there. She had been detained in another wing. Ramón Eloy López had been freed with us, and one other person. Only four were set free. In the prison the next day the beatings began.

We were taken to a delegation of the Federal Police. I was given back my belt and shoelaces, and we were each made to sign a blank page in a book. At the same time, we were told that we could not leave La Rioja. Someone in command, who was from Buenos Aires, said, 'You people must watch your step from now on; any false move might prove fatal.'

We went out into the street. I was four blocks from home. Nena Lanzilloto, Ferraro's wife, lived farther away. She was hysterical. I told her to come to my house and I'd drive her home. 'I don't want cars or houses,' she screamed. I left her and continued on my way. People appeared. The dentist Nato Pavani came out to greet me, quite surprised to see me. The names of those in custody were never made public, but word had got round.

When I reached home, my wife was crossing the street in our car on her way to see the military governor. She tried to see Colonel José Malagamba, who under Alfonsín has been promoted to general. It was he who had interrogated us and it is he who was responsible for the deaths or disappearance of sixteen Riojans. (My wife had also tried to see Pérez Bataglia, a colonel who was later taken to hospital with a nervous breakdown.) The next day, Malagamba would not see me, so I just waited for him outside his office. 'What do you want?' he shouted at me. I wanted to know why I had been detained. He said he didn't know. I wanted to know if I could leave La Rioja. 'Go anywhere you like,' he told me; 'as far as we in this military region are concerned there is nothing to stop you.'

My detention had been ordered by the regional commandant, General Benjamín Menéndez, uncle of the Menéndez who surrendered the Falkland Islands, and son of a thousand bitches. While we were in prison, he went to the barracks – I was later told this by a soldier – where he called together all our jailers, and, frothing at the mouth, screamed at them, 'I don't want prisoners, I want dead men.'

When I was told I could leave the province, I went straight to Buenos Aires, applied for a passport, returned to La Rioja, and in one week my wife and I packed up the house and we all went to Buenos Aires to wait for a ship. We sailed on the *Cristoforo Colombo*, of the Italian 'C' Line, on 24 May 1976, and on 8 June we disembarked in Barcelona. That was where I began a new life in exile.

Postscript: I had always believed we were transferred from the army barracks to the jail by bus and that, once there, I dreamed that we'd been transported in the back of a lorry and that an officer had pressed me down with his boot against my neck. For a long time I told others about this dream, then, years later, I met other survivors who had been with me on that night, and they tell me that what I dreamed was the business of the bus, that we had actually been transferred in the lorry and that they had seen how the officer had me flattened under his boot.

1988

MARIO BENEDETTI:
CONVERSATION IN MADRID

Y ou do not have to ask a Uruguayan to talk. He does it sponta-
neously. Mario Benedetti poured soft drinks and made sure that
the fan was trained on us both. It was the only way to beat the inferno
that is the Spanish capital in August. We had not seen each other
for a decade. Benedetti started with a summary of those ten years.
I had asked him what remained of the dictatorship in his country
two years after the return of constitutional rule.

A.   Uruguay's twelve-year dictatorship did everything in its power
to stamp out culture. Why? It's my impression that in Uruguay,
Argentina, and Chile there was greater communication between
artists and intellectuals and their audiences. Both sides enjoyed a
relationship of mutual trust. People looked on the artist as their
spokesman. The dictatorship was out to break that trust and to
destroy the culture.

It's hard to destroy a culture in twelve years, but it can be
seriously damaged. In the case of Uruguay it was cut in two. On
the one hand, there were those who remained in the country, some
in prison; and on the other, those of us who had to leave. Those
who stayed faced terrible problems. Censorship was crippling.
Many artists and writers were arrested and tortured. One whole
theatre company was arrested and their assets confiscated. Singers
were banned.

Q.   What did the dictatorship plan to put in place of the culture it
destroyed?

A.   That is not at all clear. This recent spate of Latin American
despots was not particularly bright – unlike their forerunners, the
caudillos of the last century, who had cultural pretensions. The new
tyrants held such a grudge against culture that to eliminate it did

26

not trouble them. When Pinochet took over in Chile all educational courses were changed. The Minister of Education, who was an admiral, held a press conference in which a journalist from *Le Monde* asked him if it were true that the government had changed the history courses. 'Affirmative,' answered the admiral, because officers speak that way. Then the *Le Monde* man asked, 'Is it true that the new history programme has eliminated all reference to the French Revolution?' 'Yes, because everyone already knows about the French Revolution.'

There is so much prejudice against culture amongst the armed forces of Latin America that the very idea of culture is considered subversive. Perhaps the dictators are right to think that culture is subversive, because culture makes people think.

In Uruguay about ninety per cent of intellectuals and artists have always been progressives. Consequently, the dictatorship found few people who would collaborate with it. There were men and women who stayed in Uruguay and couldn't work or publish for ten years but who refused to collaborate. By the law of supply and demand, the few who collaborated often had three jobs. The President of the Academy of Letters was also Director of the National Library – that is, co-director with an army officer.

Compared with other Latin American countries, Uruguay has always had a very low illiteracy rate – six or seven per cent. But I think that the whole percentage is in the armed forces. There are, of course, exceptions. Some twenty-odd high-ranking officers were in jail for years. These men were completely loyal to Uruguay's military tradition; they obeyed the constitution and they were law-abiding. For something like a century Uruguay had no military coups.

Q.   The exile's return is often as painful as his departure. How was it for you?

A.   Those who had remained in Uruguay knew nothing about what we were doing outside the country, except through tapes and books that were smuggled in. I had published twelve books in those twelve years, and suddenly the whole lot appeared in Uruguay in one fell swoop. That was not good either, because the reader looked on them as contemporary with each other, and this showed nothing of my literary development.

Those of us in exile had lost contact with the country despite the news that reached us through cassettes or letters. But letters were risky, and many people were arrested simply for something in a letter. In my own case, I had been a theatre critic for many years, but I could never be a theatre critic again in Uruguay, since I had missed out on twelve years of Uruguayan theatre. And this had been one of the most important arenas during the dictatorship. A Shakespeare or a Lope de Vega would be staged, full of hidden messages that the audience could relate to just as if it was the work of an Uruguayan author. The theatre kept on functioning, but even if one read those plays by Uruguayan authors now, it is not the same as having seen them performed at the time.

It was the same with singers. Certain songs that were approved by the censors were spiked with a line or two from a forbidden song, and the audience would roar its approval. We heard about these things, but it's one thing to hear and another to have been there. We also missed the Carnivals, our Uruguayan *murgas*, descended from the *murgas* of Cádiz, which are a Carnival-like spectacle with political satire. During the dictatorship all the lyrics had to pass the censor. The *murga* went in for metaphor. It was incredible how alert the audience was. The *murga* was much more important during the dictatorship than either before or after. The Uruguayan is very sensitive to the absurd and to the ironic. This is something common to all the River Plate. Irony in Argentina is sharper, more aggressive, whereas in Uruguay it is more humorous, more oblique. Our humour was one of the few good things bequeathed us by British colonialism. Uruguayan humour is quite English. Even our graffiti are a sort of metaphor, an understatement that was much employed during the dictatorship.

So what do we Uruguayans do now about these gaps? Each side has to find out what it doesn't know. But the problem is not like a generation gap. The dictatorship split generations down the middle. It was not uncommon in a family for grandfather, father, and son to be imprisoned. So there is a lot of political argument in Uruguay today. Though not between those who left the country and those who remained.

Q. So in Uruguay you didn't get what happened in Argentina, the 'you were all right because you got out but we stayed here and suffered'.

A. No, we didn't. Our political arguments were more ideological or literary. There has been discussion between generations, but not because one was inside the country and the other out.

The fact that censorship was so severe drove people into their own shells, and they wrote things that were more cryptic than evasive. This was truer of poetry than of popular song or the stage, because it was easier for the censors to read a book. In the *murga*, however, the verses would be approved by the censor, then changed a bit when they were sung. As the censor wasn't there, nothing happened. But change something back in a book and it's the author who is responsible. So poets learned to turn inward, and to some extent this became a habit. In Uruguayan poetry and novels today there is a tendency to less social commitment than there had been before. I think this is a phase similar to the one now going on in Spain, where a poet like Antonio Machado is rejected while Juan Ramón Jiménez is acclaimed.

Q. Despite the cruelty of the dictatorship in Chile there was much more open communication between those inside and those outside the country. Isabel Allende's novels were not read in Chile, but Chileans knew about her. Jorge Edwards did not write anything controversial, but he travelled and brought things back. Fernando Alegría has lived for years in California but remained in contact with the country. How do you compare this Chilean experience with that of Uruguay?

A. While the Chilean dictatorship treated people worse than in Uruguay, it allowed more cultural freedom. In Uruguay some writers were not only proscribed from the bookshops but were withdrawn from the National Library. Dead writers as well as living – even José Pedro Varela, a nineteenth-century reformer, who brought about great educational change and after whom plazas are named all over the country. He was the first to translate an article by Karl Marx, so the dictatorship closed the reading-room that contained Varela's complete works.

Q. In 1986 you had a long polemic in the Spanish press. What was it all about?

A. It began when Lillian Hellman died. I wrote an article for the newspaper *El País* in which I praised Lillian Hellman for her stance during the McCarthy period. She had stood firm and not denounced anyone. At that point, the writer Juan Goytisolo wrote a piece saying that everything I said was fine and that he agreed with me, but why hadn't I said anything about the McCarthyism that was going on in Cuba. Why had José Lezama Lima been refused publication? I replied that Cuba did not come into it. I also pointed out that ten books of Lezama Lima's were published in Cuba after the revolution and that the Casa de las Américas had made a record of readings by Lezama as well as having published a collection of essays on his work. Lezama had been an employee of the Casa de las Américas until his death; he never went into the office, but they sent him his salary every month. I know this, because I was on their advisory staff. He was so fat he could not get into the car they sent to collect him every day. Goytisolo did not reply to this but his poet friend José Angel Valente did. Valente got extremely heavy. He said all that was true about Lezama but that he had not published anything during the last five years of his life. I agreed that that was so, and then Valente mentioned Lezama's letters to his sister, in which he said he had been trying to finish a book. In fact, the first edition of it was published posthumously in Cuba and a second edition in Mexico. I also mentioned that Lezama was not published under Fulgencio Batista for six years. But of course as Batista was a democrat nobody cared.

This sort of political discussion had not been known in Spain for years, and the newspaper received many letters asking us to continue, because the manner in which we argued was exemplary.

Q.   But why was there such a prolonged argument about Lezama Lima? Had it to do with his homosexuality, since Castro is often accused of being hard on homosexuals?

A.   At some point I was informed that all those who were attacking me were homosexuals and that they had nothing else on their minds but the plight of homosexuals in Cuba.

Q.   I would like to explore the accusation levelled against the left that they seek solidarity from other countries. Does not the right, too, look to other countries not only for solidarity but for dollars?

A.   Why should we on the left deny that we seek solidarity with progressive groups abroad? It's always been like that. During the

Spanish Civil War writers from all over the world came to the Valencia Congress to show solidarity with the Spanish Republic. And when Paris fell, and during the blitz in London, there was always solidarity. It has been important whenever and wherever there has been aggression or injustice. Why shouldn't the Chileans look for support from Europe in their fight against Pinochet? I see nothing wrong in this. The solidarity of the right consists of dollars, arms, and the support of economists. The economies of Argentina, Chile, and Uruguay have been destroyed by students of Milton Friedman.

Q. I want you to tell me a little about your political life.

A. It was brief. It began after I visited the United States in 1959 and 1960, just after the Cuban Revolution. I had read a great deal about the problems of American blacks, and it was terrible to see them first hand. I talked to a lot of black people and found out a good deal about racial discrimination. The black rector of an Alabama university told me that in order to vote he had to pass an exam. How many windows were there in the White House? he was asked.

I once travelled on a bus from the North to the South. The bus was full of blacks and whites. After a stop in Virginia, when we got back aboard all the whites were sitting at the front and the blacks at the back. At a brand-new airport in Montgomery there was a black bar and a white bar, black toilets and white toilets. Each separate. I was struck by this, perhaps because I was politically innocent. It was this visit of mine to the United States that turned me anti-American.

Back in Uruguay, I was a founder member of the movement to defend the Cuban Revolution. I also founded one of the movements within the Uruguayan left-wing coalition known as the Frente Amplio. My political activity put me in touch with people from different neighbourhoods of Montevideo and the remotest parts of the country. At the time, I was hardly writing at all; I was in politics full time. The bad thing about this was that I had been driven into politics against my will, but I felt it was my civic duty. So often my private convictions were at odds with those of my own movement. In my speeches and in my activities as a member of the board of the Frente Amplio I had to defend positions that I sometimes did not believe in. I found myself in conflict. After I left Uruguay for Argentina I remained active in politics in Buenos Aires, but finally there came a moment when I couldn't go on. I shall always be on the left, sympathetic to the Frente Amplio, but as there are so many shades within the Frente I want to stay independent, someone who belongs to no party, to no movement.

Q. The Uruguayan army has changed its position now and has become like the Argentine army. It is a political party within Uruguayan society. How is Uruguay going to go forward democratically in such a situation?

A. Our army has a tradition of protecting the constitution. In this it was always the exception in Latin America. The United States could not tolerate this. They took a large number of Uruguayan officers to be trained in Panama. Uruguay had one of the smallest armies in the continent and was, with Chile, the country with the most officers being trained in Panama. The Uruguayan officers were brainwashed. It was not easy at first. Some officers came to blows with their instructors about what they were being taught. They were sent home; others could not stand it.

Q. Was this insubordination against their instruction?

A. They couldn't take the training in methods of torture. They were physically tortured themselves as part of the course. All this came out in a book by a Chilean, Fernando Ribas, who interviewed the officers and instructors. He had passed himself off as a right-wing journalist. The instructors practised torture on their pupils, sticking pins under their fingernails, burning their backs with cigarettes, and so forth. They were also made to torture small animals like puppies or kittens to learn about the body's sensitive points.

Q. Why didn't these officers say anything about this? They could have put a stop to it then and there.

A. It would have meant expulsion from the army. The fact is that the majority stayed and were converted into torturers. It is known that some officers were cashiered simply for refusing to commit torture. Others, who agreed to dispose of bodies but would not commit torture, were transferred to clean, comfortable jobs only to have their promotions blocked. The army is not as monolithic as it seems.

The one thing the army fears is the people. In Uruguay, when the dictatorship decided to go, there was a demonstration by a million people, who celebrated in the middle of Montevideo. Before that, when the president, Goyo Álvarez, spoke everyone switched off their television sets and the whole city went dark. There was a general strike that lasted for two weeks, and a Day of the Smile was unofficially decreed. Nothing could be done against it. Everyone came out into the streets smiling. That was all. People can't be arrested just for smiling.

Q.   In Uruguay, the tradition of the army before the dictatorship made a difference.

A.   Yes, our army was never as rabidly right-wing as the Argentine and Chilean armies. First, our officers come from a lower social class. And then, the country is much smaller; everyone knows each other. Where in Chile Pinochet destroyed the electoral rolls, in Uruguay the army didn't dare. Here, even the army is a slave to democratic tradition.

Q.   Moving on from the subject of South American armies, the problem of the whole continent today is one of colonization. Like it or not, Latin America is colonized in language and culture even down to the taste and style of the middle class, who impose their ways on the rest of society. There may be democracies and referendums and post-dictatorial intellectual culture, but the real fact is that the continent is a colony of the United States. What is the way out of this cultural and economic colonialism?

A.   In these terms, one of the most colonized countries is Mexico, but whenever anything touches on the sovereignty of their country the Mexicans strike out. Despite this colonization, Mexico is one of the most anti-American countries there is. Talk to any Mexican and he will curse the North Americans, not for ideological reasons but because he knows that his country was stripped of most of its territory.

The real colonization comes from the multinationals. If a system makes everyone poor, it is not only the working classes but also the middle classes who cannot buy televisions or refrigerators. Such an economic system is anathema even to the most reactionary capitalist. In the long run the Latin American national debt will do the international banks no good.

Q.   All this time we have been talking about politics and have not touched on literature.

A.   That's what always happens to me.

Q.   So how did your work develop in the years of exile?

A.   At first one feels very angry about the collapse of one's world. There are inner frustrations, and one has to start again from scratch. I was not a young man, but as an author I was luckier than other exiles because I was able to work out many of my conflicts through my writing.

My book of eight or ten long poems, *La casa y el ladrillo*, enabled me to get rid of many of these conflicts. I felt better after I had finished that book. One of its poems is about a time in Havana when I heard on the short-wave radio that X had been killed. It was a blow. I told myself I should write about it. When I finished I felt I had got over my grief. At first, writing was like therapy for many exiles and for me as well. After a while one began to assimilate the fact of exile and to realize that you cannot let it bring your world to an end. You protect yourself with humour. In the middle of my book *Cotidianas* there is a whole island of humour.

The subject of exile began to appear in most of my work. At first it was something bitter but not despairing, because I never gave up hope. But it was as if you had to lift many curtains from in front of you before you could see the future clearly. I next began an analysis of exile itself, particularly in a novel called *Primaveras rotas* and then in *Geografías*. I also felt that exile had robbed me of my characters, since I had always written about the Montevideo middle class.

Often the left accused me of not having working-class people in my books. Sometimes I tried to put them in, but they spoke so falsely that in the end I decided to omit them out of respect for the working classes. But all at once the dictatorship began to scatter my Montevidean middle class throughout the world. They were in different countries now, speaking different languages and confronting different traditions. This made my characters richer. Each Uruguayan exile was a new story.

The artist is like a sponge. Unconsciously, he goes on absorbing information, anecdotes, details, atmosphere. *Geografías* deals with a different aspect of exile – with what I call *desexilio*, or anti-exile. This is the process of losing the reason for one's exile. I invented the term, which has subsequently become popular. There is also a counter-exile, which is when the torturers had to go abroad.

Q.   The course of your exile ran from Montevideo to Buenos Aires to Lima to Havana to Barcelona, didn't it?

A.   No, after Havana came Palma. I lived there for three years before Madrid. I have written a book of poems about the return from exile, *Preguntas al azar*. The first part, called 'Expectations', I began when I saw that I was going to be able to return to Uruguay. In the next part, 'Recoveries', I regain my streets, my people, my mother. After that I wrote one of my longest books of poems – some eighty in all – including a few that begin to analyze the post-dictatorship period.

Q.   So these have been twelve very intensive years?

A.   This year my complete stories appeared in Spain. I still have a number of books unpublished here and others unpublished in Uruguay. I'm trying to sort this out and at the same time to write new things. I have a new collection of lectures, essays, and articles. It is called *Subdesarrollo y letras de osadía*. Everything in it is on the theme of culture and underdevelopment.

1987

JORGE AMADO: NOBODY CALLS ME MAESTRO

W herever he goes he is surrounded by admirers. Aspiring young writers want to be seen with him, women like to bask in his glamour, and the old just like the idea of being able to say that they have stood close to Jorge Amado. It is called charisma. He is short, stumpy, and in his late seventies but radiates a larger-than-life youthfulness. The phenomenon of this kind of popularity is not uncommon to Brazilian writers. Vinicius de Moraes, the poet and songwriter, was like that right up until he drank himself to death in 1980. Even the thin, frail grand master of poets, Carlos Drummond de Andrade, was venerated by Brazilians, who made him the object of pilgrimages until he died in August 1987.

Academics do not like Jorge Amado. They call him 'a manufacturer of potboilers' and say he is too popular to be serious. Academics deny him a place alongside Euclides da Cunha, author of the Brazilian literary bible *Os Sertãos*, the novelist Joaquim Maria Machado de Assis, and the experimentalist João Guimarães Rosa. But still Amado is loved – if not by academe, certainly by the man in the street. 'Nobody calls me *maestro*,' he says. 'They call me Jorge.' In 1989, Jorge received his country's ultimate accolade when he was the subject of a samba school in the Rio Carnival. Characters out of his novels had been used before in Carnivals, but this time the members of the school got dressed up like him.

'The people put far greater trust in writers than in politicians in our countries,' he told me on one occasion in London, filling the foyer of the small hotel where his publishers had put him up. 'Politicians are very corrupt and mean. I am a politician in that I am a writer. I was a political activist up until 1955. At that time I had to decide whether to remain in politics or become a full-time writer. I thought that being a writer would be more useful to my country. Poets and writers have always stood by the people.'

The novelist Antônio Olinto introduced me to Amado in Paris

in the spring of 1987. Jorge was there to attend a grand party for Brazilian authors that was being thrown by the French government. It was one of those events that culture ministers dream up to justify their office.

Amado's wife, Zélia Gattai, herself a successful writer, was with him – as she always is. Jorge left his first wife for Zélia, who followed him into exile, pregnant with their first child, in the 1940s. They married in 1947.

Q.   What do you think of Latin American literature?

A.   I don't believe there is a Latin American literature. There is literature in each individual country. Argentine literature is quite different from Colombian, Cuban from Chilean. A number of national literatures exist which together are an expression of Latin American culture and literature. But this business of Latin American literature is a colonialist label – one used by the Spanish. The Portuguese don't use it. Any Latin American who accepts the label accepts a colonial subservience. I am not a Latin American writer, I am a Brazilian writer. As such I belong to the community of Latin American authors.

They are all great literatures – Argentine literature is extraordinary; so is Colombian. Just think of García Márquez. In Peru there are four or five important writers, the greatest being Vargas Llosa. There are rich countries in Latin America – culturally speaking, that is, since we are all really poor countries. We have developing countries like Argentina, Brazil, Venezuela, Mexico and extremely backward undeveloped countries like Bolivia, Paraguay, and certain Central American countries. Then there is Cuba, whose socialist regime is seen by many as a nuisance. There is no economic unity in Latin America, how could there be literary unity?

Q.   And you?

A.   I am a modest writer from Bahia. I do not know how to dance, sing, whistle, or drive a car. I write. And I write about things I know about. I write about my life experiences. From the time I was a boy, when I started writing, I have been very closely involved with African forms of worship and still am. Here in Brazil African religions have been the object of severe persecution by the Catholic

Church. They have been the target of barbaric, brutal forms of oppression. Every sort of discrimination has been waged against their practitioners – race, blood, religion, and class. These are the people and problems that enter into my writing. As someone who has always fought discrimination, my position has been with the people, with the ritual of *candomblé*, with the great masses who constitute the population of my country.

Nowadays Brazil has become a paradigm of democratic freedom. Before 1985 we lived in a military dictatorship for twenty-one years.

Q.   What is the position of the Church in Brazil? What about your friends Monsignor Hélder Câmara and Cardinal Paulo Arns?

A.   They are great men, both of them, and extraordinary citizens. At one time, before the war, the Catholic Church sided with the rich against the poor. Today the Church is divided. Hélder Câmara and Arns, who is the Cardinal of São Paulo, are on the side of the people. As are many others as well – bishops and priests. In the fight against wealthy landowners no other agency, political party, or military group has shown as much courage as that one faction of Brazilian clergy that belongs to what is called 'the people's church'. They have shown great courage, for theirs is the hardest fight. In Brazil, you can talk about any subject, but if that subject is the sharing of land you can easily get yourself killed. The big landowners have no qualms about murder.

Q.   Does that still happen?

A.   It is impossible to prevent criminals from committing murder. With the new freedom we have now it no longer happens as often.

Q.   From the landowners' viewpoint, has the situation changed since you wrote *Cacau* back in the 1930s?

A.   Things have changed because the country has changed. Cocoa plantations were huge estates. The land belonged to wealthy families. Today in some parts of Brazil – the coffee country of São Paulo or Paraná, say – there is a kind of capitalist exploitation of the land. But in the north-east all that is different. There the system is semi-feudal, and the man who works the fields is a serf. So it is not easy to generalize about the problem of rural labour in Brazil without falling into error.

Q.   But where you come from in the north, do peasants still die as they used to?

A.   It has not changed much.

Q.   What relationship have you with an audience which may not have read your books but knows them thanks to cinema?

A.   The adaptation of my novels into film has been good, to my mind, because it makes the work available to people who cannot read. There is a high illiteracy rate in Brazil. Television, of course, reaches even greater numbers.

Q.   How would you describe your work to anyone who had not read your books?

A.   In my novels I have always tried to express solidarity with the lives and struggles of my people. All my work is a recreation of reality.

Q.   Brazilian culture is a result of wide-ranging influences, African not being one of the least of them. Is this also reflected in Brazilian literature?

A.   It is reflected in all forms of creative expression in Brazil. In music, for example, if you listen to Heitor Villa-Lobos, or to composers like Dorival Caymmi, Caetano Veloso, or Gilberto Gil, African influences are readily apparent. Our country has had three great cultural matrixes. A European-Iberian-Portuguese, which is predominantly white – although the Portuguese are not all that white; an indigenous; and an African. Brazilian culture is the sum of these, a mixed culture that is the result of the crossing of races, ancestry, and cultures. Our culture was developed in bed.

Q.   For all its richness, what future do you see for Brazilian writing in the light of the country's social problems?

A.   Brazilian literature will evolve, ever faithful to its main characteristic, which has been a commitment to the people and their
problems. There has been a unity in our literature since the days
of our first great poet, a mulatto from Bahia, Gregôrio de Mattos.
He rebelled against the Portuguese colonialists and, even way back
then, fought for the cause of freedom. This unity has come down
to us today and springs from the fact that Brazilian literature has
always been at the service of the people.

Q.   You are known to take part in the celebrations at Vieira do
Castelo, in Portugal, the fishermen's festival of Our Lady of Agonia.
What does that festival mean to you?

A.   I love Portugal very much. I feel as at home in Lisbon as I do in
Paris. I am as much at home in Lisbon as I am in Luanda, in Cidade
da Praia, in Cabo Verde. I am half Latin and half African. I have
attended the Agonia festival four times. It is a wonderful popular
phenomenon and very beautiful. I like the parade, the costumes, the
dancing.

Q.   I'd like to get back to literature.

A.   I'm afraid I am rather ignorant on the subject. I am a humble
writer, not a man of letters. As a boy, I believed I was going to be
a great writer and I used to read what critics wrote. Today I do not
see myself as a great writer, so I never read them.

Q.   I wanted to ask you what this gathering of twenty Brazilian
writers means, this homage to you and Drummond de Andrade and
Gilberto Freire. Is Brazilian literature reaching maturity?

A.   I don't think anyone could give Brazilian literature a certificate
of maturity. It has been growing towards maturity for a long time
and will become more and more mature, but we have not come
together here to be declared a mature literature.

Q.   Brazilian writing is known in other countries; your own work
is known all over the world.

A.   Unfortunately, Brazilian literature is not well known. What really matters is not the fact that one author is well known but that all Brazilian literature needs to be known. Whenever I am told that my novels have been translated into many languages I do not feel pleased. What pleases me is to think that many of my fellow authors have been translated into French and are beginning to find a readership in France. As a writer, I have always fought on behalf of my colleagues for publishers and readers all over the world. If I have achieved anything at all it has been that – to open the way by having my own work translated.

Q.   Tell me about your love for France.

A.   My love for France dates from my childhood, when I began to read French authors. We Brazilians are the spiritual children of France. Study the history of Brazilian writing and you will find France; in our political history you will find the French Revolution, Victor Hugo, the Encyclopaedists. French influences can be clearly discerned in our romantic poetry. I was born and bred to love France. Later I spent several years of poverty and exile in France that were also years of great joy.

Q.   Can you say something about the hiatus in your work – of some ten years, I believe it was – back in the 1950s?

A.   I was elected to Congress in 1946 as a member of the Brazilian Communist Party. I had been a member of the party for years, and for some ten years I was a militant party member. At the time, however, I realized that it was impossible to be both things at once, a writer and a politician. So I spent ten years without writing. Then I started again and in 1965 left the party. But I still support socialism and freedom.

Q.   So you are no longer a militant member of the Communist Party?

A.   I am not a militant of any party. I am an activist for myself as a writer and for my people. Nor have I become an enemy

41

of the party. I am very proud to have been a member of the Communist Party and to have worked with them. Some of the best men I have met in my life were members of the Communist Party.

Q. You have lived in exile but never written about it. Why is that?

A. Because I never experienced exile in a negative way – as a disaster. My exile was a consequence of my political activism but never a personal disaster. I went to live in Argentina and Uruguay in 1941 and 1942, and it was a pleasant time for me. I made some fantastic friends. I later lived in exile in France. The same thing happened. It was very pleasant. I never experienced anything in my life as a disaster. In Brazil we say if you go out in the rain you have to be prepared to get wet.

Q. What are Brazil's connections with West Africa?

A. Nowadays, since Africa is also developing, there is a greater cultural proximity. Those African nations that have become independent, especially the former Portuguese colonies, have built close links with Brazil. There are deep, meaningful cultural ties. Several African countries have established cultural centres in Bahia. The first was the House of Benin, formerly Dahomey. I hope that we will soon have a House of Angola, a House of Nigeria, a House of Cape Verde.

Q. There is some talk of unifying various elements in the Portuguese language that differ between the mother country and Brazil and the African Portuguese-speaking countries. What do you think about this?

A. Two facts must be understood. First, that the language spoken and written in Portugal, Brazil, Cape Verde, Angola, Mozambique, Guinea Bissau, and São Tomé and Principe is Portuguese. But this Portuguese is not the same in Portugal as it is in all these other places. The true Portuguese language from Portugal was that used by Camões, Pessoa, Torga, and Ferreira de Castro. This is not the same as the language of Gregôrio de Mattos in Brazil or of Carlos Drummond de Andrade. The language, while the same, has a Portuguese character in Portugal, a Brazilian character in Brazil, and so on. As for unification, I do not believe in norms established by learned men or politicians. Language is alive and changes from day to day.

1987

JORGE EDWARDS:
AFTER THE DESPOT

L ondon in May on a sunny afternoon such as London seldom sees. It was nearly ten years since Jorge Edwards and I last met in Chile in October 1980. That was on the fearful eve of my first trip back to Buenos Aires four years after my hasty, forced departure from Argentina.

Now we were meeting in London, in Knightsbridge, just around the corner from Harrods. We sat in a café with our eyes glued to the English rose who doubled as barmaid. It was mid-afternoon, and we tried to catch up on nine years of news. Edwards had flown in from Madrid for a weekend conference of Latin American artists and intellectuals at Leeds Castle.

Jorge Edwards was born in Chile in 1931, the descendent of Cockneys who went to sea and jumped ship in Valparaiso in 1806. That first George Edwards sold hens' eggs. His son, Agustín, who went from egg-peddling to copper-mining, was to become Chile's king of copper and founder of the Santiago newspaper *El Mercurio*. He amassed a fortune that won the family a place in Joseph Conrad's *Nostromo*.

'I was born in Santiago de Chile [said Edwards], and trained as a diplomat, studying law. I took a degree in law, as one did in the tried and true Latin American tradition. To be an intellectual you had to study law. I studied philosophy too, but my degree was a law degree. I entered the diplomatic service by public examination in 1957 on the lowest rung of the ladder.

'I was third secretary at the embassy in Paris from 1962 to 1967, then returned to Chile. In 1970, I was counsellor in Lima. At the end of that year I was sent to Havana as chargé d'affaires to open the embassy when Salvador Allende came to power and re-established diplomatic relations with Cuba. As a result of my association with Cuban writers I got into trouble with some of the country's bureaucrats.

44

'That was just before the crisis that is known now as the Padilla case and which culminated, in March 1971, in the arrest and subsequent show trial of the Cuban poet Herberto Padilla. My contacts bothered Fidel Castro more than anyone. This resulted in my having to leave Cuba in something of a hurry. The fruit of this experience was my book *Persona non grata*, published in 1973.

'After that – this was still during the Allende government – I was counsellor in the Paris embassy, when Pablo Neruda was the ambassador. Following the September 1973 coup, Pinochet threw me out of the foreign service. I went to Barcelona to live there as a sort of semi-exile. I had not been officially exiled, but in practice it came to the same thing. That lasted until the end of 1978, when I went back to Chile.'

Edwards and I had first met in Barcelona in October 1978, just before his return to Chile. The Catalan PEN Centre was holding its first open congress after forty years of semi-clandestine activity. We shared the lost air of accidental expatriation, of not being sure about our next step. From Barcelona, Latin Americans in exile fired a blast against dictatorships, founding their own branch of PEN. This centre, which Mario Vargas Llosa helped to start, did not last long, perhaps due to the fickle nature and impatience of Latin Americans.

Edwards today has the air of a man of the world. He wore the light summer suit of a well-travelled diplomat, and at once he radiates the qualities of the honest liberal. At the same time he displays the slightly provincial vanity of the Chilean – a cautious worldliness – which is not the same as the arrogance of the Argentine.

'I live in Chile, teaching from time to time at one or another university in the United States or Spain. I work at two things: writing fiction and writing for the Chilean papers on political and cultural subjects. Since *Persona non grata*, I have published four novels: *Los convidados de piedra* (1978), *El museo de cera* (1981), *La mujer imaginaria* (1985), and *El anfitrión* (1987).

I have been observing the situation of the Chilean intellectual under the dictatorship, and, through this medium, observing myself. Even before the Pinochet take-over the intellectual had been living a process of constant self-criticism and stock-taking. The terms for this were set by the political discourse of Pablo Neruda's *Canto general* of the 1950s, a kind of epic poem that entered the Palace of La Moneda with President Salvador Allende Gossens.

'Neruda was widely used in Allende's speeches and in those of his government. And Neruda became a symbol. But, in fact, by the time Neruda was being used in this way, the new generation of Chilean poets was already writing an anti-poetry, which was not epic but critical. Their poetry made no attempt to universalize issues, as did the *Canto general*. Where Neruda tended to be solemn, they were more humorous and ironic. In the end, even Neruda began to write that way. This was partly because of his revision of his own political position after the 20th Congress of the Communist Party, the denunciation of Stalin's crimes, the events in Prague in 1968, and so forth. I can cite examples of this from the poetry of his last years. For instance, in a poem called *'La verdad'* (The Truth), which appears in 1969 in his verse autobiography, *Memorial de Isla Negra*. It contains words to this effect: I have read so many poems about the first of May that from this moment on I intend to write only about the second of May. Everyone talks about his prose autobiography *Confieso que he vivido*, which he published in 1974. (It was called *Memoirs* in English.) But his verse autobiography is far more revealing.

'Then came Pinochet, and all this process of re-examination dried up. The situation became black and white, dictatorship and opposition. The memory of Pinochet's first years is one of tremendous fear.'

The place of the intellectual under dictatorships has worried the writer in Chile more than any other writer in Latin America. This is because the Chilean, of all Latin Americans, has always had a highly developed political sense, which has grown with the country's sophisticated constitutional evolution. I had left Edwards at this same juncture nine years earlier. We had been walking away from the Alameda, in Santiago, towards his flat, which overlooked Santa Lucía Park. The conversation then concentrated on his efforts to escape strangulation by censorship and on the need for the return to Chile of writers in exile. He had been among the first to return after Pinochet took power.

Some were to return by the mid-1980s. Among the most notable of these was Poli Délano, who had sought refuge in Sweden and Mexico. Délano became president of the Chilean Writers' Society and took delight in his ability to shock a stagnant society with a far more liberal, advanced style, which he brought from exile. Ariel Dorfman, the brilliant young author of *How to Read Donald Duck*, returned in Pinochet's latter years, via Holland and North Carolina, with international literary success. But many had been expelled by decree, and their re-entry would have been classed a crime second only to the murder of a military officer. These had to wait until the ban was lifted in 1988.

'Among the writers there was a brutal silence. It was this silence that characterized the early period of the dictatorship. One interesting young poet, Raúl Zurita, wrote a long Dantesque poem about this. Oddly enough, parodies of great works became a characteristic of Chilean writing in the 1980s. Zurita's poem begins with *Purgatorio*, which was published in 1977, and goes on to *Anteparaíso*, in 1982. When asked where his Hell was, he replied that the early years of the dictatorship were Hell. That Hell was silence.

'Zurita was arrested and held on a boat off Valparaiso. At the time, he was a leading student activist at the university. When captured, he was carrying a manuscript of poems. A naval officer took a look at the verses and found them very modern – in other words, with little on the page and text in both margins. The officer thought that this must be a code and that it might be a message between terrorists. He interrogated Zurita and tortured him to extract the key to the code. In the end a senior officer was asked to study the manuscript. "Of course this is poetry," he said, and threw it into the sea. I claim that this was the beginning of literary criticism in Chile under General Pinochet.

'I used parody in my most recent novel, *El anfitrión*. It is a Chilean Faust, in which one of the characters is Mephistopheles and another a native from Talca, in the south of Chile, called Faustino. I wrote the book in Germany in 1986.

'In West Berlin, I was caught up in the world of Chilean exile on both sides of the wall. The two are quite different. That of West Berlin was open to all influences and was made up of people from different political backgrounds from far left to centre. There were adventurers too, and some had acquired power and money. They fitted in well and had the support of organizations such as the Chilean Solidarity Committee in Germany, which was quite powerful. They had links with social democrats in Sweden, France, Spain, and the rest of Germany. They had jobs and were young and clever. Some knew the Chilean situation inside out, had been to Cuba, and were also thoroughly familiar with European capitalism.

'Then there was the exile of the other side, in East Berlin. These were for the most part exiles from the Chilean Communist Party, who lived very isolated from the world, in a disciplined, grey life.

'This is where I got the idea for a Chilean Faust. My Faust dreams of breaking out of the limits of Talca. He dreams of more power, money, knowledge, and opportunity. He is one of the East Berlin types. And then there is Mephistopheles, with opportunity galore, all kinds of power, and solid connections.

'In the novel, these two are on a semi-secret trip to Chile like the one that the film-maker Miguel Littín made in 1985 and which García Márquez wrote about. Mine is a fantasy, a journey in which the Devil is the Host. The Devil does not offer to buy Faustino's soul. Instead, in a conversation in the German Club of Puerto Montt, lunching on sea urchins and other Chilean delicacies, the Devil tells Faustino that he is worried about the Chilean political crisis. The Devil has given a great deal of thought to the qualities that will be needed by the candidate who is to become president after Pinochet. This is a bit like squaring the circle. The man must be an attractive person but not too handsome, a little inconspicuous, and have a calming effect on people. He must be someone who has not given in to Pinochet or Allende's politics. So he has to have a number of contradictory qualities. The Devil tells Faustino that he thinks the best person for the job is him. Faustino protests and says that the Devil is mad. Faustino has a Communist past; how does the Devil think that would go down in present-day Chile?

'Then Mephistopheles says, "Souls used to be bought, but now souls are out of fashion. What I buy is people's pasts. I have a large collection. In exchange, I give them a clean past for use in the democratic transition after Pinochet." It is another way of interpreting Chile's politics.

'There has been a paradox in Chilean politics all through the twentieth century. We writers were under surveillance in Pinochet's regime; we were censored and followed. But curiously, the regime had a certain respect for us. The government did not want to get involved in squabbles with writers. They gave us a wide berth. This meant that during Pinochet's rule we had more impact on the public. Up until then, the person who most influenced Chileans was the politician. The writer was marginal.

'Under Pinochet, people read us between the lines. We learnt to write in a new way. In a certain sense it could be said that we reinvented the language. We learned to write in metaphoric, allusive language; we used symbolism and parody. A number of writers invented alter egos, so as to speak through other characters.

'Nicanor Parra invented a character, the Christ of Elqui. Elqui is a valley in northern Chile where *pisco* comes from. The character is taken from real life. There was a holy man who walked the length and breadth of Chile, a vagabond in sandals and cloak and long beard, who preached apocalyptic revelations. Nicanor made up a collection of sermons and homilies for his Christ of Elqui and used him as a character in his poems to say insolent things against everyone. It is quite like Parra to fire in all directions.

'The poet Enrique Lihn made up a character called Gerardo de Pompierre, a decadent, an aesthete, who reacts against brutality, ugliness, and horror. He behaves like a *fin de siècle* aesthete, a friend of Rubén Dario's.

'I find this business rather strange. As writers, we invent characters to speak for us in times of crisis. These characters are masks who speak an invented language and say much more than we do.

'José Donoso wrote a great deal during this time. His novel *A House in the Country*, published in 1978, was his allegory of the September 1973 coup. He took a country house, which is Chile, with some children, who are the revolutionaries, some grown-ups, who represent order, and a butler, who represents General Pinochet. When a Chilean critic interpreted this in *El Mercurio*, Donoso felt afraid. He had thought that his symbolism would not be understood. So he went and hid under the bed, so to speak.

'Pepe Donoso has been very productive in Chile. He has written several novels, a quite successful play, and a collection of stories. He has written a book on exile and Chilean politics, called *La desesperanza*. It's a book that has been widely read and discussed. During the campaign for the 1987 plebiscite, he openly backed the No side, which was against indefinite rule by Pinochet. He also joined a party for democracy. He was not very active in it but he did take sides.

'Chilean writers also organized to fight book censorship. We didn't just talk about it but we actively organized the defence of freedom of expression in 1980. We had the assistance of the London magazine *Index on Censorship*. When we had evidence of censorship we informed *Index*, and in due course Chile's Minister of the Interior would receive letters from activists, politicians, and little old ladies in New Zealand, Scotland, and Canada. The minister was beside himself. He didn't know what to do.

'With *Persona non grata*, an eyewitness account of my diplomatic posting in Cuba, Chilean security did something quite absurd. The book is critical of the writer's situation in Cuba, but in my epilogue I refer to events in Chile. It turned out that a package arrived at Chilean customs, airmailed by Seix Barral, the book's Spanish publisher. An official seized the shipment after noticing the epilogue. Bureaucratically terrified, he had reacted on seeing Pinochet criticized. So he censored the book off his own bat. This gave the Committee for Freedom of Expression a legal pretext to fight back. It argued that no customs official had the right to censor, which belonged only to the Ministry of the Interior. As a former law student, I had lawyer friends who agreed to take on the case for nothing. We asked the publisher to cover nominal costs and we sued the customs. I've never seen anyone as terrified as that customs officer.

'The case went to the Supreme Court. Nothing happened. The Supreme Court ruled on a technicality. The officer should have sought authorization from the Ministry.

'As a result of the trial, everyone was talking about censorship. So Pinochet cancelled customs scrutiny. This eliminated the censorship of books. That was in June 1983. From then on, everything written by Antonio Skármeta, Isabel Allende, Fernando Alegría, and any other Chilean exile was published.

'The No vote, the referendum, is a historical landmark. Perhaps I ought to point out that a group of international writers came to Chile to support the campaign. Among them were Arthur Miller and William Styron. Miller had a good idea. When he arrived in Chile there was a relatively free press. But there was a law that if a writer referred to the army or to Pinochet, any reference whatever possibly qualified as an insult to the armed forces, which constituted an attack on state security. Under this law, one journalist, Juan Pablo Cárdenas, had been sentenced to what was known as night arrest. He had to report to prison every evening. One night, Arthur Miller, with Styron and some Chilean journalists, accompanied him. They secured cinema and TV coverage of the journalist's plight.

'At the moment, I am writing a book of non-fiction, my memoirs of Neruda. I first met him when I was twenty. That was in 1952.

From 1970 to 1973 I was with him at the Chilean embassy in Paris. We worked fifteen hours a day. Sometimes, even after working through the night, he would call me at home at six o'clock in the morning about a problem. Or I'd call him. We spent hours together at the airport with VIPs. I knew him very well. I think that of those alive today who knew him, I probably knew him best. I feel that Neruda has been made into marble or else an object of propaganda. There are not many who know the real Neruda. I am trying to make Neruda real, human, and poetic. As a model for this book I am looking into Samuel Johnson's *Lives of the English Poets*. I like the informality and humour of his portraits. The model I like most is Thomas De Quincey's *Recollections of the Lake Poets*. I am devoted to it.

'It helps having been to London to breathe some of the language as much as the atmosphere.'

1989

THE SPIRIT OF ISABEL

She is a big star now. Isabel Allende lives in California, her telephone number ex-directory in order to escape her Latin American West Coast fans. Having rapidly risen to the top of the literary scene with her three novels, her name is even emblazoned in in-flight magazines. She has arrived.

I liked her for her first novel, *The House of the Spirits*, as much as for a whole catalogue of childhood and adolescent experiences that we shared. These seem common to the middle class anywhere in Latin America. Our connection started with family parallels. Everybody in the South American extended family has eccentric uncles. Two of hers she exaggerated and used as characters in that first novel. She told me about her adolescent awakening to relationships with boys. The first naked man she ever saw was one of those uncles, a man who had once visited India and thought of himself as an inspired follower of some little-known guru. This uncle sat stark in the patio, staring at the stars. Young Isabel was left wondering why there was so much fuss about a small limp attachment which could easily fit in her pencil case.

My first view of a naked woman was that of a very thin aunt who had suddenly decided on a Montevideo beach that she would change her bathing costume under a towel. She had once seen it done in England. She struggled with the towel, her underclothes, and the bathing costume, until all at once everything fell away from her. As she cried to her daughter for help, I was left wondering why there was so much fuss about a lean ribcage on which a bra seemed an extravagance.

Isabel and I also shared such antediluvian experiences as dancing cheek to cheek to Bing Crosby and Nat King Cole – she in Santiago or Bolivia or Lebanon, where she had travelled as the stepdaughter of a diplomat, and I in Buenos Aires. Perhaps adolescent hang-ups were our common denominator. She had been flat-chested at a time when the role model was Jayne Mansfield. I thought I suffered from pubic alopecia when all my contemporaries were sprouting like bears.

She left Chile with her husband and two children in 1975, when she felt that her surname – she was only distantly related to President Allende, killed in office in September 1973 – and her outspokenness as a journalist and television presenter might prove to be her downfall. Her last experience of the Chilean dictatorship took place at the airport as she was leaving the country. In the ladies' washroom she was accosted by a humble woman who pleaded with her to help find a missing son abducted by the police.

Isabel Allende went to Venezuela, where she arrived with a handful of dollars bought on the Santiago black market. They turned out to be forged. She can laugh now at the way she had been so easily taken in. The dollars looked no better than coloured photocopies. This tells how little the people of Chile were acquainted with or needed the world beyond the Andes until Pinochet changed their way of life.

She loved Venezuela and, when I met her, wanted this emphasized. Caracas had given her a home and had welcomed her into a society without hierarchies. She had a large house on a main road just outside the city. Its only drawback was that it was hard for anyone to find. Addresses are so unclear in the Venezuelan capital – you might be told, for example, that someone lived in 'the house beside the grocer's shop that was demolished five years ago' – that she had had to install two big lamps on her gateposts. The lights were red. She called them *farolas de puta* – whore's lamps. They were what she told prospective visitors to look for.

I met her in New York in 1986, before she moved to California. She was sweet, dainty, and coquettish, with that touch of coolness of the successful, efficient woman. We talked over breakfast at the St. Moritz, where she was staying.

Q.   Many critics have said that your first novel, *The House of the Spirits*, resembles García Márquez too closely.

A.   As I am a great admirer of his, I am delighted. What is wrong with legitimate influence? It does not bother me in the least to be compared to the writer I most admire. He can't like it much, however.

Q.   Your second novel, *Of Love and Shadows*, continues the line begun in *The House of the Spirits* of reliving Chile through a family.

A.   But the second novel is quite different. It is based on a real criminal case. In 1978, in the tiny village of Lonquén, some thirty or so miles from Santiago, a secret grave was found. It was dug up by order of the Catholic Church, which had had to bypass the police to do so. A priest who had taken confession was told by his parishioner that an unknown number of bodies, illegally executed by members of the army during the 1973 coup, had been dumped in a common grave. The disinternment had caused a scandal, and the men implicated in the murders were brought to trial. Eventually they were found guilty of first-degree murder. Soon after, however, they were freed by an amnesty, and since then Pinochet has ordered their promotion.

Cases like this one were once quite frequent in Argentina, Uruguay, and Chile; they still are in El Salvador. It's terrible to say, but there was nothing original in this story. But I was moved when I read about it in Venezuela. Among the corpses were five members of the same family. They were a man called Maureira and his four sons. I tried to put myself in the shoes of the women of that family who for five years, from 1973 to 1978, searched for their missing men. These women – like a Greek chorus – had made the round of morgues and hospitals, prisons and concentration camps. They were certain that the men were dead but they could not bury or mourn them. Then one day they were invited by the police forensic medicine department into a courtyard where, laid out on some long tables, the women were shown what remained of their kin – a comb, a bit of a jacket, a jawbone, a hank of hair. And so they recognized their men, reconstructed like some hideous jigsaw.

My book is about the impunity of violence and all the horror this implies when a state condones and covers up a crime of that nature. The story is told from the point of view of the people who find the bodies, a journalist and a photographer. That part I invented. When the book came out in the Argentine, many readers asked whether I had based it on a specific Argentine case, for they had not heard of the Chilean incident. This shows how similar the tragic history of our continent is.

There was another Chilean case in the 1980s, equally horrific. Pinochet pardoned the murderers, who claimed that their victim had been a killer. The murdered man's son wrote a book to say that his father was not guilty of the death he had been accused of. The courts then ignored the amnesty and opened a case against the paramilitary police.

Q.   How long can you go on in your books trying to relive Chile from afar? How long can any writer in exile sustain a realistic relationship with his or her country?

A.   I'm not sure. I don't know about other writers but I don't think I'll be able to keep it up for much longer. Chile causes me great pain. It's always with me, always in my thoughts, in my life, in what I write. But my third novel, *Eva Luna*, takes place elsewhere and has nothing whatever to do with Chile.

Q.   If Pinochet had been forced out, would you have returned?

A.   At one time I thought so. But now, after so much time away, I cannot really say. I no longer make plans. For years I said all the things that exiles say – This year we'll spend Christmas in Chile; Next year we'll go back; If only he would drop dead we'd go back tomorrow – but in real life there are so many little things, so many complications. Even if my intention were to return, I wouldn't know when.

Q.   What are your children's feelings about going back?

A.   They aren't interested. They won't return. They belong to a generation that grew up outside Chile and has no reason to burden itself with the terrible baggage of the grief of exile. After all, it has nothing to do with them. That belongs to me, to my generation; it was my decision to leave Chile. My children adapted to Venezuela and have developed strong emotional attachments to their new country. They have put down roots and made friends. Why should they look back on a country which is nothing but a dream of a distant childhood, a cherry tree that grew in our patio and that was covered with blossoms in spring, and splashing each other with water from the garden hose? They are eighteen and twenty-two; they left Chile twelve years ago.

Q.   Jorge Edwards has said that after 1973 Chilean writers had to learn to write all over again and Chilean readers to learn to read all over again. They had to look for what was written between the lines and discover a new form of expression.

A.   That's true. It happens in all dictatorships. New keys and symbols are invented to make points, to get round the censors. But sometimes when a writer manages to elude the censor he does so at the expense of changing the language to the point that it becomes labyrinthine. In eluding the censor he may elude the reader too. Censorship is a serious interference. It is worse in journalism than in literary work.

Q.   How do you explain the great contrasts throughout Latin America – the great beauty alongside the barbarism?

A.   I don't think Latin America has a copyright on cruelty. In whatever direction we look anywhere in the world there are land-scapes that contain both the beautiful and the inhospitable. That contrast is the natural state of man. Violence is an ever-present dimension around us. Within and without. Only by consensus do we keep that beast at bay, but from time to time it rebels. It has happened in Europe, in Argentina, and in Uruguay, as well as in Chile, which is a very beautiful country. But I don't think that Chile is any more beautiful than a number of other countries. Nor do I think that our cruelty was any greater than the cruelty of others. Maybe there was more information circulated about Chile. The eyes of the world have been on us for a long time, and Pinochet's name has become a symbol, a synonym, for cruelty, brutality, and stupidity.
     Unfortunately there are dictators like him everywhere – and always will be. I believe that there is violence in us all. My life and what I write oscilate between the two poles of love and violence. They are two uncontrollable, antagonistic forces. I feel that with one and the same passion I can love someone madly or be capable of great cruelty. That frightens me.
     My second novel is about these two forces. The shadow is institutionalized violence, which is not the exclusive province of dictatorships. I'm speaking of the worst of all violence – poverty. Poverty, not police brutality or torture, is the foremost violence. Poverty's violence is that terrible disparity which allows us to be

THE SPIRIT OF ISABEL

having breakfast here, bundled up against the cold, while in Chile and elsewhere in the world people are dying of starvation. In order for us to have this large breakfast, the world has been organized in a way that condemns others to live in destitution. To me this is a brutality so extreme that it is no wonder that there are explosions of unrest and outbreaks of desperation. Because there are more and more poor all the time, one day the explosion will turn into a holocaust.

1986

ARIEL DORFMAN: A CASE
OF CONSCIENCE

When a tyrant falls, he leaves behind a society that is at pains to come to terms with his crimes, and ordinary people have to learn how to react in new ways to former despots whom they no longer need fear. The problem is restricted to no one region. From central Europe to central Africa to Central America, tumbling despots leave countries unstable and people conscience-stricken about how to deal with the years during which many may have acquiesced in the repression or even collaborated with it.

On 11 March 1990, when Chile's General Pinochet drove to the inauguration of his constitutionally elected successor, Patricio Aylwin, the outgoing president rode confidently to the ceremony in an open car, in full dress uniform, along streets lined with the men and women he had terrorized for sixteen years. But the ostentation, the arrogance, proved too much. Suddenly the crowd began to shout 'Murderer!', and all along the route thousands of mouths took up the word. To protect him from a pelting with tomatoes and rotten fruit, the general's security guard had to open umbrellas. Pinochet's power was finished.

On 24 April 1990, President Aylwin created an official body, the Commission for Truth and Reconciliation, whose twin purpose was to report on the circumstances under which some 4,000 opponents of the Pinochet regime were murdered and to determine whether compensation should be paid to the victims' next of kin. The commission had until March 1991 to report. Its brief was to act with caution, thereby limiting the likelihood of antagonizing the military. Surviors of the prisons and torture chambers would not qualify for compensation. Findings were only partially to be made public – that is, only the president would see the names of the accused. Whether or not compensation would be paid was to be decided in a closed session of parliament.

Ariel Dorfman, novelist, playwright, and popular poet – so popular that his poems had been made into posters and sold at anti-Pinochet marches and demonstrations in Santiago – returned to Chile in July 1990. Dorfman had first tried coming home from his comfortable exile at Duke University, in Durham, North Carolina, in 1983. At the time, however, he did not find the atmosphere in Chile conducive to writing and freedom of expression. In 1986, he tried a sort of part-time return, dividing his life between Santiago and Durham. Within a year, he was stopped at Santiago airport, briefly detained, and deported. Not one to give up easily, Dorfman entered Chile again in 1989, and, in July of the next year, once more attempted to establish semi-permanent residence in his country. Together with his wife Angélica and their two sons, he wanted to try to become an ordinary suburban family again. But he found that the experience of re-adapting to old habits and, above all, of coming to terms with people who had stayed on through the long dictatorship was to prove not only painful but full of unresolved personal anguish.

'In many countries today there is a kind of uneasy collusion between those who committed crimes and those who were repressed,' Dorfman told me when we met in London in November 1990. 'Such a state of affairs is a fact of contemporary society. It exists not only in Chile's transition to democracy but in Eastern Europe and elsewhere. In Chile, we call the resulting situation *la impunidad*. This impunity protects those who will never be called to account.

'In Chile, we are constrained by the past. Agents of the old regime are still in the army, armed and free to move about at will. As yet nobody had been punished for human rights violations. By imposing his own constitutional reform and appointing his own senators before he left office, Pinochet enabled himself to abort whatever legislation threatened him. Because Chile suffered so terribly under the dictatorship, we must now all be prudent. We have to say hello politely to our adversaries, and there are subjects we had better not discuss. Wherever I scratched the political surface of apparent normality, I found terrible pain immediately below. In the arts or in the theatre there was nothing that addressed this gap.

'You must remember that Pinochet was not defeated in any war; he was brought down by a referendum. The dictatorship allowed a certain amount of political dissent. It was this "space" that led to the vote. Therefore, much of the resistance to Pinochet was in place long before the dictatorship came to an end. The change, when it came, was far more gradual than the abrupt transformation that took place in Argentina in 1983. In Chile, we'd had a long preparation for our change.'

The first few months of his return in 1990, Dorfman decided, would not be a time for writing. He had a novel in progress. He was also working on a collection of essays, *Missing Continents*, about the censorship by society that affects whole sectors of the population, who have no access to the media. Both books would have to wait half a year while he settled back in with his family.

Meanwhile, all about him everyone was attempting to adjust to the new political circumstances. Yet the past weighed heavily. Dorfman sat down to work and in three weeks he wrote a play, *La muerte y la doncella* (Death and the Maiden). In it, a woman whose husband has just been appointed member of a Commission of Inquiry into the dictatorship's crimes recognizes one of her former torturers. The conflict between the three characters – woman, husband, and suspect – creates gripping theatre. At the same time, in the suspect's denial of his alleged crimes, the woman's search for revenge, and the husband's need for justice, the play reflects the seventeen years of torment and terror that the country suffered.

Like Gilo Pontecorvo's film *The Battle of Algiers*, Dorfman's play has elements of brilliant propaganda. The audience is immediately able to reach a moral judgement about right and wrong, and yet, in the play – as in the film – all the characters present reasoned and valid arguments.

Predictably, when we discussed his play, Dorfman was outraged by the word 'propaganda'.

'This is not propaganda,' he said. 'How can you call it that? It is tragedy, and tragedies are never propaganda. My position is clear. I am against torture. This is not just in the everyday way that people say they oppose torture and then in moments of anger find torture acceptable when used against those they disapprove of. I have been against all violence and against the dictatorship. I despair at the damage these years have done to the people of Chile. My play is not just a denunciation of the evil of torture. By openly debating the issues, it also aims to help people purge themselves of pity and terror.'

Within ten minutes of our reunion, Dorfman and I were arguing. We had not seen each other for years, except once very briefly at a London conference on the politics of exile. Here he was in London again, this time for a reading of his play as part of the series 'Censored Theatre' at the Institute of Contemporary Arts.

Ariel Dorfman was born in Buenos Aires, in 1942. His father, an engineer and the author of an economic history of Argentina, was dismissed in 1943 from the prestigious University of La Plata during the military dictatorship that preceded Juan Perón's rise to power. Ariel was then two years old. His father went to the United States and, in 1954, while Perón ruled in Argentina, the family – by then Ariel was twelve – settled in Chile. Ten years later young Dorfman became a Chilean citizen.

We first met in Buenos Aires, in 1973, at the Argentine Writers' Society (SADE). Dorfman, with his six-year-old son Rodrigo had just arrived from Chile, on the run from Pinochet's newly-installed government. Dorfman's book *How to Read Donald Duck: Imperialist Ideology in the Disney Comic*, published two years earlier, made him in the new regime's eyes a dangerous subversive. Within a month he left for Paris, just one day before the police went looking for him at his grandmother's home in Buenos Aires.

'The play will be criticized in Chile,' he told me. 'There are those who will say I'm attacking the Commission of Inquiry. Others will say I'm attacking the victims. The point about the play is that it works in the grey zone of ambiguity, allowing each member of the audience or each reader to ask him or herself who he or she is in relation to each of the play's three characters. Everyone in Chile has experienced this situation.'

Dorfman said that President Aylwin was bringing truth back into public administration. Sincere as Dorfman may have been, his use of the word 'truth' in connection with politicians made me cringe. However, he went on to say that in Aylwin's case one could speak of truth, because the new president was bringing Chile's past up to date after so many years of secrecy. 'Truth is merely the accumulation of facts of what happened. Many of the voices have disappeared. The idea of a secret existence, of bringing secrets out, makes for testimonial literature. This is a truth.' Dorfman went on to explain that General Pinochet was being made to obey the letter of the constitution he had created. The general's assumption that he alone was the arbiter of all national matters was thwarted by constant reminders that he could not sidestep bureaucratic channels of his own making.

The reminder of Pinochet's power brought back to me recollections of 1973. Dr Salvador Allende Gossens committed suicide during the military coup that year. He was not given a proper funeral until 4 September 1990, the anniversary of his election victory in 1971. His grave, all that time unmarked, had been shared with his sister and brother-in-law, Inés Allende Grove and Eduardo Grove, in the cemetery off Calle Uno, at Santa Inés, north of Viña del Mar. The gardeners there knew the spot. 'There's Chicho's grave,' they told visitors. 'A lot of people come here but they don't like to attract attention.' A small red stencil outline of Allende's effigy had been painted on his unmarked headstone by unknown hands, afraid perhaps to be more ostentatious but eager to leave a public sign.

'My role as an artist became clear to me on our return from exile in 1990,' Dorfman told me. 'I remember saying to myself that I must not hold back on my views. Instead, I must practise a responsible delirium. In other words, let everything out but to do it responsibly.'

Responsible delirium is what Dorfman feels he has practised at least once before, when, in 1983, accompanied by Rodrigo, he delivered 535 copies of his novel *Widows* to an equal number of members of both houses of the United States Congress. Father and son personally delivered the book to the offices of these senators and representatives in the Dirksen, Russell, Hart, Cannon, and Rayburn buildings as a briefing paper on the human rights situation in Latin America. *Widows* is a political novel set in a Greek village in 1940. All the husbands and sons there are abducted by the military government and listed as having 'disappeared'. The novel's characters are these men's widows and mothers. The message Dorfman wanted to drive home to the legislators was that in those Latin American regimes which the United States had been backing, such disappearances were commonplace and that 'an untraceable abduction is a double punishment, since it means death or imprisonment for the victim and years of uncertainty for his family.

'One of the best characters in *Widows* – because he is so real – is the orderly, with whom I disagree quite strenuously. He's a lackey, but it is people like him who make military dictatorships possible. He is one of those small men who decides he wants to serve the winner. To this extent, he obeys orders, tortures, kills. Without his type we would not have torture or censorship or, ultimately, dictatorship. There is nobody I could disagree with more than with that character, but he is the most interesting in the novel.'

Dorfman's previous play, *Lector*, like *Death and the Maiden*, contained a severe warning to dictatorships and to those who sympathize with them. Slowly, one day, the past will catch up with them. Despots are the architects of their own doom. Societies that suffer at the hands of dictators will detect that moment when the oppressor becomes vulnerable.

'*Lector* is based on the short story "Reader", from my collection *My House Is on Fire*. In the play, I take a censor in a Latin American country – it might even be in Spain, a long time ago – and follow him as he undertakes to read a novel. Immediately he sees that he must censor it, since it contains a subtle attack on the dictatorship at a critical moment when the regime cannot allow a sign of weakness. At the same time, the censor realizes that he is a character in the novel. As he censors, he wipes out his own life, and, as his effacement progresses, all the respect and obedience he formerly demanded are removed. The play is about state censorship and the self, for all forms of censorship are dependent on self-censorship. My difference with George Orwell is that there is never complete control of the human being. *Nineteen Eighty-Four* is impossible. We have seen that impossibility in central Europe as well as in Latin America. There is always somebody who will grab the controls and derail the best plans.

'The problem is how to bring ourselves out of the grey zone, how to recognize that one is acting in a climate of fear. Afraid of fear, we begin to look on it as something reasonable. Arguments to convince ourselves that fear is normal become amazingly perverse. The next step is to know what evil does to us. Unless we are willing to look at it and name it, evil will continue to haunt us.

'However, it is important to differentiate between what is fictitious and what is myth. There comes a time when people do not want to know anything about the horrors of the past. In Bolivia, when the government showed the horrors of the military regime on television, people simply switched off. It was too much for them.

'On the other hand, everybody's dearest wish is to know what has taken place. I myself have a secret longing to know what is in my dossier, which is in the hands of the Chilean secret police. This is only natural. In Chile, we all knew that secret things were taking place but we did not know what they were. One of the country's current best-selling books is the story of how a group on the left tried to assassinate Pinochet and was found out.

'In the first poems I wrote about the Chilean *desaparecidos*, in 1977 or 1978, I said that the bodies of the missing could not disappear. They would reappear even if they had to come back from the land of the dead or the land of the imagination. I was right. Ten years later the bodies are appearing in graves everywhere. The point is that if I had only written testimonial literature the dead would not be able to speak. My imagination gave them a language, created a myth, and made their return a reasonable expectation.'

Ariel Dorfman spoke rapidly, non-stop, and allowed very few interruptions. In spite of the vehemence of his words and feelings, he is gentle, loving almost, and eventually he does address all the problems presented to him. It is this combination that makes him so popular with audiences.

'The tragedy is that we must live with those who have repressed us. To repress them would be to turn ourselves into them. So unless there is a true reconciliation and repentance, during which society really opens itself up to learn what happened, we are not going to overcome the tragedy. Censorship keeps minds underdeveloped, consoling us with false solutions while not allowing us to resolve our problems for ourselves. We have to learn all over again that things are good not only when we agree with them but when we disagree. This outlook will make us review seriously every argument that justifies violence and makes vengeance reasonable, so that in the end justice becomes a many-sided debate. The defence of individual human rights is not a matter of great risk but an ordinary fact of life.'

1991

ARCADIAN PASTICHE

Paraguay is neglected by the press, by researchers, and by tourism. It is landlocked and not rich enough, not big enough to merit sustained interest from any part of the world outside. Yet it is also a nation of brave men, of devastating wars, of outrageous heads of state, of a rich bilingual culture, and it has a fascinating history. Paraguay is a country whose native people, the Guaraní, have ignored the world beyond their borders from the time of the Jesuit-built so-called Christian-Communist Republic of the seventeenth and eighteenth centuries. The country continues to lose parts of its frontier. Its River Paraná border with Brazil is soon to be flooded by the 12.5 million kilowatt Itaipú hydroelectric project, which will make Paraguay a Kuwait of electricity export but will also put seven giant waterfalls somewhere under the lake's surface.

Why go to Paraguay? First, for the history. It comes alive in a land where Guaraní life, language, customs, and festivities survive in a territory where even the Vikings were said to have settled in a remote, pre-Columbian, pre-Incan period. There is also the more recent history, a tale of nineteenth-century European court life transported to the sub-tropical village that was Paraguay's capital by the Irish wife of a Paraguayan president. His folly, which is now called an achievement, was to wage a terrible, futile war against the combined forces of Brazil, Uruguay, and Argentina. Then there are Utopian colonization ventures. Another lure was a sense of lust that I felt for a fertile soil in a sub-tropical climate – that which has prompted writers to call Paraguay an Arcadia.

I had personal reasons as well. These include the memory of sailing in a paddle boat with my father up the Paraná River, three days from Buenos Aires to Asunción, twenty-five years earlier. My memory of that time is of bushland scenery on the muddy banks, beautiful in its colour and its wildness, and of the river-boat life filled with the luxuries of an elegant first class and of rowdy, rich passengers, merchants, farmers, and propertied adventurers, who demanded service by parking a pistol on the bar-room table. I think that was why my father bought a .22 Smith and Wesson in Asunción, so as not to miss out on the drinks. It was a little of the life described by Gordon Meyer in *The River and the People*. Yet another personal reason for visiting Paraguay was to see an uncle and two cousins. The uncle, an Englishman long expatriated, had taken his wife and family three hundred miles up river into the Chaco, where he was under contract as manager and accountant of a tannin factory. When he retired, he stayed in Asunción, determined to put his savings into a string of business ventures he had always dreamed of. He started the first bowling alley in the capital, though he had to sell to meet debts; and he had been awarded the concession for the Post Office canteen. His many investments were a story of failure buoyed by unbounded optimism and a Micawberish variant; if this did not work, something else he had thought of certainly would. Had Graham Greene met him in 1968 when he visited Paraguay he might have written a book called *Travels with Your Uncle*.

Paraguay lured me in spite of all its failings. And its failings are legion, starting with a head of state dictatorially in office since 1954. He stands accused by European human-rights organizations of gross violations of the individual's entitlement to express his views freely; he has earned the world's opprobrium for harbouring war criminals out of his sense of admiration for the long-defeated Nazi cause; he is disgraced too for giving shelter to international crooks who were then fleeced by the protection rackets operated by high government officials (and in mid-August 1979 he also became host to former president Somoza of Nicaragua); and he is ridiculed for a political line that makes even the ultramontane seem moderate. And so to Paraguay because of the history, the river journeys, the uncle, and the cousins.

The name 'Paraguay' is said to have its origins in Guaraní Indian sounds: *para* meaning 'various', *gua* 'ornament' or 'crown', and *i* 'water'. Hence, 'land of the crown of waters', an idyllic land. For the Guaraní, paradise, *Yvaga*, was a land rich in fruit trees over which presided a benevolent god, Tupang. The Guaraní race, with its many tribal branches, lived between the upper Paraná and Paraguay rivers, the rich one-third of the country. Two-thirds, west of the Paraguay, is the sandy, clayey Chaco. The natives were considered a friendly people, though ferocious in battle.

Some time between the late thirteenth and early fourteenth centuries, white settlers were said to have entered Guaraní territory, having followed the network of roads which the natives had built and which extended to the Caribbean in the north and the Atlantic in the east. The roads would be used later by the Incas and, still later, made highways by the Spanish. The early whites have been identified as 'Vikings'. Three centuries later, the Jesuits found settlements with Nordic origins named 'Storting' and 'Tocanguzir'. Excavations of the ruins in 1972 appear, in principle, to justify the conclusion. And why not Vikings? The land had welcomed a long line of colonizing enterprises, such as New Bordeaux, a French Basque failure between 1855 and 1857; the utopian socialist settlement founded by 240 Australians, led by the journalist William Lane, in 1893 – also a failure; the Canadian Mennonites, in 1927, who have made a successful colony; and Germans of all kinds, who have made a Teutonic enclave out of the three-nation frontier of Argentina, Brazil, and Paraguay near the majestic Iguazú (Great) Falls.

Paraguayan history starts with the beginning of the outpost of Our Lady of the Assumption, a temporary station for boat repairs built by a lieutenant of Domingo Martínez de Yrala, in August 1537, while on an expedition in search of El Dorado which followed the trail of silver ornaments taken by the Guaraní and their white 'Viking' allies in looting forages against the Incas in the west.

Yrala, by his own example, encouraged miscegenation. 'I say and declare and confess that I have and God has given me in this province certain daughters and sons,' was the way he put it in his testament, and his confessions won him the title of 'Father of the Nation'. According to some historians, Guaraní women welcomed the Spaniards with open limbs, their mestizo offspring winning status and protection from the European invader.

The Guaraní – the word means 'warrior' – were gathered, first by the Franciscans, in 1580, then by the better organized Jesuits, in 1609, into communities called reductions. The Jesuits started thirty reductions in the region, eight of them in what is today Paraguay, R. B. Cunninghame Graham, in A Vanished Arcadia, wrote that the communities were marshalled to the sound of music at sunrise and went in procession to the fields, with a saint carried ahead. 'Along the paths were shrines of saints, and before each of them they prayed, and between each shrine sang hymns. As the procession advanced, it became gradually smaller as groups of Indians dropped off to work . . . until sundown, when the procession reformed, and the labourers, singing, returned to their abodes.' C. R. Lugon, in *La Republique Communiste Chrétienne des Guaranis*, described the attitude of the Jesuits to the Indians as excessively paternal, limiting education and development to such a point that when a royal decree banished the Jesuits from the Spanish Empire on charges of plotting to create rebel nations within the dominions, the Indians, without management, abandoned their foreign customs. Although the Jesuits' presence lasted almost two centuries, no sooner had they gone than their influence disintegrated. The Guaraní swamped the foreigner and the invader every time throughout Paraguay's history, keeping their language and customs in spite of foreign influence.

By the time Paraguay declared its independence from the Viceroyalty of the River Plate, in Buenos Aires, and from Spain, in 1811, the territory had seen a string of revolts against the Spanish which assured it a rightful claim to be the originator of the fight for South American independence.

Líneas Aereas Paraguayas, Flight PZ 801, bumped down in a cloud of dust at President Alfredo Stroessner Airport, Asunción, then taxied to a cluster of old buildings some distance from a new terminal, which had still to be completed. The temperature outside the plane was ninety degrees Fahrenheit on that sunny mid-winter July morning.

On the tarmac a group of arriving Germans jabbered to awaiting kin in Asunción *Deutsch* and passed them hand luggage in blatant circumvention of Customs. They were very much at home, of course, as well they might be, being in the same league as the nation's president, born himself at Foz de Iguazú, so the wags say, on the Brazilian side of the border, the son of a migrant Bavarian worker.

Customs clearance was quick. It entailed lifting the suitcase flap only two inches before being waved on into the near duty-free country beyond. This inevitably annoys European travellers, who proudly lug a bottle of tax-exempt Scotch half-way round the world only to find that it could have been bought cheaper on arrival.

In the airport's single telephone booth I felt watched. I turned to look up at the face of President Stroessner, smiling benevolently from a coloured print in a fly-blown frame. His pictures were everywhere in the airport, in black and white, in colour, some quite up to date, some going back to what must have been the early days after he took office, when he had more hair.

A huge border of small palms and colourful flowers awaits the traveller outside the airport building.

> I soon recognized a striking difference between the character of the country in which I now was and that of any part over which I had hitherto travelled. The open Pampa was exchanged for the shady grove; the pastures, protected by the trees and irrigated by abundant streams, were in most places beautifully green; the palm tree was a frequent occupant of the plain; hills and more gently sloping eminences contrasted beautifully with the valley and the lake. Wooded from the base to the top, those hills and slopes exhibited now the stately forest tree and anon the less-aspiring shrub, the lime and the orange, each bearing at the same time both blossom and fruit. The fig-tree spread its broad dark leaf and offered its delicious fruit to the traveller without money and without price . . .

So wrote two young Scots, John and William Parish Robertson, in their *Letters on Paraguay*, in 1811. Give or take a few kilometres from the airport to the river and omit the century and a half between us and I felt that I was in the same place. They were describing the eastern third of Paraguay, an extension of the Brazilian plateau on which I stood.

In the bus – a five-pence (twenty-five guaranies) fare for the few miles into town in preference to the seven pounds (1,500 guaranies) for a taxi – after a notice advised me that I was being welcomed to 'the happy land of Paraguay', the road sign called for respect for the leader: 'Peace and Progress with Stroessner'.

Throughout Paraguay's history as a nation devotion to an autocratic leader has been successively demanded. Soon after independence that leadership was seized by Dr José Gaspar Rodríguez de Francia, *El Supremo*, a man who had an

> acquaintance with Voltaire, Rousseau, and Volney . . . But he was most of all proud to be known as an algebraist and astronomer . . . In Paraguay, an acquaintance with French, Euclid's Elements, equations, the mode of handling a theodolite, or with books prohibited by the Vatican, was, in point of knowledge, so much the exception to the general rule that the man who had it . . . was deemed something between a magician and a demi-god.

From the letters of Parish Robertson again, in which the brothers went on to describe Dr Francia as a villain. He was brutal but claimed to love the people he repressed. He isolated Paraguay, expelling foreigners and preventing travel abroad, but in that way – though isolation ruined external trade – the national identity and independence were preserved. In 1840, when *El Supremo* died, his rehabilitation as a national hero began – and in Britain, of all places. Thomas Carlyle published an essay in 1843 that expressed doubts about the accuracy of the unfavourable descriptions of the dictator.

Dr Francia was succeeded by Carlos Antonio López, who, after a delay caused by war, opened the country to trade and to foreigners, gave it a constitution, and erected the Congress building. But still López governed as a despot with the title of first president. López's liberalization was delayed by the action of the governor of Buenos Aires, General Rosas, who closed the rivers used by Paraguay. This annoyed British and French merchants, and their anger led to an Anglo-French blockade of Buenos Aires. The European fleet, using steam-power in river warfare for the first time, forced open a route to Asunción, which prompted *The Times* to remark, on 29 January 1846, that 'This action is another instance of the advantages to be derived from steam-power in river operations.'

President Carlos Antonio López, for whom 'everybody is obliged to stop and take off their hats when he passes,' according to a scientist, C. B. Mansfield, in *Paraguay, Brazil and the River Plate* (1856), attracted British engineers, stonemasons, builders, and technicians, who were under contract not only to carry out specific tasks but to teach the natives 'the secrets of their trades'.

It was through the English that modern comfort was introduced into Paraguay ... They were the first to have fireplaces and chimneys in their houses ... in the later fifties [they] introduced the consumption of beer as everyday beverage ...

wrote the historian and novelist Josefina Plá in *The British in Paraguay* (1976). Britons organized the first hospital service, built the first shipyard, the Government Palace, and the railways.

The British presence has all but vanished. There are between two and three hundred Britons, most of them Anglo-Argentines, Anglo-Chileans, and Anglo-Uruguayans with a right to hold a British passport, though there is no British Consulate in Asunción to issue them one. There is a small number of wealthy landowners and also a number of elderly British subjects living out their lonely last years. Their diet is that of the Paraguayan – manioc, fruit, a little beef, chicken, and the local tea-like brew, *yerba mate*. This last, mixed with lemon juice and drunk cold, is called *tereré*. The old folk serve visitors afternoon tea in unmatching but treasured porcelain, the remnants of an engagement or wedding present, and talk of Britain in distant memories. Each recollection is punctuated with a chuckle and the remark, 'I suppose all that too has changed.'

The most visible British commercial presence is on the shelves in the shops. Everything is to be found from Crosse & Blackwell marmalade and Scotch whisky to Durex Nu-form. But the bigger firms have gone. In the port – where Lamport and Holt still sends its small coasters from across the Atlantic and up the river a few times a year – on the railways, and in engineering works, the British are remembered only by the metal plaque of a Birmingham or Glasgow company. Liebig's, of meat extract fame, are streamlining their cattle interests to make modern dairies. The Bank of London and South America – the oldest bank in Paraguay – keeps a low-profile competition for some of the business of the Paraguayan-Brazilian Itaipú hydroelectric project, where Germans, Italians, and Spaniards have entered in force.

The generations of journalists who on arrival went automatically to sign the book at Government House and the British embassy have long since disappeared. However, I have often found in these troubled times of unwelcome night-time searches and dawn arrests that the practice is usefully revived. Paying respects to those in public office often helps to assure that one's privacy is respected. Over lunch, I asked my cousin to request an interview with Mr Charles Wallace, Her Britannic Majesty's Ambassador to Paraguay. I planned myself to go to Government House.

We took my cousin's three children to school, St Andrew's, a neat new building behind the church, St Andrew's, which is partly staffed and financially assisted by the South American Missionary Society in Tunbridge Wells. This organization's present-day network and educational success hardly follows the failure of its founder, one Captain Allen Gardiner. He died of exposure on the south Patagonian coast in 1851 after failing in almost every attempt to open a mission in those lands. St Andrew's is the English school in

Asunción, and many Paraguayans pay the fees of approximately £40 a month, confident that their children are getting a British education and a passport to success.

The tram took us into town, slower but in greater comfort than the small buses that raced to the centre. The bus drivers and ticket collectors are fined by their managers if they arrive late. Buses cause havoc in the traffic and no end of headache to the traffic wardens, young women in grey uniforms and kepis. These ladies must be careful not to issue tickets to anyone with influence in the government or army, otherwise, for such professional folly, they risk losing their £62-a-month job. (A woman in secretarial work can earn about £350 a month.)

The wooden trams are spoken of as 'new', for they have been in service only since 1977. They are Belgian and second-hand. The Paraguayans, being impervious to all that is foreign, have blindly accepted and never bothered to remove the stickers from the original bilingual users in French and Flemish. *Sortie–Uitgang* and *Ne pas fumer–Niet Roken* were the stern indications to the passengers of this also bilingual country. Spanish–Guaraní equivalents were not posted. A guard did not need labels over the button panel to know that one button was to *Ouvrir–Opener* and the other to *Fermer–Sluiten*. He tried both until he got it right, and the passengers knew from habit that they had to move back without an '*AVIS, pour faciliter la montée au prochain arrêt, les voyageurs sont priés d'avancer–BERICHT . . .* ' It seemed only natural that such instructions as '*Défense de parler au conducteur–Verboden met de Trambestuuder te spreken*' were superfluous, unless the *Trambestuuder* was an acquaintance, in which case there was every reason to ignore a notice which could not have been conceived with the importance of a conversation in mind. Paraguayans obey rules – and the law in general – if they notice them and think that the instructions are useful or that obedience is advisable. Law-abiding follows the question, 'Is it necessary?' – unlike other Latin countries, where the law is written to offer the citizen the entertainment of finding holes in it, as in Brazil and Argentina.

The tram took us from the outskirts, along tree-lined streets, past the elegant old neo-colonial homes of the traditional rich and the new, recently-built, sprawling residences of the very rich, which had market prices of £300,000 and over. Paraguay is a financial haven for those fleeing from taxation and from the ogre of socialism – or from the law. It does not rank, however, with the offshore banking facilities or with the European principalities, largely because its economic stability hinges on the health of one man – the president.

The city is built on a grid, and a majority of the older buildings are much the same architecture as the rest of Spanish America – that is, single- or two-storey houses built on to the pavement. The windows are tall, for maximum ventilation, protected by metal bars. Inside each window is a side sill, used at times for ornaments but more often as a seat from which to look out into the narrow streets. The roofs are flat, disguised by parapets. Houses appear to have been built more for defence than for domestic comfort. In the heart of the capital, the tall, impersonal office and apartment blocks sprout like leafless stalks above the squat traditional constructions.

The tram's wheels squeal in the empty hours of the early afternoon. The halt for a siesta up until 3.00 p.m. in winter and until later in summer helps conserve the village atmosphere of Asunción. Even the country's single television channel stops for two hours at siesta time. The siesta starts at midday; midday starts at 11.30 a.m. Early rising between 6.00 and 7.00 a.m. is normal in order to make work possible before the subtropical heat of the day descends. Asunción is little more than a small country town, the capital of a nation of slightly more than two million inhabitants, with probably another half again abroad in political or economic exile. The 1977 edition of the telephone directory, including the *Yellow Pages*, fits the whole country into 570 pages.

As I got off the tram, I was offered an assortment of pocket calculators, portable radios, perfumes, cloth, and anything else which might have been imported, almost duty free, into Paraguay and sold to Argentine and Brazilian tourists. These vendors meet outside the Argentine National Bank branch, where business is discussed and *tereré* is drunk. The Maká Indians, forced into the city to peddle their goods owing to the flooding of their reservation – where the women used to lift their T-shirts and bare their breasts for a fee in front of tourist cameras in a photographic prostitution run out of business by the open sale of *Playboy* magazine – sold their belts, headbands, and bows and arrows to foreigners. What I did buy, out of greed, was a *chipá* bun, a small bread roll made of maize and manioc flour. The woman who sold it to me made a show of grabbing a small square of white wrapping paper and a pair of large baker's tongs, with which she put the roll inside the paper. Then she hung the tongs from a nail on the side of the box, on which rested a basketful of *chipá*. A child, who sat with an older woman on the pavement, stood, picked the tongs off the nail, and flung them at a small dog that came sniffing at the basket. The short, attractive woman who had served me and whom I took to be his mother remonstrated only for the short time it took her to pick up the tongs and return them to the nail. She shooed the dog away.

Many of the women vendors had children with them, reflecting a fact of Paraguayan life that the woman is the head of the family. In forty per cent of families there is no man, desertion being accepted by the children and womenfolk as normal. This tolerance of the absence of the male partner has its origins in the war of the Triple Alliance, between 1865 and 1870, when Paraguay fought the combined forces of Argentina, Brazil, and Uruguay, as a result of which the male population was decimated. When eventually the balance of the sexes was established, custom let the male off family responsibilities.

Government House was a narrow, squat building with long galleries, shuttered windows, and a square turreted tower on which flew the Paraguayan flag. Through the building the river could be seen from the main entrance. The place had been designed and built by a Mr Taylor during the Carlos Antonio López regime. Outside on the front path, hearing my request to see the press secretary, a soldier told me to wait. He used the familiar *vos* form of address rather than the formal *usted* normally used by Paraguayans. First he consulted another soldier, then together they sought an NCO. Finally all three came back to say that they did not know what a press secretary was and that public offices were open only in the morning. Under a bust of Paraguay's most famous general, Marshal Francisco Solano López – famous for leading the country into the Triple Alliance war – who had a large, elaborate spider's web stretching between his brass curls and decorated shoulder, the three men in uniform assured me that there was nothing they could do to help. They suggested that I walk back along the path through the neatly clipped garden, round the huge shrubbery clock, across the street, and ask at the red-brick building on the corner.

The building there, its open doors level with the pavement and its high barred windows shuttered, belonged to the eight-page Colorado Party broadsheet *La Voz Nacional*. This national voice is a paper devoted to drawing parallels between the heroism of General Solano López and the heroism of President Stroessner; to proclaiming Paraguay's brotherhood with such regimes as that of Nicaragua under Somoza; to berating the opposition Liberal Party in some line of every article; to calling Paraguay's only independent newspaper, *ABC*, a lying rag; and to upholding Paraguayan freedoms by claiming 'the indisputable freedom to think, to have opinions, as long as this does not tend to cause discord and dissension among Paraguayans.'

The chief reporter was there. He said that if I wanted to talk to the president I should go to Government House at 7.00 a.m. and ask to see him. 'Just like that – anybody can go. This is a free country, my friend. But what I think a foreign journalist should be asking himself is how this man has remained in office for twenty-five years, a quarter of a century, leading the country out of anarchy – both in the armed forces and in civilian politics – peacefully. Twenty-five years is a very long time in politics, and during that time we have had peace. Before he took office there were barrack revolts every week. Since he took over . . . ' The reporter lowered his two raised arms and moved his hands horizontally, palms down indicating that the political pandemonium had been quietened. 'I think that is what a foreigner should ask.'

But I asked my colleague what was being done for the flood victims. The floods are an annual winter disorder caused by heavy distant rains swelling the rivers. In 1979 they were the worst in almost seventy years. The water had begun to rise in May and had risen by eight metres. From a course of two or three kilometres, the Paraguay River had grown to span thirty-five kilometres and was not expected to return to anything resembling its normal width until October or November, the latter month, with March, the time of the country's heaviest rainfall. Water lapped at the back walls of Government House, immediately below which were the roofs of dozens of slum dwellings, some of them lopsided after the flood had undermined their wooden or metal-sheet sides.

There was a cruel contrast in the passage of a small cabin cruiser, its sportily-dressed occupants inspecting the damage done to the inundated homes, and even greater cruelty in the entertainment of the driver of a speedboat towing a skier, whose wash ran over the roof tiles of a small house. There was only a soldier on the corner of *La Voz Nacional* to notice the insult. 'Must be a *cambá*' the soldier said, using the Guaraní name Paraguayans give Brazilians – a 'black'. (The name for Argentines is more derogatory – *curupí*, or 'pigskin'.) He was summing up the traditional contempt Paraguayans hold foreigners in, particularly the two giant neighbours who defeated the country in war over a century earlier.

Evenings, a block away, lights and music were switched on full force in a fun fair at the flood's edge below the square around which are strung the Congress building, the cathedral, the old military academy, the former Cabildo – in colonial times the seat of the city council – and a huge statue to another great general. The general gives his back to the river, as if in disgust, and an outstretched arm points accusingly towards Government House. Around the fair, which stood on dry solid tarmac, were wooden huts, their floors under water and surrounded by a thick green vegetation that floated on the surface. Pigs snorted and rooted in the puddles, and men and women were packing earth at the base of their homes against the still rising flood waters.

The chief reporter at *La Voz Nacional* said that the whole country had united to help the flood victims, who had been housed by relatives, fed by the government, sheltered by the army, given metal sheeting and timber and blankets by Colorado Party officials and the police. 'Everybody helps. This country still works in unity. You can walk the streets at night without harm coming to you. You can't do that in Brazil or in Argentina or even in England. Here we are still clean; corruption is starting, we must admit, but it is not like what you see in Brazil or Argentina. We are not very corrupt and we are free.' This last seemed rather an exaggeration in a country where smuggling is almost a recognized occupation and where members of the Supreme Court have been photographed wearing red sashes and scarves in solidarity with the Colorado (Crimson) Party. 'And this healthy, stable life is all thanks to the president. I don't know how he does it, and I hate to think what will happen when he is finished. You know, don't you, that under the constitutional reform he can be president for life?'

There is a perplexing contradiction in the simultaneous sympathy shown for Stroessner, who bullied the country into political submission, and the veneration shown for López, who plunged the country into such turmoil that Paraguay has never recovered either physically or morally. Official propaganda has fostered the idea of a parallel between General Stroessner and Marshal (the rank to which he promoted himself) Francisco Solano López. All they have in common is a stranglehold on the country's affairs.

George Thompson, an English engineer who served Marshal López, described him in *The War in Paraguay* (1869) as a very stout man . . . He is short, but has a commanding presence . . . He is careful of appearance, fond of military finery . . . He is of very indolent habits . . . He is extremely fond of Mrs Lynch's children, but not of his other ones, of whom he has a number by different women. He entertains friendly feelings for no one, as he has shot almost all those who have been most favoured by himself, and who have been for years his only companions . . . López speaks French fluently, always conversing in that language with Mrs Lynch, who was educated in France. He knows a little English, and of course Spanish well . . . however, he never spoke anything but Guaraní to the men and officers . . . López is a good speaker, especially in the kind of oratory likely to inspire his troops with confidence . . .

Mrs Lynch – Eliza Alicia Lynch – born in 1835 in County Cork, had been a highly regarded courtesan in the Paris of the Second Empire. She met López when she was nineteen. He had ambitions to become a Napoleon of South America; she aimed to be his Josephine. She was despised in Asunción but feared. When widowed she was imprisoned by Brazil and later deported to Argentina and returned to Europe.

Marshal López had inherited Paraguay's age-old border disputes, which in 1865 led him to declare war on Brazil and its satellite, Uruguay, as well as on Argentina. The war against the Triple Alliance did not end until López was killed by a lance at the battle of Cerro Corá, in 1870. Paraguay lost large areas of borderland to Brazil and Argentina; the country's poets and politicians have written hymns, homages, panegyrics, eulogies, and patriotic prose to the heroism of the soldiers who died in that useless war. But never have Paraguayans recovered from the humiliation of that defeat, which, by 1871, had reduced the population from 525,000 to 221,000, of which 106,254 were women, 86,000 children and only 28,746 men.

Not only is Marshal López venerated today but so is his consort Eliza. She died in Paris in 1886, in poverty; her remains were shipped back to Asunción half a century later and on arrival received every possible honour, finally to rest in the Pantheon of the Heroes, in the capital's central square, a beautiful plot decorated with tropical plants, huge palms, and trees and shrubs with large leaves in many shades of green.

With the tributes to Stroessner from *La Voz Nacional* packed into my notebook and with the confusion of historical controversy spinning in my mind, I set out for Paraguay's National Archive. Much of written history in the country is an emotional appendix to events rather than an analytical record based on fact. The National Archive, housed in the grey fortress-like building used by the sparsely endowed Fine Arts Museum, was just beginning the gigantic task of compiling a card index. There was no catalogue, no copying service, and some sections – court files and criminal records among them – had never been touched by investigators since the day they had been deposited there. Of course, many valuable papers were missing. In 1870, at the end of the war of the Triple Alliance, what documents the Brazilians did not burn or carry away were packed into hessian sacks and sold as wrapping paper. A travelling Spaniard, one Señor Bravo, bought as many sacks as he could and with them started the Bravo Archive in Spain.

At mid-afternoon in the street, a feeling of historical moment was growing. It was yet another battle which this nation of very brave men would fight with great courage. Inside a bar, a television set drew attention from patrons and passersby. The cameras focused on the announcer, who gazed at his invisible audience, took a deep breath, and then said, 'A decisive moment in Paraguayan history is near, and the people must be united to meet the challenge.' Other such patriotic phrases were emitted by radio broadcasters, political personalities, and members of the sporting world and the acting profession. Paraguay's champion soccer team, Olimpia, was playing in Buenos Aires against Boca Juniors in the final for the Liberators of America Cup, the South American Championship, with the winner to play the European victor.

Paraguay had only once before in the nineteen-year history of the Cup entered the finals. Now, after a home victory, Olimpia needed not more than a tie away to become the champions. The country had recently been put on the world's sports pages by a tennis player, Victor Pecci, who had left Asunción to star in tournaments in Wimbledon, Paris, and the United States. But that had been an individual's performance. This soccer match represented the team metamorphosed into the national army going forth to vindicate the national image. The idea of overcoming the humiliation of history is ever-present in the Paraguayan mind.

In 1932, Paraguay went to war with its third neighbour, Bolivia, following an invasion of Paraguay ordered by the La Paz government in pursuit of land thought to be rich in oil. Bolivia was confident of rapid victory but met the resistance of a people who were united – which the Bolivians were not – and brave. Paraguay, however, did not win the three-year Chaco War. Its troops, physically equipped to traverse the hostile forest and scrub of the Chaco, were unable to thrust into the Bolivian high plain. Neither did Paraguay lose, however. It won just enough land and self-esteem for its people to believe that they had reached a point marking the end of over half a century of inferiority. Paraguay's neighbours, acting through the League of Nations and other bodies, determined the course of the post-war borders, and Argentina's foreign minister won the Nobel Prize for Peace for leading the negotiations. The Chaco War also marked the end of a liberal period of government, when writers, poets, and historians held the highest offices in the land. Their literary output is, moreover, mostly unknown, for many wrote in Guaraní, whose beauty and musicality is lost in translation. The problem of the Paraguayan writer remains much the same today. He cannot cross his literary borders. There are exceptions, of course, such as the internationally known Augusto Roa Bastos, who has been translated into English, French, and German and most of whose work is written in Spanish. The most important book on that forgotten war was *The Epic of the Chaco, Marshal Estigarribia's Memoirs*, published in English in 1950.

I was invited to a barbecue supper and to watch the match on television in the patio of the grocery store that my cousin Richard was to inaugurate the next day. Within three minutes of the start of the Olimpia–Boca match, two men were ordered off the field, one from each side, which made our Paraguayan guests fear for the country's great future. But Olimpia held its Argentine opponents to a scoreless draw, thus winning the privilege of playing the European champions, Nottingham Forest. Great and universal was the public's joy. No sooner had the match ended, when car horns sounded in what rapidly grew into a city-wide cacophony, and a few fireworks briefly lit the sky. Whistles blew, and all kinds of musical and less musical instruments came out of storage to increase the volume of noise. Cars jammed the centre as drivers and their families and friends congregated there to be seen to be taking part in the revelry.

The Interior Minister announced his support for the merry-making and at midnight he lifted the 1.00 a.m. 'drunk's curfew', a year-old decree which ruled that every business catering to the public must close at that hour. The curfew had been celebrated by the middle class as the right way to discipline the lower orders. The ruling affected all forms of business, including the many small brothels scattered about the city and its outskirts. The women had to finish work at 00.55 so that they had time to wash and dress before the house closed its doors to the public. A taxi driver claimed that the decree had caused Paraguayans a few embarrassing moments at the outset, but more often it was tourists who were caught – literally – with their pants down. More recently, according to the driver, two senior army officers had been found in a brothel visited after curfew by the police. The officers argued that their uniforms gave them immunity. They had been politely reminded that in the circumstances they were not wearing their uniforms. I heard the same story on several occasions, each time with new and amusing embellishments.

I went early to Government House, only to be told that General Stroessner had travelled to the city of Encarnación to open a supermarket. José Bernabé, who went by the title of Chief of Information and Director of Public Relations of the Presidency of the Republic, took me to his small office, where, among yellowing certificates for loyalty and attendance, hung a photograph of a small sailing ship, the M/S *Albatross*, built in Gothenburg in 1941, but which had nothing to do with Paraguay. There was also a childish pastel drawing of a youthful President Stroessner. The dedication underneath, from a women's section of the Colorado Party, was full of spelling mistakes. Before he showed me in to see his chief, Mr Bernabé supplied me with a stock of newspapers, government statistics, Colorado newsletters and weeklies, to which he often contributed articles. When I left the building I noticed that I had been given at least two copies of each of the papers and four copies of the speech by the President of the Republic and Commander-in-Chief of the Armed Forces, General Alfredo Stroessner, to the national congress in April 1970, on the occasion of the centenary of the War of the Triple Alliance.

I had met Mr Bernabé in an official capacity almost a decade before, which is not an unreasonable occurrence in Paraguayan government circles. Why should anybody change in an administration that dislikes change, which has kept cabinet ministers in office for twenty-five years, and which has nonagenarian officials holding some of the country's highest posts? Mr Bernabé answered each one of my questions about the activities of the president in a long, enraptured, high-pitched monologue. When I had first met him years before, he had informed me that in order to get an interview with the president one had to go to Government House very early any morning 'because the president starts work before the lights of the city go out.'

On that previous visit, in 1971, I had been granted the opportunity to meet the president and I keep a photograph of the occasion. I had been cautioned that I could not take notes of the conversation as the meeting was a *saludo*, a greeting. The conversation had been more personal than a formal interview. Stroessner thanked my wife and me for our visit and asked mechanically what we were doing other than visiting relatives. He looked at my beard, which he would have associated with Fidel Castro and Communism, and told us that there were many lies being told abroad about Paraguay, a nation of brave people with a great talent for music and song. The manner in which he rejected criticism was not in the angered voice of the autocrat, but he seemed genuinely bewildered that anybody should question his method of government, unless, of course, one were a Communist. A member of this breed, he said, he had never met and was unlikely to as the annihilation of every suspected specimen had long ago been ordered. I asked him what his favourite pastime was and he said fishing. He had a house on the river, where he liked to go and spend a weekend on the bank, rod in hand, alone.

Ten years later, the pastime had not changed. Stroessner, now in his late sixties, thickset though not stout and with receding fair hair, which betrays his origins, is in his sixth five-year term of office. He makes solitary fishing the one escape from public duties. The security patrols that surround him are instructed to stay out of his sight while he sits on the river's edge, alone with thoughts and rod.

Normally Stroessner rises before dawn to read the newspapers, which he combs for reports of public and private blunders. Then, promptly, he reaches for the telephone to bawl out the ministers responsible. Often they receive rough treatment from him by being made to wait at length in *la amansadora*, the softener, the waiting-room outside the presidential office. Veteran members of the government have to sit and watch as their juniors or a friend of the head of state – a lady who lives down the road and is a friend of Captain So-and-so and wants a job in the bank for her daughter, a local Colorado chieftain bringing a *saludo* to the president – go in ahead of them.

In what he has made the third stage of his morning, Stroessner goes, still very early by anybody's standards, to inaugurations of new works, clubs, cooperatives, and banks. The international business community and diplomatic corps have to trot into line behind him at these early hours so as to be present at his more important public performances. Stroessner occupies only two centimetres in *International Who's Who* but he is a vote at the United Nations and he is an importer of foreign goods. Hence he has to be humoured. His birthdays are remembered by diplomats, who queue at Government House each year to offer him their best wishes, a *saludo*, and often an elegant gift. He, in turn, makes sure that reward is generous when the birthdays of such foreign guests occur.

The fourth stage of the morning, and by then it may be as late as 9.30 a.m., takes General Stroessner back to Government House, where he signs decrees and discusses matters of state and military affairs with his aides or visits the army command to give a pep talk.

He leaves his office for an early lunch and after that, at the official presidential residence – Mburuvicharoga (Guaraní for 'house of the chief'), on Marshal López Avenue – he enjoys a long siesta. After that, barring official evening social engagements, his time becomes his own, and nobody seems able to pinpoint a schedule. It is said that he has been seen driving his own car in Asunción. Inevitably, there is the anecdote of the motorist who, swearing at the driver who did not signal at a turning, then spotted the president at the wheel and fled in terror. The terror must have been heightened by the knowledge, or the rumour, that the president has a good memory for faces and pictures and has been known to recognize persons or landmarks years after a first encounter with them.

He is said to enjoy the company of several women and neglects his wife. At the homes of these women, he often spends an evening, feet up, watching his favourite television serials. To accommodate this fancy, advertising breaks have been eliminated from such broadcasts. He has a passion for chess, which he plays at every possible moment. Among his inner circle – men he has helped throughout their lives with business opportunities and career advancement – a number are kept on a string, required to advise the president of their whereabouts at all times and only to visit places where there are telephones and rapid access to transport in case he may urgently require their company for a game.

But this image of the whimsical, rather naughty grandfather has been achieved only after years of well-established autocracy. Stroessner came to power as a young captain in May 1954, with a reputation won as a determined lieutenant in the Chaco War against Bolivia. After the end of a succession of military uprisings that led to near civil war in the late 1940s and early 1950s, the conservative Colorado Party, founded in 1874, chose him as an interim leader. From there he moulded the party into his own tool and by 15 August 1954, when he took office as elected president for the first time, he was firmly in control. It is now the younger ranks of the Colorado Party, the educated professionals – with no memory of the civil upheaval that preceded Stroessner's government – who criticize his unrelenting sclerotic leadership. Naturally, these young men are described by the party hierarchy as infiltrated Communists. The epithet – in Paraguay it is worse even than the more Latin aspersions cast on an individual's mother – is extended to younger officers in the army. Their promotion is increasingly difficult in view of the accumulation of senior officers in the highest posts after a quarter of a century of unchanging command. These junior men complain about the state of affairs, thereby unleashing the wrath of the old leadership.

Over breakfast one Sunday morning, a leading opponent of Stroessner, Domingo Laino, said that conditions had improved in the prisons. The system of repression is unchanged, but inmates are no longer treated so brutally. The attitude of the police towards a prisoner also remains unchanged. 'The detainee is not a person, he is a detainee.' In September 1979 the United Nations Human Rights subcommittee classified Paraguay among the worst offenders. But by the time of my visit, there were only a handful of political prisoners. The police and security forces prefer to take people into detention for a few days to administer a good beating and a taste of hardship, then release them. The foreign minister, Alberto Nogues, was heard to remark with a feigned note of regret to a European visitor that he no longer got much mail from abroad about prisoners. Censorship too has been relaxed, although in 1979 two newspapers, *Última Hora* and *Tribuna*, were closed for three months for having reported in too great detail on corruption in government. But amid my interlocutor's anger and frustration there came again the amusing anecdotes, this time about censorship. On one occasion a friend, Mrs Lara Castro, had given an alternative name and address for receiving correspondence. Within weeks, her clandestine letters were deliverd by the postman to her own home. To her protestations that there had been a mistake, the postman said simply, 'Open them; you will see that they are for you.' On another occasion, an opposition MP was advised by a colleague, a government member, not to gum down his letters too much because if they were damaged in the opening they would be destroyed, while a light lick would insure that the letters would be resealed and delivered.

The anecdotes about President Stroessner as a Germanophile are also legion. He has admitted privately and shown publicly that he is an admirer of the Nazis. All over Paraguay are tales of Germans with strange behaviour. Colonel Hans-Ulrich Rudel, the most highly-decorated fighter pilot in the Nazi Air Force, who represents some US and West German business interests in South America, is said to be a fairly regular visitor at Government House. In August 1970 Simon Wiesenthal announced a reward of £25,000 for the arrest of Josef Mengele after his Paraguayan citizenship was annulled, at Germany's request, probably in acknowledgement of the considerable West German investment in Paraguay. A visit to the countryside leads inevitably to German rest houses and restaurants, each with mysterious patrons who make a hasty exit whenever strangers arrive.

The plight of the Guaraní population is a cause of endless argument and, among those more sympathetic, of research into their customs and culture that might help lift the native Indian out of his wretchedness. In the north, the enslavement and murder of the Aché and Guayakí Indians was given international publicity, and this criminal activity was reduced. The Maká Indians, tall, elegant men and women, whose reservation on the outskirts of Asunción suffers the ravages of every flood, peddle their crafts in the streets of the capital. All this, Domingo Laino told me, was a cause of embarrassment to Paraguayans who were concerned about their heritage. The South American Missionary Society and the Catholic Relief Service run aid programmes for the native tribes, but there is hostility between the two organizations over the methods used in the promotion of the welfare of the sixteen language groups of the Guaraní.

Before my interview at the British embassy I went for a shoeshine in the Plaza de los Héroes. It is a beautiful concentration in the city centre of tropical luxury, and I enjoyed sitting and looking at the vegetation, although my thoughts were constantly interrupted by shoeshine boys, lottery ticket vendors, portable radio and pocket calculator salesmen, and a variety of other such ambulatory merchants. On this occasion, as usual, I was accosted by half a dozen small boys, many with the fair hair of obvious European ancestry, most of them barefoot, all with their little boxes of polish and brushes.

As one of them went through the process of working over my footwear, I watched his mates play with wooden tops, making them spin at high speed in the dust on their iron nail points. Others threw coins in an endless game of heads or tails. A young man in his twenties approached me, producing out of a folded newspaper a badly printed coloured pornographic magazine. I was surprised at his quite classic undercover offer of 'dirty pictures'. Asunción's news-stalls were stocked with copies of *Playboy*, *Oui*, *Hustler*, and several other elevators of the male inclination. The local equivalent, in which breasts and buttocks have at least an inch of cloth discretion, is called *Fotosex*.

The Pakistani ambassador to Brazil and Paraguay was the last visitor to sign the book at the British embassy before I entered my name. The British ambassador, Charles Wallace, welcomed me into a small office, which transported me back over many thousands of miles to London. It was neat, the furniture smelled like an English office, and the ventilation, unlike any Paraguayan offices I had been to, was by air-conditioning. The ambassador gave me the essential briefing needed to face the country's statistical records. Without Britain's diplomats, most British journalists would be lost. Mr Wallace was annoyed, however, with the *Guardian* because of an item published in the Diary column a year earlier. It had portrayed him in plumes and livery, presenting a birthday gift to President Stroessner. He denied ownership of any such costume.

Like other Britons, he was enthusiastic about Paraguay's economic boom, a new-found wealth which, while insignificant to the world outside, is revolutionizing (if President Stroessner will allow the word) life inside the country. Three main factors account for this. First, general stability, a symbol of which is an exchange rate of 126 guaranies to the US dollar, unaltered for nineteen years; second, agricultural expansion and increased exports of cotton, soya bean, and tobacco; and third, the Itaipú hydroelectric project, which pours money into Paraguay at the rate of half a million pounds a day. Inflation, according to official figures, is fifteen per cent and rising with a growth rate of 11.7 per cent in 1977 and 10.8 per cent in 1978.

Paraguay always manages to be bewildering. I asked Mr Wallace if he had read Roa Bastos. He said no in the manner of the Foreign Office functionary who claims he has not read Marx. Protocol demanded a denial. But then my wife and I had asked Stroessner if he knew Roa Bastos. He had replied, 'We have great writers, but sometimes it is better not to read them.'

1979

AUGUSTO ROA BASTOS
IN SEARCH OF THE SUPREME

Ten thousand people stood waiting in Asunción airport in March 1989 to welcome home their most famous exile. Augusto Roa Bastos had been trying to return to Paraguay for years. Now a military coup had removed General Alfredo Stroessner the month before, allowing Roa Bastos back.

Stroessner had been in government – had *been* the government – six months short of thirty-five years, and for every month of those three and a half decades Roa Bastos had remained his most famous enemy. For all those years, the subject in Paraguay, in Buenos Aires, in Montevideo – or wherever you found two Paraguayans – had been how long would the dictator last.

Set the scene. We sat in an untidy flat which doubles as a study. The apartment downstairs doubles as home and is filled with the sound of small children, three of them, the youngest only months old. As Rubén Bareiro Saguier, the poet and critic from Paraguay who lives in Paris, says, 'Augusto Roa Bastos is a prolific writer – and not only prolific in the production of books.'

How can you set a Paraguayan scene in the south of France, in Toulouse? The first Concorde supersonic airliner flew out of Toulouse in 1969, and I want to set here the Paraguayan scene when Paraguay itself has barely arrived in the jet age.

When had we last met? In 1974, at one of the parties given by Susana 'Piri' Lugones, in Buenos Aires. Some time in the 1970s she had been abducted, murdered, 'disappeared'. In September 1976 Augusto Roa Bastos fled from Buenos Aires. Many fled Buenos Aires in that terrible year. Augusto took a job at the University of Toulouse. His Spanish wife also teaches there. He retired a few years ago to concentrate on his writing and on politics.

Saturday, 13 June 1987, the author's seventieth birthday and the eve of the anniversary of the truce that ended the long Chaco War between Paraguay and Bolivia in 1935. Roa Bastos had taken part in that war as a fourteen-year-old stretcher-bearer.

After the war, Roa Bastos called himself a foreign correspondent and decided to go to Europe to report on the 1939 European war. It took him nearly a year to get there, stopping first in Buenos Aires and then travelling by Liberty ship to New York. After much waiting, he raised the money to cross to England, where he spent nine months. He later entered France shortly after the liberation of Paris. On his return home in 1946, he published a small book called *La Inglaterra que yo ví* (The England I Saw).

He left Asunción for Buenos Aires in 1947. There he wrote short stories and did odd jobs. He also adapted a samba to tango and wrote the tango '*Venganza*' (Revenge), which became quite famous. In 1951, for about eight months, he was employed as a waiter in an assignation hotel, where he kept a score card with the frequency of the visits of people he knew but who did not recognize him. Some of them were writers, but, not believing their eyes, simply did not see him. In 1960, he published his first novel, *Hijo de hombre*, with which he made his name. From time to time, he returned to Paraguay for short visits that General Stroessner's satrapy overlooked.

Roa's long masterpiece *Yo, el Supremo* was published in Buenos Aires in 1974. I had taken to Toulouse the copy of it he had signed at the time, and now he endorsed it. In 1982, Roa returned to Paraguay to have his young son baptized and registered as a Paraguayan. He was only there a day before he was bundled out and dumped unceremoniously on the Argentine border without a passport. From a Buenos Aires friend who owed him a favour, he obtained a second passport. He was in a hurry to get out of Argentina, but Argentina was too busy losing the Falklands War to notice him. The *Belgrano* had just been sunk.

A.   In my article, 'Fragments from a Paraguayan Autobiography', I had the rare opportunity to show the symbiosis in myself between the writer and the man with social concerns. I'm not talking about politics now, nor am I talking solely about Paraguay. Consciously or unconsciously, I have always acted on a broader scale. My interest has always extended to the whole Latin American experience and to the long-range problem of Latin American integration. At some point, concrete measures will have to be taken towards integration, otherwise Latin America will go from bad to worse. There are definite signs that things are moving the right way. This is especially so in view of a closer relationship with Spain. Spain is spending a good deal of political energy and money to help Latin America. The Spaniards have become involved in Nicaragua and Chile.

By the end of the century, the Hispanic-American community will have a population of 600 million. This is a social, political, and historical fact that may help bring about Latin American integration. Within this broad canvas of utopian vision, we now have to face the details.

Q.   Paraguay, which remained isolated for so long, is now threatened by a class of people known as the *brasiguayos*. They are those who left Paraguay in search of land and a better life in Brazil but are now returning and find themselves on the fringe of Paraguayan society.

A.   What you're talking about is those Brazilians who have been buying land and settling in Paraguay. The term now also used is *portuñol*. They are Brazilians living along the border with enough money to have bought land – in some cases, sizeable tracts – and there are some 350,000 of them. These settlers have peacefully invaded the whole east and northeast of Paraguay from a bit below Iguazú all the way to the Altos de Guairá and even farther north. It is an expansionist movement; Brazil is an expansionist country. It's a land rush rather than a gold rush, and it extends right up to Bolivia and the iron mines of Tumi. These vast expanses of land were bought very cheaply from members of the new Stroessner oligarchy, mostly army officers and land speculators, such as a certain Chilean who bought up huge tracts and carved them up into lots for resale. As a result of so much foreign settlement, Paraguayan troops were moved in, and all this is creating a problem. The situation is something like the Israeli colonization of the West Bank of the Jordan. At the moment, people are too caught up in daily survival to worry about this, but with the number of new colonists equalling the number of landless Paraguayan peasants a painful and politically volatile situation is in the making. These rich outsiders are buying up the most potentially fertile land in Paraguay. Almost all of it was virgin forest, which was cleared for the Itaipú dam. Nothing of this is known outside Paraguay, and it is a much more serious problem than our local political difficulties.

Q.   On the subject of your novel *I the Supreme,* would a bit more publicity in the English-speaking world have helped?

A.   Call it retirement to winter quarters, if you like, but I find myself less and less interested in literary politicking. I know it has a certain promotional value, but there is also the ethics of it. I am talking about the fact that we have Latin American writers today who are dollar millionaires.

Q.   Thanks to Carmen Balcells.

A.   Yes, she is my agent but she hasn't made a millionaire of me yet. I'm a maverick. I keep telling Carmen that I want to stay poor, that I want to be in control of my own personal and ultimate freedom. But there are writers who are getting rich, and they are on a dizzying pinnacle and no doubt find it hard to look down. Nor are they interested in anything that does not keep them up there.

Those of us who take another view are few. It's no good pretending we are revolutionary writers. We are grounded in the Western world and are *petits bourgeois* writers. This means that, consciously or unconsciously, we are cultivating literary forms to say something new. This makes me reflect on the future of the bourgeois liberal writer in Latin America today. The problem is serious. It involves a good deal of soul-searching and has its risks. One of these is that of jumping on a political bandwagon – something I am not about to do. I am still a free lance but with a very clear idea about the world I come from.

The situation of the Latin American fiction writer is becoming problematic in the social sense. This does not happen anywhere else. The publishing industry is in the hands of multinationals, who don't give a damn about discovering new talent or finding any coherence in the oppressed field of culture. The philosophy of big money is not at all helpful.

Q.   At present these multinational publishers are on the increase. The writer who can find his way into them is going to be financially rewarded. But the chances of any Third World writer going farther than his tiny publisher in south India or Sierra Leone will be slim.

A.   The day of the independent writer is over, that's obvious. As long as the multinationals hold all the cards, he can't compete. I am published by multinationals. I know of no independent publisher in Latin America today apart from Nueva Imagen in Mexico. But houses like Orfila or Siglo Veintiuno or Losada or Sudamericana, in Buenos Aires, which used to be independent, have been taken over in stock market deals. This is part of the nightmare of the *petit bourgeois* writer, who now finds himself in a system that is completely closed but that still preaches independence and austerity. Someone in my situation is caught in a hopeless contradiction. I have written articles about it, I have even studied the market research of the French multinational publishers. Each of them has a hand in the country's eight annual prizes. This seems to me a sign of utter decadence. The writer in France must work for one of the annual prizes, otherwise he can't sell his books. He has to choose a prize, he has to choose an audience, and he has to choose a subject for that audience. He has to have files on all this. If I had to work under these conditions I'd rather plant potatoes in Patagonia.

Q.   You could get rich doing that now that Argentina plans to move its capital there.

A.   There is no solution to this problem for the individual writer like myself. Of course, I can't compare myself with the princes, who number some ten or twelve. The rest of us are mere acolytes, and our incomes are in proportion. Not that this bothers me much; one can always manage one's finances. But how much writers earn affects their moral state.

When the so-called boom in Latin American writing got international attention, we had to take advantage of it. That boom is now over, but it left a permanent mark. Those who did well are now financially secure. At the same time, we have a huge mass of people in Latin America who have no acquaintance with culture and don't even know what a book is. I don't think a writer should cut himself off too much from the spirit of his time, but he should not lower his standards. The one thing I have learned in all these years is not to lower mine. Somehow, I must make *El fiscal* (The Public Prosecutor), the novel I am writing now, a better book than *I the Supreme*. I have been incubating this new novel for several years now.

Q.   You have begun writing it?

A.   I'm working on it. I'm trying to find the form to cast it in. My chief problem is always that of finding the right form. I am constantly told, 'You keep writing in a different style; every one of your books is different.' This is because I am always searching. In Paraguay we have no literature, so I have no tradition behind me, no design to take off from. I have to be my own magician every day.

Q.   You remarked somewhere that it was strange that the English reader should first come to your work with *I the Supreme*, which you regard as your most difficult book. Did you actually say that?

A.   I don't remember saying it. As you know, the book was first published in New York and then in London, twelve years after it was written. By then I was quite well known in American and Canadian universities, especially in comparative literature departments, but not in England. Besides, my only other book in English was an early novel, a rather bad translation of *Son of Man*, published by Gollancz in 1965.

Q.   Then you were passed over by the boom?

A.   I wasn't part of it because I came before it. The only book of mine that might have been involved in the boom was *Son of Man*, but that came out in Spanish in 1960, and by then the Latin American novel had taken another path. *Son of Man* simply didn't fit in. That's when the boom peaked, not only financially but in terms of a whole process of absorbing influences and models from the English-speaking world. Faulkner above all.

Q.   Yes, I remember your having spoken of Faulkner long before publishing *I the Supreme*.

A.   He was the master of a whole generation and of the boom as well. Hemingway, Faulkner. Someone else I read – I don't know whether he influenced me but I read him – was Salinger. But the significant thing is that our literature, our Hispanic-American culture, only produces anything new when we turn to a culture quite different from the Spanish. Modernism and romanticism, for example, diverged from the influence of Spain towards France.

The whole creative strength of the boom was that it assimilated Faulkner's model. García Márquez shows this influence not so much in *One Hundred Years of Solitude* as in his stories. So too do anti-baroque writers like Rulfo, himself a Faulknerian, or Benedetti, the Uruguayan. We are all in a way followers of Faulkner, or at least we find support in him that we have not found anywhere in Spanish literature. Something similar happened to Spanish intellectuals like Ortega and the philosophers. They left Spain and quickly found that Spanish was two or three centuries behind.

Q.   Are your books sold in Paraguay?

A.   Yes, they are. In Paraguay, literature is not regarded as subversive. Years ago, before I began my head-on battle with Stroessner, an independent publisher called El Lector published an edition of *Son of Man*. My books are sold, but they are extremely expensive. Every school textbook has passages from my work.

Q.   That surprised me when in Paraguay – not only that you are studied but that books are so expensive.

A.   It should be pointed out that Paraguayans don't read fiction. History or chronicles, yes, but not stories or novels. Paraguayans simply are not in the habit of reading, not even if you give your books away.

Q.   This form that you are searching for, did it lead you to *I the Supreme*, which in many ways is a historical recreation rather than fiction? I remember our speaking fifteen years ago in Buenos Aires about Parish Robertson. You were looking for correspondence of his, knowing that I was writing my history of the English in Argentina. You have depicted the two Robertson brothers in *I the Supreme* exactly as they were. This is fiction but it is also an historical recreation without being an historical novel. Where does the balance fall?

A.   It's not easy to answer. I can tell you what my intention was but I am not altogether sure about the result. I did not want to write history; I set out to transform it into fictional characters. Like *Son of Man*, in its way, *I the Supreme* is anti-history rather than history.

I was deliberately going against accepted Paraguayan history, which was written by the conquerors – Bartolomé Mitre and his followers and in turn by Paraguayan historians. Paraguayans make a lot of noise about the war of 1870, and this is what my book *El fiscal* is about. It's an attack on the historians.

Q.   Can you tell us something about *El fiscal*?

A.   The background is this: when I began reading that Paraguayan history had been written by Argentine historians, I found it had not described either the facts or the reality of Paraguay. As victors in the War of the Triple Alliance, the Argentines had their own view of their triumph over the backward country they had set out to free from a tyrant. This too was a kind of fiction, far more advanced than true fiction, the pure novel. Argentine historians had created a work of historical imagination. I had to destroy that, or bring it to a breaking point. I work with a great deal of apparatus – notes, quotations, and so forth – and not only with this literary phenomenon of the intertext, by which I mean original texts that I use in my own way. What I am doing here, then, is not writing a new work but stealing outright. That's why – as in *I the Supreme* – I am the 'compiler', the person who collects other people's words, which belong to nobody. All these quotations, the fragments of intertext which make up a tapestry are also distortions. What I did in *I the Supreme* was to make a sort of pastiche, a bit like Valle Inclán did in his *esperpento*, and with it saturate an historical idea and then destroy it. For example, take my texts. None of the quotes attributed to the Robertsons is verbatim; they were all deliberately falsified. So too with Mitre and everyone else, including ancient classics.

Q.   But these interpolations, such as Robertson's descriptive letter, are direct quotes, aren't they?

A.   No. If you compare the two, you'll see they aren't.

Q.   I know the Robertson text and I thought when he shoots the bird –

A.   Yes, the episode is true, but the text itself I changed. I deliberately distorted it. My object was to distort all my primary source material, to put it in a blender, a particle accelerator, and come out with something different. I don't know whether I managed it.

Q.   I think you did.

A.   My current book is taking a considerable effort. After the last one, I was traumatized by the plight of my readers. The book is very difficult. At least it was for me writing it! Afterwards, friends came up to me and said, 'I bought your book', as if to say, 'I had to begin somewhere; I now have the book, but reading it is another matter.' And I would say, 'Don't bother reading it; I'll tell you the whole story in ten minutes.' I was worried stiff about anyone having to kill himself reading the book. After that, armed with patience, which for me is a minor form of desperation, I said let's see how it goes. Starting another book right away did not appeal to me, as I was fairly written out. So I began developing the story of *El fiscal* and telling it to myself day by day, because that's how I work. I don't know how to take notes or make plans. I tell myself the story in my head, hearing the sound of it, even asking myself what language it should be written in. A mixture of Spanish and Guaraní, or an older, pure Spanish, or in a neutral sort of Spanish like Valle Inclán's in *Tirano Bandera*? There are no answers to these questions except as they are resolved in the work itself.

Even after I finished *I the Supreme*, I found myself in a state of nightmare and anxiety. I kept dreaming I was in an enclosed space without even a chink. With my fingernails I kept feeling for a crack, and when I woke up my nails were broken and bleeding. I had been scratching the bedstead and the wall.

One of the basic problems in my new book was to decide who I was writing for, since I was never going to be read by any Paraguayan. A book implies a message, communicating with someone. What it came down to was that I had nobody to communicate with. This made things hard, but with no particular reader in mind my worries about the reader vanished. I no longer write for anyone, which I think is the way to write for everyone. Nor do I think in terms of large printings. All this is my answer to your question about whether *I the Supreme* is an historical novel. It isn't; it's an anti-historical novel, written to explode the false myths of history. The same goes for *El fiscal*. They'll shoot me in Paraguay when they read about López, who is Paraguay's national hero, though I don't depict him as really bad. But I'll be condemned anyway.

I'm not just doing it out of literary bravado; I'm doing it out of a deep-seated need.

Q. Who is this public prosecutor?

A. He's not López nor anyone else; in fact, López is very much in the background. Nor do I touch on the war, except that the novel begins at the end of the war when López is killed, run through with a spear and shot. The period of the story (not the historical chronology) is from that moment until the Itaipú turbines are switched on.

There is no conventional narrative line but there are several narrative nuclei. It's not until the end of the novel, for instance, that we find out who the public prosecutor is. He is the son of one of the attorney generals under López at the time the war ended in 1870. Born with a physical disability, he constructs an organization in his mind which is a repeat of everything that has ever happened in Paraguay and every disaster of his own period. Another theme is the search for the Lynch treasure. But it's not really the Lynch treasure; the book deals with the whole myth of the search for gold in the Americas. We are always looking for things like the city of the Caesars in Patagonia – it's that type of myth. And ultimately it is the attempt to discover the treasure that each of us has within. The story is not told quite that way but is reflected very simply through the action. It has none of the difficulties of I the Supreme. I want it to be read like a serial; it is a serial. I had to invent something new, a completely normal Spanish with internal subtleties which will not be noticed. I have reverted to a taste for classic storytelling.

Q. Going back to I the Supreme, there is an anecdote about Carlos Fuentes and Mario Vargas Llosa's idea of getting together several Latin American authors to write long stories about dictators. Is that how you arrived at I the Supreme?

A. I had the idea for I the Supreme long before that, in fact, from the time I first thought about writing. I had actually written about the Supremo in a story called 'Lucha hasta el alba' (Struggle Till Daybreak) when I was only fourteen. I lost the story and came across it again years later. Two pages were missing, but I restored them. There is even a murder in which someone's head is cut off with a stone. Then there's a rabbi, although a Paraguayan rabbi is inconceivable; there was also a man called Zachariah. In my village there was an old man we called Zachariah. He wore a tiny straw hat that he never took off. It was really just the crown of the hat stuck to his head. My mother once told me he was a rabbi. Both this experience and the Supremo are in my story.

What Fuentes goes around saying with a sort of ingenuous, adolescent pride is that Latin American literature exists because of him. That's what he said in a long newspaper or magazine article that I once read somewhere. He had written me a letter saying he was thinking of putting together a collection of stories about dictatorships and was I interested. There have been a number of dictators in Paraguay – López, for example, who, being a bit of a folk hero, is much more palatable, and then there was Francia, the Supremo. I answered Fuentes, saying I could write about Francia, who had been a bogeyman for us as children. Cortázar was going to write not about Perón but about Evita Perón, and so forth.

Q. It's a wonderful anecdote, because so much of Latin American writing is about the subject of dictators.

A. But we Latin Americans did not invent the dictator; our forerunner, in a certain sense, was Valle-Inclán and, in my case, Conrad's *Nostromo*. Like a great deal else in Latin America, the dictator was brought in from outside. You can't make claims for any literature's being completely indigenous.

Q. In the review Fuentes wrote of *I the Supreme* for the *London Review of Books* he talks about a pub crawl with Vargas Llosa in the course of which this idea about dictators came to them. The anecdote introduces the review of the book.

A. Carlos Fuentes also reviewed it in the *New York Times*. It was a long review and very helpful as far as sales go. I can only be grateful to him. Later, in London, they referred to the book as a prodigious meditation not only on history and power but also on nature and language. This from one of the best-known London critics, who even read *I the Supreme* twice in one weekend.

Q. He was obviously a fast reader! A comparison has been made between Cambodia and Paraguay, which arises from Francia's idea of closing the country to the outside world and beginning all over again just like Pol Pot with his zero year. Have you ever come across this comparison before?

A.   No. I haven't, but Francia's stroke of genius was knowing that if Paraguay was to stay an independent republic – which was his intention from the outset – the only way to do it was to seal the country off. Not only was there chaos all around Paraguay, a kind of orgy of blood, but there was an understandable attempt on the part of the Province of Buenos Aires, which was at war with the other provinces of the Argentine Confederation, to drag Paraguay into the conflict. From the point of view of centralist Buenos Aires, Paraguay was a rebel province. In this they were right, but from Francia's viewpoint the only choice was to cut the country off completely. He did so because he knew he had scant forces, and to have sent them abroad would have laid him open to the risk of invasion.

Within the country, he could manage with his three thousand men, which was barely an army. They could scarcely fire a gun, even though he had taught them to. What could a small army of yokels do against Argentina's seasoned troops and caudillos like Paz or Quiroga or Urquiza or even Rosas himself? Francia could not have held out for long against such a monstrous enemy once the other neighbouring countries were lined up in the fray. Once he had created the myth of an impregnable fortress, he began oppressing the country itself, destroying everything. This is where history takes issue with Francia. As a matter of fact, Francia was an elected dictator, voted in by a show of hands by a thousand deputies. He was a dictator in the ancient Roman sense, as Bolívar had also been. When Francia was made head of the government, one of a Triumvirate of Consuls, he said, 'Very well, but I won't accept the post unless I am given half the arms.' And he took them – but the half that worked. All the other heroes of independence were out on a spree. The only one who functioned was Francia, who had grabbed most of the guns and turned the Congress into a temple ringed by his private army.

What I find interesting is that, whatever Francia's aim, self-determination was achieved in Paraguay for the first time in Latin America. Oddly enough, this self-determination was brought about not by the armies of Liberation or by Bolívar or by generals but by a civilian. Having established independence, territorial sovereignty, and self-determination, Francia got around to feeding the hungry population.

Q.   So it could be said that, for better or worse, Paraguay exists today thanks to Francia. Otherwise it would have been cut up and divided between Brazil and Argentina. What remained of the country created by Francia, then, provided the foundation for Paraguay to emerge from one war and, sixty years or so later, to plunge into another – the Chaco War.

A.   That's true, but the country was completely destroyed and half its territory was taken away. I think that back in 1870 the whole country should have been shared out among the victors. What prevented this? There was nothing left, absolutely nothing, and everyone would have welcomed this measure. Two hundred thousand square kilometres were lopped off each side of the country, and occupying Brazilian troops remained in Paraguay for seven years.

Q.   But as long as he lived, Sarmiento, who was president of Argentina at the time, was opposed to the splitting up of Paraguay.

A.   That's because Mitre and after him Sarmiento wanted to annex the whole of the Chaco. This became a problem between Argentina and Brazil, who nearly went to war over it. The carving up of Paraguay was exactly like the partition of Poland by the Soviet Union and Germany in 1939. There had been such rivalry between Brazil and Argentina that the Argentines pulled out of the war leaving the work to the Brazilians. In the end, when the final defeat came with the death of López, the two victors reached an agreement over reparations that left Paraguay with war debts so huge they could never be paid. We were paying off these loans, made to us by London, right up until the Chaco War in 1932. Paraguay's destiny has been tragic; I suppose this aspect of it is what's comparable to Southeast Asia.

Q.   Tell us a bit more about what is in *El fiscal*.

A.   Madame Eliza Lynch, the younger López's Irish mistress, bought herself a piano in Paris said to have belonged to Chopin. This piano was hauled along in the great retreat, four hundred wagonloads containing the national patrimony as well as Madame Lynch and López's personal treasure. They buried it in remote spots and then had the wagon drivers shot to keep them silent. This was what gave me the idea for the book.

Q. In your book, do they bury the piano too?

A. No, the piano ends up in an immense dune. They can't carry it so they leave it behind in the sand, and it gives birth to a myth of its own. Somehow the wind blowing over the piano wires turns it into a magical piano.

Q. I've got a story about Madame Lynch's furniture as well. I came across it in Government House in La Rioja. A certain provincial governor acquired these pieces, Empire chairs and sofas, which once had gold braid, when Madame Lynch's belongings were dispersed after she left Buenos Aires. I saw them in the governor's waiting-room and office.

A. The wagons were retreating to their last capital, a beautiful little village in the middle of the mountains, where they set up a large field hospital. When the Brazilians entered, they bombarded it and burned it to the ground. But a few hours before the Brazilian attack, an Italian, an apothecary by the name of Parodi, was put in charge of the retreating wagons. He was very efficient and was made guide of the wagon train; having escaped with their lives, they continued their exodus. As they could go no farther, they began burying the treasure out in the marshes. I learned all this from one of Parodi's grandchildren – it's an incredible story and almost worth a novel in itself – who had married a doctor friend of mine who lives in Buenos Aires. I even have Parodi's papers. After the war, this family took advantage of the offers of various provisional Paraguayan governments, whose only aim was to raise money from anywhere. They sold off what had been common land, and for a song the Parodi family bought a stretch of land as big as a European country. It was full of the richest maté plantations of the north. This land sale was a terrible thing, because Paraguay had managed to establish a system of common lands, which had become a completely accepted, popular institution. This is how the new oligarchy arose; it followed on the one that had been destroyed, the one López set up after all that sort of thing had been abolished by Francia.

Q. Then there's the story about the sale of the papers of the National Archives, which the Brazilians got their hands on and sold off for kindling. And is your public prosecutor going to go on until the Chaco War?

A. No, at a given moment he disappears. What I'm trying to work out is how to tell the story. There's a story within a story, one of extortion that concerns the Parodi papers. I don't tell the story myself but present it through various characters, trying to pick up the threads of what is a very secret story. A number of families of the first rank are involved, and even though I give them other names they are all identifiable. This is a story of the Atridae, a very narrow society where everyone is related.

Q. Which would be only natural in a country closed off for two or three generations.

A. And with total inbreeding. This novel is the main thing in my life. I find writing very hard, so I only write when I can't hold back any longer. But I very much wanted to write this book, because it's a good story and also because the source material is history that's been lived, not written.

Q. Let's jump ahead in time now. What position did you take in the big split among Latin American writers over the Heberto Padilla affair back in 1971? García Márquez went one way, Fuentes and Vargas Llosa another. Were you on the sidelines?

A. I stayed completely out of it. First, it seemed to me a very minor business. Second, I later found out a number of other things, such as Padilla's domestic problems with his wife. Besides, I was never in that clique of top writers, especially during the boom years. I don't know Cuba; I've been invited there every year since the Casa de las Américas was founded but I've never gone. And yet my expulsion from Paraguay in 1982 was over my supposedly having been to Cuba twice. I'd been reported as being a raving Communist, which was untrue. Later I saw the files. They were the sort of thing that embassy intelligence services keep on their countrymen who visit Cuba, only these were forged. It was a list of names with the points of entry and exit from Cuba.

Q. So your name is on a list for having done something you did not do.

A. Yes, it's this sort of thing that makes you angry in Paraguay or in any dictatorship. They give no explanation for anything they do; they just say this guy is some sort of a grey eminence, so we'd better get rid of him. I have never committed any kind of subversive act, and whatever I've said I've always said knowing I could be shot for it, but I have never been politically active. I can't even have the luxury of bragging that I've been involved in underground political activities. I have, of course, always had my own fairly consistent political viewpoint.

Q. What do you think of the debate between Mario Vargas Llosa and Günter Grass? Despite what's been said about Vargas Llosa's having moved to the right, there is some truth to his criticism of European intellectuals who promote and support revolutions in other countries that they don't want to see in their own. This is the basis of Vargas Llosa's defence of capitalist democracy, the kind of democracy he wants for Latin America. What Günter Grass says in his support of left-wing revolutions against Latin American dictatorships is fine and his heart's in the right place. But Vargas Llosa criticizes him, as a German, for supporting revolutionaries in other countries while wanting bourgeois peace in his own.

A. I don't think these things can be reduced to such simplistic terms. What other kind of revolution can Günter Grass want for Latin America, where there are only dictatorships and authoritarian governments set up by imperial democracy? That's what Vargas Llosa doesn't take into account; he justifies all his arguments on the grounds that as a German Grass has no right to express an opinion on Latin America. The fundamental issue in Latin America is not the fact that the Soviet Union has Cuba planted there, a little Communist island, and Nicaragua, another island of Communism. What should concern us is the struggle against dictatorships like those of Pinochet and Stroessner and all the other military juntas that have come to power, in coups against their respective peoples, in order to guarantee the interests of imperial democracy – in other words, the United States. If Vargas Llosa is going to leave out this factor, which to me is the central issue –

Q. He does.

A. Günter Grass can be allowed to make mistakes about Latin America, but people like Vargas Llosa and I, whatever interests we may be defending, must not. Here in Latin America we have an imperial power, on which we are totally dependent and which is the cause of all our ills. This imperial power has intervened with military force in the affairs of Latin America and the Caribbean more than two hundred times. The last occasion was Grenada, but it goes all the way back to the war with Mexico. I consider Mario Vargas Llosa a friend, but I would take issue with him. I don't deny him the right to change his mind and his political position. As a middle-class writer, an individualist, a liberal, he can do this. But he should not deliberately lie – that's what I criticize him for – nor should he make a career of gaining public opinion abroad about the situation in Latin America. You can't compare Fidel Castro's regime, with which I am not in complete agreement, or Ortega's, with those of Stroessner and Pinochet. The former are popular revolutionary movements that arose out of struggles against the dictatorships of Batista and Somoza, those old crooks and murderers of Latin American so-called democracy. If we are going to say that Castro and Stroessner are the same, then we simply can't have a serious discussion. Here I agree with Günter Grass. I also take issue with Vargas Llosa over García Márquez. I applaud García Márquez not necessarily for his political views but for his total commitment to them and to Cuba.

Q. What is the current illiteracy rate in Paraguay?

A. Sixty per cent. Official figures lie about the extent of bilingualism. There is an extensive rural area where only Guaraní is spoken, and people there don't know a single word of Spanish. In what category do you put them? Literacy programmes promoted by present-day officialdom are aimed towards integration into society, which means they are in Spanish. Compared with Cuba, our situation in Paraguay, both as writers and revolutionaries, is limited. Moreover, I do not believe that revolutionary literature can appear all at once or by decree.

My novel *El fiscal* will make no concession to socialist realism or to any of the inventions of world-weary people. I am very interested in Cuba and Nicaragua not because I wish to defend their revolutionary regimes but because they are part of Latin America. If we share the concept of the integration and sovereignty of Latin America, then we cannot allow it to be fragmented. If a Communist revolution were to take place in Paraguay, what would the orthodox political reaction be? To cut Paraguay out and send it to the United States to be put in a concentration camp? We are Latin America and we must stick together. The minute the United States sets foot in Nicaragua, we all know what will happen next. They'll shoot first and ask questions later.

I know I have the freedom to say anything I want, whether I am listened to or not, and I know this isn't so in Cuba or Nicaragua, but I still feel morally obliged to defend those countries and their people. This does not imply taking political or ideological sides. I find that in my work I must go on defending my personal freedom against all incursions. But this also involves my taking social responsibility.

1987

MARIO VARGAS LLOSA:
FROM PARIS TO POLITICS

On 10 June 1990, Mario Vargas Llosa was defeated in the Peruvian presidential elections. He had to go back to being a writer. During the long campaign he drew world political attention to his country, which had previously been noticed only for guerrilla activities. For a writer in Latin America to aspire to or reach the highest levels of public life is not at all surprising. The novelist Rómulo Gallegos became president of Venezuela; Jorge Amado was a member of the Brazilian congress; Pablo Neruda was Chile's ambassador to France; Octavio Paz once represented Mexico in India. The list is long and runs from the last century right down to the present. Such postings and appointments seem quite natural.

This is why it was not unusual in 1988 for Mario Vargas Llosa to begin campaigning for the presidency of Peru, though he looked a bit too clean, too suave, for the cutthroat business of politics. The rumours about his sexual encounters seemed more in character, and his critics faulted the man for his great vanity. Whether the rumours were true or not does not matter. Never stop a good rumour; in some ways it helps an artist's career. In Mario's case there were so many rumours. Such is the risk for handsome men.

But whatever has been said about him in the back-biting, insecure corridors of academe, Mario Vargas Llosa has to his name some of the great novels of twentieth-century Latin American literature. He is honest in his aspirations and in his beliefs, insofar as they appear in his writing. History, if not the book reviewer, will only be able to judge him on that. The approach of European journalists to the subject of Vargas Llosa during the election campaign was sometimes amusing. While he was in front they fawned on him and agreed that he must be a good writer. When he failed to win the first round, the same press which had praised him turned against him. All those free air tickets to Peru that the newsmen of Europe hoped to get from Vargas Llosa had he won were now in doubt. The tone of the articles was suddenly different and shabby.

Mario Vargas Llosa's books as much as his charm and ability to deal with the most controversial issues have made him a household name both in Peru and far from his home in Lima. This combination has also won him cover stories in *Newsweek* and the Spanish weekly *Cambio 16*, as well as in *Caretas*, the Lima weekly for which he wrote when he and the editor were young friends starting out on the road to success.

Mario and I met in Barcelona at the first post-Franco congress of the Catalan Centre of PEN. It was a time for celebration and endless social rounds, as Catalan writers could at last meet openly. This was in 1978, some years before the Peruvian novelist went to live for part of each year in London. In England it became easier to keep in touch. We would meet two or three times a year. International PEN was one of our links.

The last time we met as ordinary citizens, before he began running for the presidency, was for dinner at my home in London. It was prior to the launch of his Libertad Movement in Peru, which started him down the long political road. Salman Rushdie was there too, a little embarrassed because he had just given Mario's novel *The Real Life of Alejandro Mayta* a bad review in the *Guardian*. It was October 1986. George Theiner, the Czech-born editor of *Index on Censorship*, who died in July 1988, was present, as were the journalists Neal Ascherson and Isabel Hilton, and a former Tanzanian cabinet minister, Mohamed Babu. A few days earlier, I had chaired a talk of Mario's at one of English PEN's quarterly dinners.

Odd how relationships change. The dinner party was a meeting of friends. After that evening, it would have no longer been possible for me to interview him. Somehow, you do not interview friends. But thankfully there had been interviews in 1981 and 1982.

The latter of these took place in March 1982 at a service flat in London when Vargas Llosa was in town on a short visit. Latin America seemed very far from Sloane Street, though only three or so months later it would loom large as the Falklands/Malvinas conflict drew closer to war. What Mario and I talked about was exile and estrangement among the community of Latin American writers.

Q. Do Latin American authors need exile as an incentive to their writing? Is exile good or bad for them?

A. I don't think there is a rule that applies to all exile. Extraordinary literary works, both historically and socially, have been stimulated by exile. It is worth pointing out that some of the most important books in Latin American literature were written – and often published – abroad. One of the pillars of Peruvian culture is the Inca Garcilazo de la Vega's *Royal Commentaries*. Garcilazo was an illegitimate half-caste and Latin America's first native-born writer of distinction. He wrote his book twenty years after leaving Peru and settling in a small village in the south of Spain. These seventeenth-century commentaries are not only a literary monument but they place the mestizo squarely in Peruvian history and culture. Domingo Faustino Sarmiento's *Facundo* is another example. First published in Chile in 1845, this book is vital to the understanding of Argentine history.

Nostalgia obviously played a strong part in the writing of *Facundo*, so we can't say that distance always makes for a clear perspective and more objective writing. Exile can even usefully distort an author's vision. So there is no rule. Sometimes exile is productive and stimulating, but for writers who need the living presence of their native reality to be able to write about it, exile can be crippling.

Q. Where were your books written?

A. *Los jefes*, a collection of short stories, was written in Peru. But my first novel *La ciudad y los perros*, translated into English as *The Time of the Hero*, was written in Spain. *The Green House* was also written in Europe. The draft of my third novel, *Conversation in the Cathedral*, was done in Peru, but I finished the book in London. *The Cubs* belongs to Paris, and most of my books after that, up to *The War of the End of the World*, were written outside Peru. In my case, expatriation was beneficial. I have almost always written on Peruvian subjects, but I found it easier to write when I removed myself from the everyday concerns of Lima.

In spite of this, I regret having lived outside Peru for nearly eighteen years. I left the country with the firm idea that I would not stay abroad long. It was a voluntary exile, made possible by a scholarship to complete a Ph.D. in Spain. I spent two years there. Then I went to France and stayed for many years. I found a way of life in France that allowed me to write for several hours a day, something I could not do in Peru. And the years slipped by.

But although I do regret the long absence, I was never cut off from Peru. On the contrary, I think those years gave me a closer tie with my background. Paris gave me time to understand what about Peru was important and what was secondary to my own reality. Above all – and this is what I have to be grateful to exile for – it made me feel more Latin American than Peruvian. I came to understand that Latin America was itself a cultural community. Without this context, it is difficult to understand what it is to be Peruvian, Bolivian, Ecuadorian, Colombian, or Venezuelan. In Peru I could not see that. I needed the distance of exile.

Our countries often give us all good reasons to go into exile, not just writers and those who leave for political reasons. For them exile is not chosen but imposed. The rest of us may find that our native circle is too small, too constricting, and offers no stimulus for creativity. Then it's time to leave, to seek out an atmosphere where literary aspirations can find a meaning and justification. Often this is a matter of landing a job that will pay for food and board and the time to go on writing or painting.

When I left Peru, to make ends meet I had been doing seven different jobs. I had married young, so my writing, which for me was the most important thing, I could turn to only on Sundays or weekdays between 9.00 and 11.00 p.m., when I was dead tired. That was an aberration, because what I felt was the justification for my life took up an insignificant part of my day. My time was filled with activities which had nothing to do with literature.

Q.   What were those jobs?

A.   I worked on the news desk at Radio Panamericana, some of the experience of which went into *Aunt Julia and the Scriptwriter*. I worked at the library of the Club Nacional as a research assistant to a Peruvian historian. I wrote for the Sunday supplement of *El Comercio*. I wrote for *Turismo* magazine. Quaintest of all was a job for the Public Charity, which was trying to compile records of the old cemeteries in the Spanish colonial parts of Lima. We had to remake the original register, which had been lost. There was no record of who had been buried where. I had to check the inscriptions on the tombstones and fill in cards. I was paid for each death recorded. All these were different jobs, which I carried out at different times of the day. I was also teaching part time. My life was completely devoted to alimentary employment. There was no time for what I wanted to do most, which was to write.

Q.   So exile marked the beginning of your literary career?

A.   Yes. In Paris I was lucky to find work, first in one news agency, then at the Agence France Presse, and later at Reuters in their French-language service. Those jobs took up part of my day but left me time to write. That was what weighed most, I think, in my decision to stay on in Europe. It seemed vital to be able to give the greater part of my time, energy, and concern to what interested me most.

Q.   Were you ever forced into exile for political reasons?

A.   No, not into political exile. I returned to Peru in 1974. Up till then I had been abroad of my own choice. Although for as long as I can remember I have always been against military regimes, I never had to flee one. I went back to Peru at the time when the military government had nationalized the mass media – newspapers, radio, the lot. This was when the dictatorship had become more intolerant and intransigent. It was a bad time. I had many arguments with the regime, but I did not have to leave.

Q.   When you cast your mind back to the mid-1960s, a time when Latin American writing was just beginning to break out of a limited circle of readers and find audiences abroad, what do you remember?

A.   Those were very beautiful years. I remember them with nostalgia. There was a kind of coming together of Latin American writers – those who were living abroad or simply travelling abroad. We met in Europe, and our paths kept crossing. A number of strong links were established among us and with Europe, all this at a time when Latin American writing began to gain an audience it never had before. People were beginning to talk about Latin America and its literature; writers were being translated and published. A cordial, fraternal relationship between the writers of our different countries grew up.

There was a project, which in the end came to nothing, that seemed to crystallize that spirit of union. Carlos Fuentes had the idea one day during a pub crawl in London. He thought of putting together a book for which each contributor would produce a piece on a dictator of his country. Fuentes was going to write about Antonio López de Santa Anna from the last century. I was going to write about Luis Sánchez Cerro from the beginning of this. Augusto Roa Bastos was going to write about Dr José Gaspar Rodriguez de Francia. I think Fuentes may have been going to write about Argentina's Juan Domingo Perón as well but I'm not sure. Gabriel García Márquez was going to write about Gustavo Rojas Pinilla. Borges did not come into it. There was a Brazilian – I can't remember if it was Jorge Amado – and from Chile there was either Jorge Edwards or José Donoso. Anyway, for Chile there was to be a story about José Manuel Balmaceda, who committed suicide in 1891. He was not a dictator like the others but more of a caudillo. In Chile it was difficult to find dictators, so we had to make do with a caudillo. Of course, since then, Chile has more than made up for this omission. But, as I said, the project came to nothing. Oddly enough, later there were novels which seemed to have had their origin in Fuentes's plan. I am thinking of Roa Bastos's *I the Supreme*. I do not know if Gabriel García Márquez's *Autumn of the Patriarch* arose from that, but to me the original idea had a lot to do with the great closeness and fellowship of the time, with an identification with what was Latin American. Subsequent political events were to break down this unity. But then, in the 1960s, it was easy to feel united. We were all against the same things. At some point Cuba was our common bond, just as later Cuba became one of the elements that caused our split and the deep disagreements that followed. The case of Heberto Padilla was a main factor.

Q. Do you see any prototypes among Latin American exiles? One comes to my mind – that of William Henry Hudson, the naturalist and novelist, who was born in Argentina and went to live in England, never to return to the River Plate. He spent his life in Britain longing for the wide open South American spaces of his childhood and youth, yet he was aware that there he would never have had the writing career or the success that he had in London.

A. I think that what is said of children is also true of writers. They want what they cannot have. Only with writers the attitude is more sophisticated and subtle. Distance is an important source of stimulation. What would the novel be without those experiences, those adventures, which are far away – exotic scenery, events that memory enriches?

You mention Hudson. I think of Joseph Conrad, a writer I greatly admire. What would Conrad the writer have been without exile? All his work is immersed in a strong nostalgia for a world he knew as a young man, a world of adventure, which he preserved in his memory and which is the great driving force of his writing.

To my mind, such a force is very much present in Latin American literature. The Latin American writer was always being forced to leave, or deciding to leave, his country – especially since the modernist days of the last century. Our writers really move about the world and have become much more universal than European writers, who tend to be deeply parochial. Europeans have a totally provincial, narrow vision.

Don't you find this interesting? Look at the underdeveloped world, with its often quite primitive cultures. Yet in literature it has produced universal attitudes with great simplicity and with much greater frequency than have European societies. Take the British. England has an extremely rich literature, but its modern literature is parochial, one which hardly goes beyond the island's shores. The British can be extremely ignorant of and indifferent to all that occurs beyond their borders. This is the exact opposite of Borges, who appears to be interested in everything in the field of culture the world over. Or Octavio Paz. He can write about Tibetan art or Japanese poetry or a picture in the Tate Gallery. There is a universality which seems to be at the heart of this sort of vocation. This impresses me about Latin American culture, and it must be encouraged and preserved. Such universality is our defence against great distortions, such as nationalism, which cause considerable damage. It is paradoxical that at times primitive countries can produce open, enquiring, absorbing minds.

It is an illusion to believe that a writer starts from scratch, that he works from entirely new ground. In fact, his childhood, his reading, his education, and also the linguistic system in which he operates exert pressure on him which can be enslaving and paralyzing. Here – in conditions which are more favourable, let us say, than those of English, or German, or French writers – is where the Latin American writer begins. The European literary tradition is very rich but at the same time it is crystallized and works in one predetermined direction.

To attempt to innovate deeply in the literary language of a country like England, where the language has such a clear and well-worked tradition, is much more difficult than to attempt to innovate in a medium such as that provided by Peru, Bolivia, Nigeria, or the Ivory Coast.

In finding his way out of a relatively uncultivated field and out of a mass of confused traditions, the Latin American writer runs the risk of one day discovering what has long since been found or following paths which have already been thoroughly explored. This sometimes seems to make the literature of the Third World appear ingenuous, lacking in novelty, repetitive or anachronistic. But it also allows for an ingenuous, innocent approach to the language, to the reality of invention. This gives much of Third World writing a freshness and a boldness in both form and subject, something unusual and hard to find in the great literatures of Western Europe.

1982

GABO IN BOGOTÁ

The front page of *El Espectador* of Bogotá showed Gabriel García Márquez waving to the crowd in the bullring. Six ears had been cut and were offered to him.

At his house in El Retiro on the Monday afternoon that I visited, Mercedes, his wife, answered the door. Sorry, the interview could not take place. Gabo was ill. The doctor was with him. It was a result of the outing to the *toros* on Sunday.

On Tuesday morning he telephoned to explain that he had been unwell but had gone to the *toros* anyway. It had been a special event, organized by journalists in his honour. He could not stay away. It had rained, and he had caught a cold in that almost English weather of Bogotá at nearly 7,000 feet above the tropics. The doctor had ordered him to rest for a week. 'The trouble with rest is that it is exhausting – so terribly boring,' García Márquez said.

Why had he gone to the *toros*? A duodenal ulcer had acted up again, but 'the doctor and I tried to decide what was worse – to go and risk a relapse, not go and let down the press, or not go and say I was ill. Since the last would have prompted rumours that I was dying, we agreed that it was best to go and risk a relapse. Now, let us see if we can cheat the doctor.' A date for my re-visit was set.

García Márquez returned to Bogotá in March 1983 a celebrity and a guest of the country's new president then only four months in office. It was just after Easter, just after an earthquake had destroyed the ancient city of Popayán. Behind García Márquez lay nearly two years of self-imposed exile in Mexico, where he had gone to escape threats against his life which had much in common with the story of his *Chronicle of a Death Foretold*. His death had been foretold. He had not waited for it.

He seemed quite settled. He was living the life of the writer as

113

public figure that seems the destiny of Latin American intellectuals. It had been the same with Pablo Neruda; it was still the same with Mario Vargas Llosa and Ernesto Sábato.

Unlike the colonel of his story, García Márquez has too many people writing to him. He does not answer. 'Some ask for work,' he told me, 'so I send those letters to the ministries or to other public offices that might help. Some are requests for jobs in journalism – those go to *El Espectador*, where I have a weekly column. The commercial propositions go to my agent in Barcelona. And then there are those like researchers and others who just want to write to a well-known author. I can't be bothered with them.'

Conscription into the Latin American establishment of literary lions has not made his views less radical, though perhaps he has become more cautious. He is still obstinately convinced that the Gurkha Regiment went on a rampage in the Falkland Islands during the advance against the Argentine army in June 1982. 'I believe my source,' he says. 'Others may wish to believe a British officer's denial. Okay. But why should I accept his statement?'

García Márquez has been surprised that the Opposition in Britain never made more fuss about his allegations. I said I thought that it was because nobody took them seriously. On the other hand, I was surprised that Argentina had not extracted more publicity value from his accusation after it had been published in *El País*, of Madrid, on 6 April 1983. García Márquez's explanation was that no Latin male would ever admit publicly to buggery. Only the British, he remarked, seem to regale readers with that kind of information in their memoirs.

'I am tied by a commitment not to reveal the name of my source. He will not come forward. I cannot ask him to. I have given my word. One source is secret, the other common knowledge – Daniel Kon's book *Los chicos de la guerra*.' But Kon's collected interviews, in which conscripts were quoted reporting the Gurkha outrages, were all second-hand accounts. Kon, an Argentine journalist, never found a single soldier who had personally suffered the indignities related.

Of all the recent small wars, the Falklands conflict became the most bewildering, García Márquez said. Britain's reaction to Argentina's invasion had been the most surprising factor. 'It was Thatcher's war. She did not care what it cost. No man would have acted like that. An English gentleman would have made peace and been pleased with the bargain.'

And yet, if Britain's reaction was surprising, how much more was that of the United States. 'It has always made such a fuss about extra-continental intervention against small countries – in its attacks on the Soviet Union, for example – and then it joined one of the world's powers against one of its allies on its own continent.'

García Márquez said that at last he could begin to rest now that Golding had succeeded him in the Nobel Prize. Of course he had ideas for novels. But these ideas had to be developed, and that would require time.

As I entered his flat, decorated in white, set in the hillside – my mind on that mystery world of Colombia, of guerrilla wars and drug dealers, and of the contrast between the country's particularly brutal violence and its historical position as one of Latin America's oldest and most stable democracies – García Márquez's welcome was warm, but he was peremptory in his demand for information on his successor, the new Nobel Prize winner William Golding. García Márquez had to write his weekly article for *El Espectador* on Golding. As it turned out, I had to get my Aunt Betty out of her bath at 11.00 p.m. English time to answer my telephone questions at 5.00 p.m. Bogotá time about her neighbour in nearby Bowerchalke, who happened to be Mr Golding. This was for the benefit of my host, who was overwhelmed by the coincidence that his visitor had an aunt living in a village close to the new Nobel laureate. Aunt Betty and I were a little more famous after that, but it soured my interview, because García Márquez only wanted to talk to me about the call to my aunt.

He made no secret of it that his candidate for the Nobel Prize for Literature was Graham Greene. But García Márquez was polite about it. 'The Swedish Academy,' he said, 'cannot forgive Greene's use of the language for his pleasure and entertainment.' García Márquez admitted that his annoyance was tainted by personal acquaintance with Graham Greene. The two shared a close friendship with Fidel Castro and with the late General Omar Torrijos of Panama.

'Graham Greene is the last of the English writers of this century,' claims García Márquez. 'He is good. I often think that there must have been more to his going to Panama than just a social call on Torrijos. Some use must have been made of his old experience in intelligence work, enabling him to establish links with the Sandinistas and take their message to prominent personalities in Europe. I don't know. I just suspect.'

García Márquez cannot suppress his admiration for the English writer. 'I like Greene because he says to hell with everybody. That pamphlet of his on Marseilles – there was something Quixotic about it. It has all the determination of a nineteenth-century exposé.'

He supposed that his own friendship with Castro had won him enemies. 'Some critics cannot forgive not just my support for the Cuban Revolution but my friendship with Fidel. I can pick up the telephone and call Fidel, and what is more he will answer.' Nobody else outside Cuba can do that.

Gabriel García Márquez stretched out in his white leather arm-chair grinning contentedly. 'Good luck to Nobel Prize winners. I want to get back to writing. I am pleased to pass on the crown. The spotlight is on somebody else. The social whirl that came with the prize forced me to grant myself a sabbatical for a year. Living in a village may protect Golding from some of the pressures.' There was a sense of relief in the congratulations he offered William Golding. My Aunt Betty had been the essential link to help García Márquez find out that Golding lived quietly.

'How different it was for us,' the Colombian said, looking at Mercedes. 'It's been a hell of a year. Enjoyable, but hell. At six o'clock in the morning the day the prize was announced, we were invaded by friends carrying bottles of champagne. At two o'clock in the afternoon we abandoned the house to our guests and took rooms in a hotel.' He had been in Mexico then, in exile.

'How wonderful it must be for William Golding to be able to live quietly. How wonderful that an Englishman got the prize. Britain has given the world the great novels of the twentieth century. Not recently, of course, but just think of Conrad, Lawrence, Huxley, and Joyce. Why were they overlooked? This was the century of the English novel, as the nineteenth was of the Russian.'

The telephone rang. For a telephone that was unlisted and the number of which changed every three months, it rang with great frequency. He explained that it was journalists asking his advice or consulting him on a variety of issues. He sounded impatient with the newsroom devotion to *la chiva*, the scoop. 'They hear that a meeting is to take place, and it is enough to report that it will. They do not care about the damage this might do – or bother about the outcome – which may be a better story than just saying there will be a meeting.'

The cause of his impatience did not become apparent until the next day, when the leading newspapers of Bogotá bannered the news that President Belisario Betancur was planning to meet leaders of two guerrilla groups, the M-19 and FARC. When García Márquez discussed progress in the negotiations for peace in Central America, he sounded proud of the efforts of the Betancur government and he was full of praise for the foreign minister, Rodrigo Caicedo Lloreda.

'What I still cannot understand is the remarkable transformation he has undergone. He was, after all, quite reactionary. His family owns a right-wing newspaper, *El Colombiano*. He was a visibly right-wing university dean and a reactionary minister of education. Either he has suffered a change in character or else he is interpreting Belisario Betancur so well that he is working as a progressive.'

As an active observer of the Central American peace process, known as the Contadora Plan, García Márquez wrote in an article: 'Contadora is a Panamanian island in the Pacific Ocean so named because pearls from the neighbouring seas were stored and counted there. At the turn of this century it became a secret paradise for US millionaires, and it became one of the world's most famous refuges when the Shah of Iran went there for a few months before his death. It has required ant-like workers, besieged by opposing interests, to make the new Contadora advance. At present the achievements of Contadora have been too subtle to be regarded as important news. Colombia's press has not given it the attention it deserves.'

Now he remarked, 'Colombia is doing the work that Mexico cannot because of its proximity to the United States.' His regard for Colombia's share in the Contadora group effort makes him withhold criticism of the government and of Colombia. 'Here violence is something you learn to live with. It is part of life – you live with it or leave it.'

Journalists, three of whom have been killed in recent months, had to acknowledge death as part of the profession. The conversation moved to his own idea of a return to journalism, not just as a columnist but as a publisher. His desire to have his own newspaper was newsroom gossip throughout Latin America.

'All that remains for the launch is for me to decide if I can do it. All our market studies show that it is feasible to found a paper on the style of *El País* of Madrid, *El Diario* of Caracas, or *La Opinión* of Buenos Aires. But the studies also say that if I am going to be the editor, I have to work on the paper – be there every day until late at night and not just top the mast-head without ever appearing. I have to decide if I am prepared to sacrifice my own writing for several years to start a newspaper and make it a success. I am not sure I want to make that sacrifice.'

It seemed a very honest remark. The subject slipped, inevitably, to contemporary writing in Latin America.

Carlos Fuentes was leaving the United States, returning home to Mexico. 'Have you seen him?' García Márquez asked. 'He says he wants to be home for the apocalypse. He says these things waving his arms about, shaping the explosion with his arms outstretched.' Fuentes was, however, a worried man, according to the Colombian. The Mexican novelist had just told Henry Kissinger's committee on Central America that the United States, not the Soviet Union, might destabilize Mexico in the process of trying to preserve it from contamination by revolution.

'He is going home for the apocalypse,' García Márquez repeated.

The Colombian had stayed out of Fuentes' and Vargas Llosa's fictional encyclopaedic project of the late 1960s, a volume on the dictators of Latin America.

'I was too involved with *Autumn of the Patriarch* – even before *One Hundred Years of Solitude* – and was not prepared to give up what was a major project for what would have been of limited use to me. It was to be called *Los padres de la patria* (The Fathers of the Fatherland), but it came to nothing. Fuentes accumulated information on Antonio López de Santa Anna, but then did not use it. Julio Cortázar toyed with the idea of doing something about Juan Perón, but then I think he wanted to follow the wayward path of the body of Eva Perón after her death in 1952. I think the political circumstances were not favourable. That is a story that remains to be written.

'I know Naipaul did something on that subject,' García Márquez continued, 'but I find him a very bitter man. I don't know why. He sounds so bitter that it damages his writing. I met him in London, when Mercedes and I were there working with the translator of *Autumn of the Patriarch*. Naipaul sounded bitter then and he sounded bitter now in a recent interview.

'Something of Fuentes's project is to be found in Augusto Roa Bastos's *Yo el Supremo*, on Paraguay's dictator, José Gaspar Rodríguez de Francia. And I think Alejo Carpentier used some of the life of Gerardo Machado y Morales, who was overthrown by Batista in Cuba, for *El recurso del método*. But I can't swear to that.

'Mario Vargas Llosa wanted to write about Miguel Odría, or was it Luis Sánchez Cerro, of Peru? I don't remember. Mario and I have not exchanged a word for ten years. He became very aggressive at the time, suspecting me of wanting to go to bed with his wife Patricia. I did not want to. Still, he is a good writer, though he has tremendous obsessions.'

Mario Vargas Llosa and García Márquez had argued in 1977, in a Mexican cinema, and Vargas Llosa had landed a punch that is now famous in Latin American literary gossip.

García Márquez regretted the ill-feeling that had rent the Latin American writing community in the 1960s and he said he did not understand some of the causes of the discontent. For example, Guillermo Cabrera Infante, the expatriate Cuban who sniped at Castro from Gloucester Road, in London, had made a virulent attack on García Márquez in a fulminating review in the *London Review of Books* of *The Fragrance of Guava*, a book-length interview between the Colombian novelist and the journalist Plinio Apuleyo Mendoza.

'Cabrera has no reason to be so bitter. He is a good writer, his books are read everywhere, even in Cuba. I did not think much of *Three Trapped Tigers*, but *Infante's Inferno* is very good.'

But then some things about writers, Latin American writers, he concluded sadly, were beyond comprehension.

1983

WILLIAM GOLDING GLIMPSED
BY HIS NEIGHBOURS

By Gabriel García Márquez

I have always been curious about people's reaction to news that may change their lives. In the case of a writer, I had always asked myself what almost every journalist and friend asked me a year ago. 'What do you feel when you win the Nobel Prize?' In almost every case I have given a different answer, depending on who was asking, for the truth of the matter is that I no longer clearly remember. There had been so many rumours in the days preceding the announcement (just as there are every year) that by the time I got the news I really didn't know what I felt. All hearsay to the contrary, I had the irremediable confirmation on 21 October 1982, at home in Mexico, when the telephone rang at five minutes past six in the morning. Mercedes answered, half asleep, and passed the receiver to me, saying, 'It's Stockholm.' A male voice, speaking perfect Spanish with a slight northern accent, identified itself as that of the editor of Stockholm's most important newspaper and said that the Swedish Academy had made the official announcement five minutes earlier. I am not sure what he said next, because at the moment – thinking about the speech I would have to make two months later when I received the prize in Stockholm – I was over-come with fear. This terror was the one clear feeling I had, not only during the endless days and sleepless nights while I wrote the fifteen hardest pages of my life but right up to the moment I finished read-ing them publicly in the Swedish Academy's lecture hall. Everything that happened after that – up until today – has been mere routine.

I am reminded of this because last Thursday, when I learned that the Nobel Prize for Literature had been awarded to William Golding, I asked myself again, in all sincerity, 'How did he feel when he got the news?' I spent the whole day reading news agency

120

bulletins to see if they would provide an answer. But these reports lacked those details of human interest that do not seem important but that are in fact the ones that move us. That afternoon, however, there occurred one of those events which are far too incredible to be called mere coincidence and which writers steer clear of in the fear that they will not be believed.

At five o'clock on Thursday, as had been arranged for over a week, Andrew Graham-Yooll, from the *Guardian*, in London, called on me to talk about mutual friends and perhaps to interview me. Since he was a fellow countryman of William Golding's, we talked about the topic of the day. We knew everything about Golding that could be learned from books, and I had followed his career closely since, when living in Barcelona, I first read *The Lord of the Flies* in Spanish. *The Scorpion God* and *The Invisible Darkness* came later, but I think that Golding appeared in Spanish long before he wrote these books. So the new Nobel laureate was not as unknown in Spanish as was at first claimed. Moreover, as Graham-Yooll confirmed, in Great Britain Golding is a widely-read, prize-winning author. Still, as we two talked, I kept wondering how William Golding had received the news of his prize and how he had spent his day in Bowerchalke, a village of 600 inhabitants, near Salisbury, where he lives. It was then that the incredible happened. 'An aunt of mine is a neighbour of his near that village,' Graham-Yooll said matter-of-factly. 'If you like, we can telephone her.' He took an address book out of his pocket, and two minutes later Mrs Betty Graham-Yooll heard her phone ring at eleven o'clock at night and had to get out of her bath dripping wet to speak to a nephew over six thousand miles away, who said, 'I'm here with the winner of last year's Nobel Literature Prize, who would like to ask a few questions about this year's winner.' His very British aunt showed no sign of surprise but asked politely for a minute while she dried herself.

My curiosity was satisfied. Unlike us writers from the Americas, who find out the news at daybreak, Europeans hear it at one in the afternoon, the hour when the solemn Lars Gyllensten, the Secretary of the Swedish Academy, makes the official announcement. So that William Golding was not wakened by anyone but heard the good tidings along with everybody else over the air on the midday news.

As glimpsed by Mrs Betty Graham-Yooll, the new Nobel Prize winner is surprisingly like the picture of him that a reader might have formed from reading his books. He is a white-haired, bearded man, who lives with his wife Ann and their two children – a boy and a girl – but who at seventy-two cannot be considered old, because he leads an active life. His second vocation is music, not only as a listener but also as a performer on any of the following instruments: violin, viola, piano, or oboe. His third passion is sailing – as his readers might have guessed and as seems natural in a man who is such an admirer of another great writer of the sea, Herman Melville. Golding's fourth interest is Egyptology. Recently, however, he has taken up a fifth – riding. He had bought a horse, and on fine afternoons he can be seen galloping about the countryside with the air of one who has done it all his life.

Someone I had spoken to before the telephone call to Mrs Graham-Yooll rightly said that it was easy to invent the life of a seventy-two-year-old English writer who lives in the country. 'He is bound to have a dog and to work in his garden on Sundays,' I was told. Golding, who gets up to begin writing at five o'clock in the morning, thereby making time for his other four interests, is not a great flower enthusiast, unlike his wife, who grows orchids which are the envy of the village. Mrs Graham-Yooll affirmed that the Goldings' garden is one of the most beautiful in England. She concluded by saying that she enjoys watching the new Nobel laureate, with his magnificent Viking looks, out riding his horse, and she hastened to add that he is not an unsociable man but that he keeps his distance from the neighbours out of a certain shyness.

Anyway, that Thursday in Bowerchalke passed like any other. Nobody disturbed the Virgilian peace of Ebble Thatch, the thatched cottage where the Goldings received telephone calls and telegrams from all over the world. They and the other 600 villagers are not English for nothing, and they know that while a Nobel Prize does not fall from the skies every day neither is it so important a matter as to warrant disturbing the privacy of a good neighbour – he too doubtless terrified by the speech he will have to make in Stockholm sixty endless days from now.

1983

Editor's postscript, 1989: In revising the above translation, I wrote to William Golding, who now lives in Cornwall, for verification of certain facts. He answered my queries and added: 'Despite García Márquez's amusing guesses, I don't get up at five o'clock and I don't have a dog!'

COLOMBIA WITHOUT GARCÍA MÁRQUEZ

Gabo returned to Mexico City at the end of 1983, and Colombia is a little emptier without him. That is always the feeling prompted by the departure of a friend and hero, even if nobody else leaves. García Márquez did not stay long in Bogotá – about eight months – then left his house up on Carrera Primera and took his duodenal ulcer, his notes, and his plans for a daily newspaper that was never launched, and together with Mercedes moved back to Mexico.

He had tired of Bogotá, and Bogotá of him. The adulatory articles about Colombia's Nobel Prize laureate, short and shallow compositions which only provincial scribblers can write, were printed no more. At the Academy of Letters, the elderly Anglophiles in three-piece pin-striped suits, who had played cricket and read English poetry in English in their youth at the Gimnasio Moderno School and once organized fox-hunts, had ceased to make Gabriel García Márquez feel welcome. After all, he wore the *guayabera*, the open shirt of the people from the Caribbean coast, who lived in tropical heat seven thousand feet below Bogotá. Nor did he ever wear a tie. But because he had won the Nobel Prize, academy members thought it their duty to invite him into the inner circles of official obscurity and so share in the academy's formal favours. But some considered that he had 'lowered the level and quality of the language'. The same sort of people said the same sort of thing about President Belisario Betancur. Colombia's president had 'taken all kinds of people, any old *pata-ancha* into the government. Many of them don't wear ties either.' A *pata-ancha*, or flat-foot, is anyone too poor to afford shoes.

It was Betancur who had invited García Márquez to return from self-imposed exile in Mexico, where Gabo had gone in 1981 to escape death threats attributed to the drug mafia. This was a few days after an earthquake had destroyed the ancient Andean city of Popayán.

The poet Maruja Vieira, the Colombian PEN Centre's secretary, said she would always remember the quake for the terror it gave her to see her house moving with the fragility of a leaf. She had run into the street in her nightdress just after her bath. Another poet, Nestor Madrid-Malo, editor of a remarkable Bogotá literary magazine called *El Café Literario*, said he would always regret having missed seeing Maruja in the street in her nightdress.

But the attitude of Bogotá and the praise of pursed lips were foreign to García Márquez, and he returned to the refuge of Mexico to write a novel.

Ernesto Sábato, the Argentine novelist, author of *On Heroes and Tombs* visited Bogotá in February to talk about Argentine letters and new-found democracy in Argentina, and he was criticized for damning Colombia's democracy with faint praise. Sábato said that he was not politically in agreement with García Márquez, because, unlike the Colombian writer, Sábato was against all dictatorships, while his colleague was only against right-wing tyrants. Sábato had the same disagreement with Julio Cortázar, the expatriate Argentine novelist, who died in Paris at the age of sixty-nine just as Sábato reached Colombia. Perhaps one story has nothing to do with the other. But writers find journeys and demises occasions for praise or slanging. Claude Couffon, the French poet, called Cortázar a 'master of fantasy'. And Sábato, in spite of ideological differences, had praise for Cortázar and then for García Márquez – both friends of Fidel Castro – as valuable representatives of Latin American writing.

At the same time, in Rome, Jorge Amado, the Brazilian writer, told the Communist Party newspaper *L'Unità* that there was no such thing as Latin American literature. The tag was merely a European simplification. Europe liked to see Latin America as André Malraux had seen children. Malraux said that there was genius in the art of children, but it was the same genius in all children. Europe looked on Latin American writing the same way. The pages of its novels were interchangeable – a war, a dictator, a country surrounded by a palisade of rotting bones, and a voluptuous siren who swallowed her lovers. Perhaps such stories had crossed boundaries, because they portrayed Latin America as the confused continent Europeans thought it to be.

*

After recovering from the *soroche* – the crushing ill-feeling brought on by the altitude – travel can be considered. Colombia is a time-machine. From Europe the plane descends in the 1940s, in Bogotá; later, the southern *llanos* may be guaranteed to impart all the discomfort of nineteenth-century travel in bandit country; while in the lost city of Taironas, north of Santa Marta, a pre-Colombian experience seems just around the corner.

Geoffrey Matthews, *The Times* correspondent, leads the way every Saturday to Doña Herta's German restaurant, through the market, where he buys a three-day-old copy of the *Guardian* from a second-hand bookstall that keeps stacks of remaindered volumes of essays about García Márquez.* The English paper is delivered by El Dorado airport ground staff, courtesy of the passengers arriving on the Friday flight of British Caledonian. Copies of *Le Monde* are obtainable from the cleaners on Air France. Reduced prices apply, of course.

Doña Herta's restaurant itself seems to have been remaindered from an age before *Mein Kampf*, from a time when a large German community settled in Venezuela and Colombia. Beggars come into her eating house and are tolerated as a necessary evil. They pick up a coin or two among the patrons, a piece of bread from the proprietor, and if they hang around too long their attention is drawn to a clock that turns the time back as its hands move anticlockwise on a reversed face.

In the street, from every food stall, paper stall, toy stall, and even the clandestine cocaine stall, comes the sound of *ballenato*, the mixture of Cuban and African rhythm which, with *cumbia*, belts out of two radio stations twenty-four hours a day. The stalls of fortune-tellers said they were fully booked for the first two months of the year, but after February trade slackens and the customer off the street can always be fitted in.

Does a Latin American visiting Europe find a sense of unreality everywhere? Why, then, is ordinary, day-to-day reality so different in all the Latin American cities for the European? Take the way a colonel can decide the fate of a society because he disapproves of the way others live their lives. Why would it be extraordinary for any European parliament to authorize the re-introduction of

---

* Matthews died in Bogotá in March 1990, aged forty-four.

cock-fighting? Why is no one in Latin America held accountable for the history he or she makes? Even though I was born in a Latin American capital and am accustomed to its realities, I still often come across public statements – a road sign, political declarations, a list of rules on the conduct of a visitor in a church – that drive me to want to explore the mentality of their originators. In the capitals of Europe a motorist or pedestrian does not wonder at the civil servant who ordered signposts reading, 'It is dangerous not to stop at the red light.' In Europe nobody thinks of not stopping. Another sign – I saw this in Bogotá – reads, 'It is best not to drive when drunk.' Not even in Spain are there trade union graffiti, as there are in Colombia, that tell us, 'Bullfighters fight for their rights.' From October 1983 to February 1984, the length of my link with Colombia, signs and graffiti like these just quoted set me thinking that however much the novels and stories of García Márquez test the limits of the imagination, they are in fact portraying reality. What seems extravagant, or even surrealistic, in Latin America to an outsider is to a Latin American as natural as a simple misunderstanding is in London. It is the same in Peru with Mario Vargas Llosa and in Paraguay with Augusto Roa Bastos. However far their books stretch reality, they often fall short of what is happening all around you every day.

A long white wall yelled in large scrawled letters at passing pedestrians, 'The "disappeared" are the dead without corpses.' How do people in modern societies disappear? They may be arrested, they may be shot, but to disappear? Yet in Latin America 90,000 have 'disappeared' in ten years – 35,000 in Guatemala, nearly 30,000 in Argentina, 2,500 in Chile, maybe 1,000 in Colombia, and 500 in Paraguay. In Argentina, when a person 'disappeared' it was a relief to discover that he was under arrest, even if tortured. In Colombia, it is a relief to learn that a captive is held for ransom by guerrilla bands; the army and the drugs gangs murder their captives.

In Colombia, endemic criminal violence is known as *la inseguridad*, the uncertainty. The word 'violence' is reserved for an event in recent history. A civil war, known as *el bogotazo*, began in 1948 and over the next decade claimed 200,000 lives – this is remembered as *la violencia*. 'The uncertainty' is the name for the current wave of crime that is reflected not just in muggings and snatches but in some twenty kidnappings each month, usually unpublicized abductions inflicted on middle- and even working-class families, for which a ransom of £2,000 might be demanded and paid. Thieves rob the poor because the poor have no defences, no fences round their homes, no alarms on their cars, and only old guns that jam. García Márquez described *la inseguridad* as a sword of Damocles that you got accustomed to living under. Then he left.

For years, the British community of Colombia managed to stand aside from local events, as did the French and the Germans of long residence – unless they were like Doña Herta, who turned the clock back so as to reverse events. It is not out of indifference but because they are somehow different and do not get involved that accounts for the British aloofness. All over Latin America the British are still merchants, not poets or writers or statesmen. It is hard to imagine how the British here manage to be Colombians yet still stay British. There are a thousand of them in the country, perhaps half in Bogotá. In Colombia and Venezuela – as nowhere else in the Americas, not even in British-influenced Argentina – British troops fought for and helped win independence from Spain alongside the army of Simón Bolívar in a manner which earns them special honours to this day.

Whatever is left of their bones lies in the British Cemetery – subscription, 5,000 pesos for British subjects, 15,000 for non-Britons – next to the capital's main burial ground. A railing fence that separates a path for the living from the place of rest of the dead was built with the muskets and bayonets of the British Legion. An archway is inscribed in memory of the last commander of the Albion Battalion, Colonel John Mackintosh, a Londoner, who served in Colombia between 1818 and 1823 and died on 30 May 1846, in Bogotá, aged fifty-seven; in memory of Colonel John Bendle, who died on 5 February 1831, aged fifty-one; and in memory of Captain Charles Smith, an Irishman who died at the grand old age of sixty-three, on 3 April 1853. All around them, in the neatness of an English garden, lie the remains of their youthful officers. Much later came the bodies of many a young Scot who, in the 1870s, tried to make a fortune on the numerous short railway lines built to reach the gold mines of the interior and died in the attempt. Their story is told throughout the old empire.

Somehow, García Márquez left the British out of his fiction. All over Latin America, many say they never understood the British.

1984

Postscript, 1989: García Márquez's latest novel, *The General in His Labyrinth*, about the last months of General Simón Bolívar's life, brings in examples of the great friendship and support that existed between the Liberator and his British officers.

REUNION IN CARACAS

The Venezuelan poet and novelist Arturo Uslar Pietri was awarded one of Spain's most prestigious literary prizes, the Principe de Asturias, in April 1990. He was eighty-three years old, and it seemed late recognition – or was it recognition before it was too late? Venezuela has seldom been in the mainstream of Latin American writing. Caracas's literary exports seem to have stopped after Rómulo Gallegos. Arturo Uslar Pietri is well known in Latin America for his journalism. For the past thirty years his by-line has been an almost daily feature in the serious newspapers of the continent. But he is little known outside the region or elsewhere outside academe. He is a bit like Caracas. The city was a red-roofed village until the late 1930s but, with some help from the oil boom, became a city only in the 1970s. Since then it has reverted to something of a backwater.

My recollection of Uslar Pietri is of a man dedicated to serious art; the serious is underscored. In Venezuela, at the time of the new wealth, he was on a par with the president, and the president was panting to keep up with him. Uslar Pietri had been a cabinet minister several times, a vice president of the republic, and an exile in New York during the Marcos Pérez Jiménez dictatorship of the 1950s. He walked with the step of a literary lion. In his mid-seventies at the time of our meeting, he towered over younger men. Unconsciously, he had fallen into the manner of his literary subjects, the looming figures of nineteenth-century Venezuela, who, because nothing was known abroad of the environs of Caracas, were considered in Europe to be Colombian heroes. Oil money, however, had now made them Venezuelan. These were odious dictators, like Juan Vicente Gómez, or uncompromising conquistadors, like the Basque Lope de Aguirre, and advisors and hangers-on in the court of Simón Bolívar. For Uslar Pietri, they were men of flesh and blood and much fire. He described himself to me as unable to create – and uninterested in the creation of – fictional characters.

129

His talent is peculiarly Latin American. He can describe the most ferocious personalities and explain their historical context without justifying their excesses; he can dramatize their lives yet condemn their actions. Between explanation and condemnation, Uslar Pietri's own humanity and gentleness come through. It is this contradiction that makes him uncomprehended in Europe outside Spain. His only book in English is the novel *The Red Lances*, written in 1931 and published in New York in 1963. Its main character is a caudillo, a leader of rabble and founder of anarchy. In his attempt to mix literature, politics, and history Uslar Pietri has much in common with Mario Vargas Llosa, who is also able to look on five centuries of upheaval in Latin America and effectively to distinguish beauty from brutality.

In his own country, Uslar Pietri is a hero, which is as it should be. He represents a continuity between the old Venezuela and the new Latin America. His years and his durability as a literary figure have helped him bridge the gap between history and literature. When we were introduced by the poet José Ramón Medina our three-way conversation quickly became the perennial one of Latin American literary circles. We talked about the desire to achieve the worldliness of Europe, which runs counter to the shallowness of regional nationalism. Venezuela, a place caught between the two worlds, is a clash between rootlessness and the deeply rooted nationalities of Europe. In the end, the conflict remains unresolved, but the charm of Caracas is permanent.

To be in love with Caracas, with this uninteresting, oil-boom town that stretches along the flat bottom of a smoke-filled valley with a lid of cloud, between the Ávila hills on the sea and the *cerros* on the other side, where Germans came in the last century and made an Alpine toy town in the green hills that overlook the traffic-clogged, overcrowded streets! A reunion of friends for a writers' conference transformed the city into the laughing, lively, capital of the tropics that it liked to think it was.

The city became Chefi. She was short, smiling, and shaped like men's dreams of women. Born of an Italian immigrant father and a Venezuelan mother, Chefi's lips were full and her eyes large. She moved confidently, notebook in one hand, pen in the other, swiftly subjugating the celebrities, whose vanities she wanted to shrink into a short article for *El Nacional*.

The 46th International Congress of PEN, the world association of writers, was meeting in Caracas. But there had been congresses, symposia, conferences, meetings, encounters, reunions, and semi-nars all year long, for 1983 was the bicentenary of the birth of Venezuela's national hero Simón Bolívar.

There had been medical conferences and gastronomic jamborees where it was not enough to be against dieting but delegates had also to discredit thin people. There had been a congress on the preven-tion of suicide. The best attended was the congress of art critics. Where there was art, everybody liked to be seen – talking about it or touring the Visual Arts Biennial in the Contemporary Arts Museum in the city's Parque Central. I watched an old couple admiring the museum's polished copper plumbing. The woman looked for a label that would tell her what this piece of sculpture was. Such are the difficulties of understanding what is art, and in Caracas everybody had been obliged to learn overnight. Throughout the 1980s, oil money had been poured into culture. When the oil cash dried up so did the arts funding. Jorge Romero Brest, the Argentine critic whose dicta were instant law in Latin America, flashed his large, shaven head under the spotlights and said that the biennial contained noth-ing of interest. Caracas had been proud and now was hurt.

And Chefi took notes with a little pout. 'It is ingenious without depth,' Romero Brest told her. As a consolation, he said that the phenomenon was universal. There was nothing of interest in Italy, France, or the United States either. 'Haven't you noticed that all the art movements of the twentieth century are neo? In art we have made no progress since the nineteenth century; we have not moved from the horse and cart to the motorcar. Artists nowadays have taken refuge in geometry. The only strong art comes from the people; the upper classes have stopped having any links with a country's culture. They believe in nothing. But the lower classes have an appetite for art and culture, yet nobody can interpret this need, this power. Architecture will become the leading art form because architects are the only people duty-bound to interpret the needs of the people.' He went on to say that writers might be able to report these needs but that they could not interpret them.

Chefi wrote as fast as she could, no doubt wondering whether the wisdom that Jorge Romero Brest was imparting to Caracas was genuine or whether she was being used to convey the latest dictum of the vain critic, which she was obviously reading into his words, 'Innovate to entertain me – so that I may bless you and make my blessing valuable.'

Then there was the writers' conference. The Swedes came in silent bewilderment, unable to find where they were going, because, owing to the city's recent haphazard growth, there was no convenient A–Z. The streets bore no names. The Dutch came, angered that the Third World they patronized in Amsterdam was offering them only a Dutch treat – they had had to pay their own way. And then there were the Japanese, who arrived in numbers that other countries reserved for describing their foreign debt. All came equipped with theories of rapid development as recommended by Western agencies. The Ecuadorian poet Jorge Adoum had said in 1968 that Europe sent such beautiful coffins that it was a pleasure to get into them.

Chefi wrote it all down and, steered firmly by the arm of José Pulido – a science-fiction writer, fellow reporter, and raconteur, who at the age of thirty-seven was the father of eight and grandfather of two – went back with him to El Nacional to get their copy into the early pages. Outside, the strange scents of the tropics floated on the pavements, and the cumbia beat blasted out of record shops. Pedestrians picking their way between ice-cream vendors' tricycle boxes found themselves blocked by begging cripples with thigh stumps like mortadellas.

An election campaign was under way, but after the vote there would be three months before the transfer of government. It was a time in which to tidy up, when no decisions were taken and assurances were offered only within the realm of political expediency. Corruption had grown in the overcrowded civil service, which was padded by appointments in payment of political favours. Government employees struggled to find a desk. They stood around in corridors for a while each morning and if there was no vacant chair they left.

The devaluation of the bolívar in February 1983 from B4.30 to B12.00 to the dollar was a shock. Spending had to stop. A way of life – which included shopping trips to Miami and cheap Trinidadian maids – had to change. Corruption became the real force behind the economy. 1983 was an important date in the calendar of recession, just as 1973 had been in the calendar of economic boom. Members of the exchange-control committee, set up after devaluation to arbitrate in circumstances where businesses had bought currency at unfavourable rates, demanded a bribe of one bolívar per dollar supplied at the pre-devaluation rate. The radio stations broadcast frequent messages on the need for public morality in the struggle against offering or taking bribes for supplying public services.

President Luis Herrera Campins, in his bedroom slippers at one end of the long tiled verandah of his official residence, La Casona, laughed a slow, full, fat man's laugh. 'Venezuela lives in a world of fantasy,' he said. 'That was the economy of delirium. Everybody borrowed. The rich borrowed millions, the poor borrowed thousands.' Caracas was a rich man who had become impoverished but could not give up spending. The streets were cluttered with toys – huge American cars, fancy shop windows. The president was overweight. In the last lethargic months of his constitutional rule, which would end three months later, in February 1984, eating had become his main interest; that, going to the theatre, and opening conferences.

The president's speech at the start of the PEN congress was a catalogue of literary quotes, pocket philosophy, and remarks about freedom of expression. Then he held a reception for writers in the courtyard of the presidential residence, where Grand Marnier was poured liberally into a mix of strawberries, cream, and ice. The kick was unnoticed until men began to cling to their ties for stability and women gripped the brims of their hats. Later, they were half carried out. It was all part of the Venezuelan fantasy – a president who showed an interest in writers and whose predecessors in the high office had included a novelist. It was part of living in democracy, President Campins said.

Rómulo Betancourt, Venezuela's president from 1959 to 1964, who survived guerrilla attacks and two military murder attempts, had once quoted Winston Churchill to the effect that 'The nice thing about democracies, compared to police states, is that when the bell rings at 5.00 a.m. you know it's the milkman, not the police.' Betancourt died in comfortable retirement in September 1981.

'Is not so essotic, yes?' remarked a Scandinavian writer at the congress. 'I mean, Caracas – well, I do not know what I esspected.'

To find the exotic, he could go to the state of Carabobo, a short distance west of Caracas, where in the enclave of blacks who had once been slaves he could drink Scotch whisky, two or three bottles in a night among four people. Or he could drink six bottles of the local rum, which was much cheaper since the imports crash. But Black Label went down better.

Venezuela had been proud of being the third largest importer of Scotch whisky in the world before devaluation. Now imports had fallen by nearly half. National rum was taking over, but at one time middle-class Venezuelans would not be caught dead with rum on their breath. It was Scotch that kept them high on the social scale.

Out in the suburbs of Caracas men wore guns in open holsters that hung from their belts. It was a show of manliness which, like other displays of being manly, entailed a lot of Scotch, and often somebody got killed when voices were raised to the height of the spirits.

The Scandinavian writer was told that he might like to travel to the southeastern *llanos*, where he would find native Amerindians herded into compounds by North American missionaries. The Indians wore T-shirts that said 'I love New York' and 'University of Ohio'.

Out there, where the European mixed with the native to make Venezuela more surreal than anywhere else in Latin America, people had lived for the parties, which had sometimes lasted for days. Wakes made the best parties; the mourning drew people from everywhere, provoked good fights and sometimes another death, which would give rise to yet another wake and another big party. It was never difficult to find supplies of beer and food, but often a long time went by without anybody dying, and so there were no parties. Of course, there was always someone who could be found to provide the body – by going out on to the road and picking a fight with a traveller.

Chefi laughed and said that such customs had disappeared years ago and visitors should not be frightened by that kind of story. Caracas had acquired European customs. The muggers were mostly motorcyclists, who snatched handbags and jewellery, and in one good haul they could make more than a month's wages.

The city had been built and destroyed by Europeans. The Spaniards had called the country 'Little Venice'. Caracas was flattened by an earthquake in 1812, then devastated by Spaniards trying to defeat Bolívar in 1814. Foreigners fell in love with her even then. Sir Robert Ker Porter, the British chargé d'affaires, painted the city meticulously in 1825; Jean Baptiste Gros, the French diplomat, portrayed her in soft colours in 1839; so did Ferdinand Bellerman, a German artist; then a Danish painter, Fritz George Melbye, who arrived in 1852 with Camille Pissarro.

The British, afraid of the foreign city, introduced the watchman, who lives on in the language as *guachimano*. If the native was friendly, he became a chum, or *chamo*; a fat man's gut was a *guata*; and in the port, the early wire hawsers, which replaced ropes, became known as *guaira*. After the French passed through, all foreigners were called *musiú*.

The Germans laid the foundations of Venezuelan commerce and their descendants still run it. In 1902, in alliance with the British and supported by Italy (with the keen interest of France), Germany declared war on Venezuela, blockaded the coast, and shelled the ports of La Guaira and Puerto Cabello in an attempt to induce President Cipriano Castro to pay his country's debts.

Venezuela accepted all kinds of Europeans. Federico, a German expatriate, came to the writers' conference and offered participants the opportunity to take back to their European publishers his new theory of evolution. He gave traffic police a copy in lieu of a fine whenever he was stopped for an infraction. Federico had flown in the *Luftwaffe*, fled to Buenos Aires in 1945, then to Venezuela. He had married an Amerindian woman and referred to her as an ignorant savage. In evidence of his liberality, however, he had married her and allowed her to bear his child. He enjoyed contact with the visiting German writers – even though they rejected his theory – and they answered his questions about the country he had left half a century before. They heard him in his nostalgia. In Germany they would not have addressed a word to him.

After World War II the North Americans had made Caracas into a boom town. Now the developed nations' banking crisis would help to reduce Venezuela back to Third World proportions – a small country, rich in oil, that imported most of its food and all of its commodities. Even the crickets in the Central Park, where the arrogant Hilton Hotel exuded imported comfort, were foreign and had been introduced by the Brazilian planner Roberto Burle Marx, who thought that the sound of a Mexican cricket was best suited to Caracas.

The capital's French-built Metro had caused a silent revolution. It was clean and so quiet and smooth that it affected some of the customs of the tropics. In the train, people spoke in low voices and did not throw litter on the floor, because noise and litter contrasted sharply with the spotless coaches. The first grafitti noticed on a Metro wall, some scrawls by the Bandera Roja guerrillas, made a two-column story with pictures in *El Diario de Caracas*.

PEN's congress, organized by José Ramón Medina, the Venezuelan poet – and library director, journalist, lecturer, lawyer, former prosecutor general, later to become procurator fiscal in the Lusinchi government – became the biggest gathering of Latin American poets that Latin America had seen in years. Chefi enjoyed their company, many of them exiles on their way home, some just out of their hideaways in the improved political air that was blowing away the military regimes of the 1970s. Impossible to name all the poets: Oswaldo Trejo, Silva Otero, Vicente Gerbassi, and Arturo Uslar Pietri, of Venezuela; Nicanor Parra, of Chile; Enrique Molina, of Argentina; José Miguel Oviedo and Jorge Rufinelli, of Mexico; Pablo Antonio Cuadra, of Cuba; and Jorge Justo Padrón, of Spain.

The president of the Venezuelan Writers' Society, José Ramón González Paredes, wanted to meet them all. More a retired bureaucrat than an artist, he basked in the praise which his guests lavished on the organizers of the writers' conference. His own fifty-year-old society had 570 members in Caracas.

Among those attending the conference was the Uruguayan critic Angel Rama, laughing, joyful, at times patronizing, but looking much younger than his sixty-one years. He was back in Caracas to offer his literary wisdom to an assembly of friends. Caracas had given him refuge when he had left Montevideo in 1972; now he had been expelled from the United States after three years as a professor in Maryland, on grounds that he had a subversive past. Rama was making his life anew in Paris. Who would imagine him dead just a few weeks later, killed in the most foolish of deaths, strapped in his seat in the Colombian plane that crashed in Madrid on 27 November 1983. With him died his wife, the Argentine novelist Marta Traba, and Manuel Scorza, the Peruvian novelist, who, at fifty-five, was making his return to Lima after more than a decade of exile and expatriation. Angel Rama, poet, lecturer, a large, lovable, lanky man, enjoyed the warmth of Caracas, where in 1978 he had been among the founders of the Ayacucho Library. This was the city that had made sure he would never be forgotten.

Every visiting writer to the conference was laden with books, beautiful goods, published by the government, which must have spent a public fortune to enhance a number of private vanities. They were books intended to show the world the culture and history of a country that thought it had none. The culture minister, Luis Pastori, moved among the writers at the many receptions telling guests that he was a good poet.

As a farewell, José Ramón Medina and his friend, the translator and poet Jaime Tello, presided over the launch of an anthology of Venezuelan poetry. It was done in local literary tradition; they poured a bottle of rum on the book and then asked every guest to sign the soggy pages. A German said that back home the people would have sucked the pages dry rather than see so much spirit go to waste.

1983 & 1990

CLARIBEL ALEGRÍA: THE SMILE AMID THE SADNESS

S he had the look and style of a fighter. Claribel Alegría does not shy away from trouble and is delighted to enter into an argument. A mother of four and a grandmother of ten, she is a staunch feminist with a strong undercurrent of humour. 'Whenever I see the titles "Women and Democracy", "Women and the Environment", and so forth I wonder, what are they accusing us of now? I like the idea of "Women and Literature". It is a theme that attracts me very much. Here I feel it represents another feminine incursion into a field which, with few exceptions in Latin America, has been an exclusively male domain.'

Her childhood in El Salvador took place in what she describes as an aggresively macho society. She was born in 1924. Her generation in Central America had two options. To marry and become a husband's housekeeper or to wither away as an old virgin. 'The working-class woman had no choice,' she says. 'Her family made sure that she became some man's slave and the mother of his children.'

Until only a few years ago, there were not many women in Latin America who had distinguished themselves in literature. Alfonsina Storni, Delmira Agustín, Gabriela Mistral, Juana Ibarbourou, and Claudia Lars, points out Claribel Alegría, were not just the best known but were the only ones. 'Of course, Sor Juana Inés de la Cruz was the greatest of them all. She threw down the feminist gauntlet 500 years ago.'

Claribel Alegría says that the audacity of these women to write and publish under their own names provoked astonishment and panic in their male-dominated societies. 'Most of the girls of my generation, whose families could afford their education, didn't even finish high school. In those days, you could count on the fingers of one hand the Salvadorean girls with a university degree. I wanted to study medicine, but my father, who was a doctor, looked at me in horror and said, "Don't you realize that medical students play obscene jokes with anatomical scraps?"'

She spent three years learning how to sew, to cook elaborate dishes, and to play '*Für Elise*' on the piano. Then she rebelled and threatened to become a nun. Her parents sent her to study literature in the United States. For some time before that she had been secretly writing poetry. Had her girl friends found out, they would have thought her mad; had any young man found out, he would automatically have assumed that she was a loose woman.

The main influence on her as a writer was Juan Ramón Jiménez, with whom she studied in Washington. Under his guidance she read all the Spanish classics. She later developed a lasting love for Emily Dickinson. Once she told her husband Darwin Flakoll that she was sure that she had plagiarized the Amherst poet and hoped the critics would not find out. What Jiménez taught her was that the poet is like the shoemaker. The craft improved by working at it each day.

Six of her books appear in English, at least two of which were translated by her American-born husband. In 1962, they also produced an anthology, *New Voices of Hispanic America*, which heralded the arrival of many outstanding new Latin American writers. They edited a second anthology, this time of poetry, several years later.

My first visit to Central America started in Panama back in the early 1970s, when General Torrijos was still alive. Journalist and writer friends of mine from Argentina were enjoying diplomatic posts in the region, and it was easy to move around cheaply with the benefit of their hospitality. In those days, politics seemed far more important than literature in Guatemala, El Salvador, and Nicaragua. The Sandinista revolution brought to international attention the volume, quality, and history of writing in the area. On later visits to the region, when I stayed in Costa Rica, this literature became a source of interest to me as great as that of politics.

I met Claribel Alegría in London in 1985, when she and Bud Flakoll were visiting publishers the year before her book *They Won't Take Me Alive* appeared. They had come from their house in Majorca, where they spent part of the year when not at home in Nicaragua. They had bought the house in Palma in 1966.

'That was where we could write and be at peace. Palma was very beautiful, but I began to feel guilty about living so comfortably when there was untold suffering and injustice in our real homes in El Salvador and Nicaragua. As Bud wanted to write a book about Central America and I always have speaking engagements there, we decided we wanted to be part of political events back home.'

Q.   Which country are you a native of?

A.   I am a Nicaraguan by birth, but my mother was a Salvadorean. When I was quite small, my father, in opposition to the landing of US Marines in Nicaragua, took us to live in El Salvador. He had actually been persecuted for his stand against this North American invasion. I never went back to Nicaragua until after the revolution in 1979.

Q.   Tell us about those early years in El Salvador.

A.   I have to admit that I am directly connected to some of the notorious fourteen families who control El Salvador lock, stock, and barrel. One of my first cousins was recently the country's defence minister. In fact, there are more than fourteen now – they have built up their strength. Ours is one of the fiercest oligarchies in all Latin America. They hold real power, and are multi-millionaires even by US standards. This oligarchy is unique to El Salvador. The coffee planters present a frightening image. They dress like Wild West cowboys and look very threatening.

My father was a doctor who served this oligarchy. I will never forget one of his friends, who had a daughter my age. As a child she was a millionairess. Years later, I was invited to her wedding lunch. The plates were not porcelain with gold fillet but solid gold. It was actually grotesque. One of her aunts would travel regularly to Europe on a shopping spree. As she always took her dogs, she would buy them seats on the plane.

Why do you think there is a guerrilla war going on in the country today?

Q.   Is any of your work published in El Salvador?

A.   No, my books are banned. But there is something strange about this. Bud and I wrote a novel together about the Salvador massacre of 1932. The National Guard killed some thirty thousand peasants. I was seven or eight at the time. And you know how it is – some scenes remain in the mind of a child for life. Our house was just across from the National Guard headquarters, and I can remember hearing people scream. Then I saw many *campesinos*, tied by their thumbs behind their backs. I heard shots right through

140

the night. It was horrific. I remained obsessed with this memory. The government had most of the issues of the newspapers that ran the story destroyed.

Bud suggested that I write all this down. And with his help I wrote *The Ashes of Izalco*. Izalco is a volcano in permanent eruption. My mother and father approved of the novel, but my various aunts and uncles were outraged. The book was published in Spain. My relatives burned as many copies as they could lay their hands on. News of this got about, and it helped the sales considerably.

Q. But was the novel available in El Salvador?

A. Yes, in 1976 the dictator Molina decided he wanted to assume a liberal appearance. One way to do this without much risk was to publish Salvadorean writers. There were two progressive young men at the Ministry of Education, and they chose *Ashes of Izalco*. Not only that, it was made a high school textbook. It ran to ten printings. Having been published by the ministry and so adjudged to be safe, nobody higher up in the government had read it. The book was even authorized for reading in the local prison. I found this out years later when I went to interview long-term political prisoners.

Q. And your poetry?

A. One of my books of poems was published in 1970 by the University of El Salvador. But the whole edition was destroyed by the army.

Q. Latin America has produced a lot of good political and revolutionary poetry. How much do you identify your own writing with that category?

A. I was a very subjective, even lyrical, poet. But I became more and more anguished by what was happening in Central America. The abductions, the murders, and the injustice became another of the obsessions in my writing. I think that everything I do and write now is political. And yet I consider my poetry love poems to my people.

Q. Was the change in your writing brought about by the war in El Salvador?

A. One of my most crucial poems was written in Palma. It is called 'Majorca, My Paradise'. In it, I contrast my beautiful surroundings with the ghosts that fill my room every night. They are phantoms that persecute and tell me of suffering. I do not think this is good poetry. I call this work emergency letters and testimonial poetry.

Q. Do you feel more comfortable writing poetry or prose? After all, you have published four short novels.

A. I am a poet more than anything else. But I firmly believe that eye-witness books are of inestimable value, because they record events as they happened. Look at the book *They Won't Take Me Alive*. It is the story of how political prisoners were treated in El Salvador. Some of what I had to report made me physically sick when I was writing it. An earlier book, *Para romper el silencio*, put on record a series of prison rebellions. For that, I interviewed former prisoners in Mexico and Nicaragua.

Q. How do you account for the abysmal oppression in Central America?

A. The brief answer, I would say, is that it is the result of the system of land ownership, whereby vast tracts are concentrated in the hands of very few. This is a constant in El Salvador and Guatemala. In Nicaragua, the Somoza family owned eighteen per cent of the arable land. Revolution has spread recently because there never was a transition from a feudal land-ownership system to a developed economy. There is no other way to bring about change now than by violent revolt. Anything short of that will inevitably allow repression to prevent reform.

We always have been repressed in Central America. When the Spaniards came they wanted to abolish our indigenous culture. In Guatemala more than half the population is still Indian and still fighting for the right to keep its culture. In El Salvador most of the population is mixed; ninety per cent is Ladino, which means Spanish and Indian. By the way, that 1932 massacre that I was witness to was caused because the dictator Martínez thought that everything that was Indian was Communist. Anyone who was Indian had to be killed. Men started to dress as women to escape from Izalco. They denied they were Indians and said they were Ladinos. They even refused to speak their native language.

Q. The account by the Guatemalan woman Rigoberta Menchú of the plight of the Central American Indian is quite moving.

A. Yes, I met her in Spain. Her book, *I, Rigoberta Menchú*, makes me cry. She is only one example. There are dozens who share the same story. They have been treated like animals all their lives.

Q. Are you able to visit El Salvador now or is it unsafe?

A. I started to go back in 1979, when we went to spend Christmas with my mother. I am allowed in but I have to be careful. As a matter of fact, one of my cousins – whom I hardly ever talk to – sent me a message to say please do not come back to El Salvador, because it will be embarrassing for the family. I wanted to return again when my mother died. I was told she had called for me. But my brother phoned me and said, 'Please do not come or there will be two funerals.' My family does not want me to write or telephone them from Nicaragua. They live in utter fear.

A. Did you know the poet Roque Dalton?

A. Yes, I did, and his death in 1975 was awful. It was terrible that a faction of his own organization committed such a crime. We used to correspond frequently years ago. He lived in Prague and I in Paris. We exchanged Salvadorean recipes. Bud used to laugh at us and say, 'Some revolutionaries! All you two write about is *tamalitos*.'

When I was invited to Cuba for the first time, in 1968, Roque was at the airport waiting for me. We liked each other very much. He wrote a poem about our friendship. For some reason, he told everybody that I was a dancer and that I knew the rumba and the mambo. Years later, I wrote a poem in his memory called '*Salto mortal*'. Roque's poems are published in El Salvador now, probably because he is dead. But the people know him and read him. They consider him a martyr. The literary community places him with the novelist Manlio Argueta in the so-called Generation of 1958.

Q.   What has happened to the protagonist of *They Won't Take Me Alive*?

A.   Margarita spent nearly two years in Milopango women's prison, until she was released in May 1983. Only then was she able to tell Bud and me the whole story of that experience. She is out of El Salvador now and she is still working for the resistance movement. She is one of the lucky ones. Over 60,000 Salvadorean citizens were not so lucky. They are merely statistics in the books of the death squads.

Q.   Can you tell us something about Margarita's story?

A.   Margarita is not her real name. That was what her jailers called her. Bud and I met her when we were writing the book about political prisoners in El Salvador. Margarita had joined the revolutionary university students' movement in 1979. She was a second-year student at the school of law when the army closed the university in June of 1980. Margarita went into hiding but she became very ill and was forced to return home. She was discovered and captured in June 1981 by naval police and found to be in possession of compromising documents. She was still convalescent when arrested but nevertheless was made to suffer torture during interrogation. When a Red Cross official visited the prison in search of missing political prisoners, Margarita managed to draw his attention. But before he could come back for her, her jailers smuggled her out and took her to the National Guard headquarters in San Salvador.

Her new guards there in the capital told her quite honestly, 'We would have preferred to kill you, because we really feel sorry for you. Here the boys are going to tear you to bits and never let you out alive.' On her first night, the sentry on duty tried to rape her but desisted when she began to scream at the top of her lungs. One of the torturers came next, with a small electrical appliance. 'Here come the little wires!' he said cheerfully. Margarita was tortured for eighteen days. Her weight fell to eighty pounds, so that she managed to slip the handcuffs off her wrists. This prompted another beating, because her guards could not understand how she had managed to get free.

Every other day, her guards would hide her in a truck or outbuilding so that the Red Cross inspectors would not find her. But during the days she spent in the torture chamber she memorized

144

the names of her tormentors whenever they were mentioned. When eventually she came out, she published each of their names.

Our book collects all her memory of that period of torment. It is one book for one woman. But remember, there were thousands of women and as many men who suffered the same horrors, and each one deserves a book.

Q. Have you any fear that people outside Central America will one day soon stop listening to these endless stories of horror?

A. I won't blame people from other parts of the world if they tire of reading about us. They have their problems too. This is a long war, and we cannot give up. But I feel that outside support for the Salvadorean struggle must continue.

1985 & 1990

THE LATIN AMERICAN GREENE

Graham Greene is Latin America's favourite Englishman. His good-humoured appearance and his political statements have endeared him to people all the way from Haiti and Mexico to Buenos Aires. Championing the cause of the under-privileged, he has written a book about his friendship with the late General Omar Torrijos, of Panama, and has admitted to a liking for Fidel Castro and a certain admiration for Cuba's revolution. Though he has an old acquaintance with West Africa and Southeast Asia, his longest running fascination among Third World places has been with Latin America.

Greene once told the *Spectator*, a magazine he has always supported, that his doubting faith had led him to give half the royalties of one novel, *Monsignor Quixote* (1982), to a Trappist monastery and the other half to the guerrillas in El Salvador. You know that this was done out of deep feeling, but when an Englishman like Graham Greene makes such a gesture there lingers a suspicion of mischief. He says he is an angry old man.

At eighty-one, he is tall and a little stooped. His large eyes open wide in permanent friendly surprise. His apartment in Paris, where I met him, like his flat in Antibes overlooking the port, was sparsely furnished. Among piles of books were a few luxuries. A number of small antique pieces and ornaments, including a small stone sculpture of a warrior by Henry Moore, sat on the mantelpiece above the fireplace. The walls were decorated with Haitian paintings. In his toilet in Antibes, he told me, he had a poster of Baby Doc Duvalier dressed in a child's clothes and holding a pistol to his head. It had been sent to Greene by an unknown correspondent following Baby Doc's forced departure from Port au Prince. Other letters from Haitians at the time asked the English novelist to go back and write a sequel to *The Comedians* (1966), and still other Haitians wanted him to protest against Duvalier's presence in France.

Greene drank in small measures. He had been out to supper with his girlfriend to a cellar where they had drunk several good wines, one of them a 1945 white – all of which he remembered with delight and a slightly pained expression in his watery blue eyes.

Politics and his sympathy for Latin America took up much of the conversation. I had first seen Graham Greene in the flesh in July 1968 in Buenos Aires, at a press conference at the Villa Ocampo, the home of his friend and publisher, the late Victoria Ocampo. He was on his way to Paraguay, researching for his novel *Travels with My Aunt* (1969). He described himself then as an admirer of Fidel Castro and said that Ernesto 'Che' Guevara was too important to use as a character in a novel. The *Buenos Aires Herald*'s report of the press conference was headlined 'Greene favours revolutions'. The next day the *Herald*'s editor Bob Cox was chastised at a drinks party by a socialite with a surname as long as a litany and told that Greene was a Communist.

Did he remember anything of his visits to Buenos Aires? 'They are very much in the past. In fact, all I've seen of Argentina is Buenos Aires. I've been to Mar del Plata with Victoria Ocampo. I saw a little bit. Then I went to Asunción by river boat.' Asunción is still very much as he saw it. Later, he went back to that part of South America to write *The Honorary Consul* (1973). It was set in northern Argentina and dedicated to Victoria Ocampo, invoking his days with her in Mar del Plata, where she had her summer home. I asked if the honorary consul had been one Stanley Sylvester, a meat-packing plant manager in Rosario, kidnapped and held for one week in 1971 by the People's Revolutionary Army. The kidnappers thought they had a diplomat and only got a minor figure, an honorary consul.

'I'd never heard of that. I would have been very depressed if I had. I do remember that in March 1970 the Paraguayan consul in Argentina was kidnapped in Buenos Aires during an official visit by General Stroessner of Paraguay to General Onganía of Argentina. Stroessner had gone fishing or shooting in Argentina and said that he did not mind; the kidnappers could keep the consul if they wanted him. So the guerrillas released the man. It did not become a world-wide story. The consul had been kidnapped to embarrass the Paraguayan dictator.'

Was the priest in *The Honorary Consul* modelled on the Colombian, Father Camilo Torres, who had died fighting alongside the guerrillas in February 1966? 'Not really. Torres was a much more romantic young man. My man is an orthodox Catholic. I had to invent a little personal theology for him.'

Greene went on to say that he had last been in Buenos Aires on his way to see Salvador Allende in Chile. 'Pablo Neruda had arranged the visit when he was ambassador to France in 1972. I liked Allende very much. He was very kind to me and gave me a little aeroplane to go north, to the desert, and a car driven by a Communist lady with a guide to go south. I had only two meetings with President Allende. On my way to a third meeting there was some trouble in Argentina. The Argentines had quite an agreeable general as president at the time – General Alejandro Lanusse. The tanks had moved against him or something, but it came to nothing. He had been arranging a conference with Allende, and they were on the telephone all the time.' It had been a strange association, the socialist president and the army general who had been involved in a number of coups. When they had finally met they had walked arm in arm in one of the provincial capitals as good friends.

'It was a rather delightful sight,' Greene said. 'I suppose General Galtieri seemed one of the slightly better ones too. But he got mixed up in that war. I was surprised during the conflict, just about the time of the sinking of the *General Belgrano*, to receive a letter from a woman journalist in Buenos Aires asking what I thought about the war. I wrote back to her saying that one of the things that separated us was that she would not be able to publish my letter while I could have published anything she wrote. I said it was all a silly war, and the only good which would come out of it was the fall of the military junta. She published my words while the fighting was going on. She sent me the cutting from *Clarín*. She said she did not understand how it was published. Probably as a result of a disagreement within the forces.'

Our conversation moved on to the Argentine writer Ernesto Sábato, who had chaired the inquiry in 1984 into the *desaparecidos* and produced the report *Nunca Más (Never Again)*, which led to the trial of the military junta. 'I last saw Sábato in Buenos Aires when I was going to Chile. He told me he was carrying a revolver because he did not feel safe returning home late at night. He showed me the gun. Perhaps he was not so blind then as he is now.'

Blindness was a reminder of the late Jorge Luis Borges, who had died in Geneva in June 1986. 'I liked him very much,' Greene said. 'I once went to fetch him from the National Library, where he was then director, and as we crossed the street I said I thought that

Robert Louis Stevenson, whom he admired and I was interested in as he was my mother's first cousin, had written at least one good poem, "Requiem", about his ancestors. Borges stopped at the edge of the pavement and recited the whole piece.'

Borges it was whose genius led him to describe the Falkland/ Malvinas war as two bald men fighting over a comb. I told Graham Greene that I had seen Borges at the time. He had invited me to his house just as Pope John Paul arrived on a visit to Argentina.

'I would have gone to see Borges. I don't like the Pope.' I admitted that I had chosen Borges.

In Latin America Graham Greene is seen as a Catholic writer. He converted to Catholicism in 1927 and once told reporters in Buenos Aires that he had done so only to marry a Catholic woman. 'But I don't like to be regarded as a Catholic writer. I always say I'm a writer who happens to be a Catholic. Nobody knew that I was a Catholic until I published *Brighton Rock* in 1938. Then they discovered it and tried to make me into a Catholic writer, which I am not. Besides, I take a very independent line about Catholicism. I've been attacking the present Pope quite a lot.'

The writer John Mortimer has said that Graham Greene's favourite meeting place was the point at which doubting Catholics and sceptical Communists join in questioning their loyalties. Latin Americans, however, had seen in *The Power and the Glory* (1940) a Catholic writer, and this suited their conservative view of devotion and pious doubt. Then came *The End of the Affair* (1951), which had caused them to swallow hard but not alter their view.

Greene said his writing after that became more political. '*The Quiet American* [1955], set in Indo-China, was more political than religious. And *The Honorary Consul*, though mixed up, was also more political than religious. *The Human Factor* [1978] was not religious. Even the adventures of Monsignor Quixote were political.'

He spoke of being invited to lunch by Mrs Thatcher. 'I suppose that *Monsignor Quixote* was the reason I was invited to 10 Downing Street for lunch with the King and Queen of Spain. There were a lot of people there. One only went there to shake the king's hand. There were no speeches. I'd had to go over to London anyway, because I had a dinner date with the Nicaraguan ambassador and a surgical examination which I have to have every year since my operation for cancer in 1979. Ten Downing Street was more of a joke than anything else.'

Greene returned to religion. 'The Church is the mirror image of Communism. They ought to get on better. The Communists have a politbureau and we have the Curia.' He said he goes to confession once a year and occasionally to mass.

Graham Greene had written a book about Omar Torrijos, *Getting to Know the General* (1984). He had served as a member of the Panamanian delegation to Washington for the signing of the Canal Treaty, and five years later the government of Panama awarded him the Grand Cross, Order of Vasco Núñez de Balboa. But how close had he been to the Panamanian leader?

'I was very fond of him. I really loved the man. He first invited me to Panama in 1976. Then I went again in 1977 and 1978. In 1979 I didn't go, because I had to have an operation, and I think I went for the last time in 1980. I was packed to go in 1981 when the news of his death came.'

From Torrijos he had learned a lot about what was happening in Central America. 'He introduced me to some of his Sandinista friends during the civil war in Nicaragua. He had very good information on what was happening there. You see, he was helping them. Not with arms, I don't think, but he provided them with uniforms for the storming of the national palace. The clothes were indistinguishable from those of the Nicaraguan national guards. Torrijos wanted me to go along in a plane to Managua to fetch some released hostages with his aide de camp, who was my friend. But my friend was drunk and did not get the full message, which was that I should sleep at an airport and wait for the plane there. Torrijos was a remarkable man. He would have had a big influence today. We might not have had the Contra business in Nicaragua. He might have been strong enough to face Reagan. Before the US election, he told me, "I want Carter to win, but if Reagan comes in it may be more fun." He was really contemplating confrontation. He was an extremely nice man and a human person. He wasn't at all a typical general. I don't like Panama nearly so much now. But I won't speak about General Noriega's regime, because I don't want to offend my friends there. I miss Torrijos very much.'

Graham Greene was last in Panama and Nicaragua in 1985. 'The curious thing about Nicaragua is that everybody there writes poetry. It's most mysterious. Tomás Borge, the minister of the interior, writes poetry. Old Cardenal is a poet. Even Ortega writes poetry. His wife, Rosario Murillo, certainly does. I liked his wife very much. I knew her in Panama, when she was in exile. I also met her in Costa Rica once, when Torrijos's aide had to meet Daniel Ortega to discuss arms or something of the sort. She and I sat at a table well away and were not allowed to hear what they were talking about. Everybody I spoke to in Nicaragua I would ask what he did. And they all said, "I write poetry." Both women and men.'

What did he think of the accusations of press censorship against Nicaragua? 'Well, there is a war on. In England we had censorship during the war. I don't think you can avoid it in wartime. It is the same with conscription. France has conscription even in peacetime. It always had. And England had conscription in wartime. I don't see how it can be avoided.'

How did he look on Cuba now? 'I was one hundred per cent for Fidel at the beginning. I can't help liking the man, and still did when we met again two years ago. But I don't really know the conditions in Cuba now. I want to go back for a good period so that I can drive around the country. I used to go to Cuba during the Batista period. It may have become too much of a bureaucracy now. I don't know. But it amuses me to see that Fidel has written a book on liberation theology with the help of a Brazilian friar. I'm glad to see this rapprochement and that he's getting on well with the Cuban bishops. The Pope has accepted an invitation to go to Cuba. I hope he will behave better than he did in Nicaragua.'

Greene went on to speak about Ernesto Guevara. 'Poor Guevara, he was betrayed by the Communists in Bolivia. I never met him, but I was amused once on a later trip to Cuba. I was travelling about the country in a car with the minister of education. We stopped at a village to look for a cigar factory, just as the children were coming out of school. The minister stopped one of them and asked, "Do you know" – this was when nobody knew – "where Guevara is?" The little boy said yes, and the minister's face fell. He thought there was going to be an awful disclosure in front of me. He cautiously asked where. The little boy answered, "Fighting for freedom." There was an audible sigh of relief from the minister.'

Did he still keep in touch with the Colombian writer Gabriel García Márquez? 'I used to see a lot of him when Torrijos was alive. He was a great friend of Torrijos's. Sometimes we would meet in Panama. But I haven't seen much of him since then. We've corresponded a bit and spoken on the telephone.'

García Márquez had been an ardent advocate of the Nobel Prize for Graham Greene, an award the Colombian thought had been devalued by Greene's not receiving it.

'Well, he speaks as a friend. It's not a thing I would worry about. I would like to have the money.'

The last time I had seen Graham Greene before our Paris meeting had been at the Garrick Club, in London, when he was clutching a cigar box. It had contained the Order of Merit, which he had just been to Buckingham Palace to receive. It was the same day as the memorial service at Westminster for the Swedish prime minister Olof Palme.

In Paris, Greene told me, 'One is rather pleased because there are only twenty-four holders of the OM. Except that I did become depressed. I was momentarily pleased when they wrote and asked if I would accept it. But afterwards I felt as if my writing had finished. It was the end of the manuscript. There is a poem by Mathew Arnold on old age. It ends with the line, "To hear the world applaud the hollow ghost/ Which blamed the living man." I suppose I've got to go on being blamed as much as I can.'

He looked relieved when I switched off the tape recorder. The questions were over, and his conversation became more lively. He poured drinks, measured his Martini in the bottle top, and then sat down and relaxed.

1986

PINTER AMONG THE POETS

T he television camera moved from scenes of Prague, where Harold Pinter had been to visit his fellow playwright, and now president, Vaclav Havel, to focus finally on Pinter in his London study. The English playwright looked at the camera and delivered a blistering attack on the United States for its recent role in Central America, and specifically the US bullying of Nicaragua. Pinter was a high-profile friend and supporter of Nicaragua and of its former Sandinista government. The televised address was broadcast at the end of May 1990, after the election defeat of the Sandinistas and shortly before English PEN's International Writers' Day. This is perhaps the only date when writers in England become publicly political in their statements.

Pinter is one of only a handful of English writers who speak out politically all the year round. Two years before the broadcast we had met in his study for an interview. I wondered then why there was so little political motivation in most of Western Europe's writers. Could life and society be so comfortable that there was little incentive to sound off? I said that one difference between British and European writers and Latin American writers is that the Latin Americans have become political figures mainly because they can read and write. Why don't writers in Britain speak out on political issues?

'We don't understand the extremity of our own position [Pinter said]. In England it is assumed that there is nothing really to be very concerned about. This country is full of American bases, full of nuclear bombs, but people prefer to blind themselves to that reality. In Central and South America everything is thrown into much sharper focus.'

But isn't there an intellectual responsibility to be far more vocal about what is happening in places like Mrs Thatcher's Britain?

'There is an intellectual responsibility. But there is a failure of moral nerve in terms of vigilance and a proper scrutiny of what is taking place. It is part of our responsibility as citizens to understand what is taking place. That is the view that I find is part of my life now.'

I recalled that Carlos Fuentes, the Mexican writer, had once stated that the Nicaraguan revolution had to be supported. Even though Fuentes could hardly be identified as a revolutionary, he was sympathetic to Nicaragua as a humanistic project. Fuentes had said that there had to be an intellectual rallying round Nicaragua. But how do you bring this about?

'Men like Fuentes, Eduardo Galeano in Montevideo, Arthur Miller, and Donald Freed in California – and in Britain there are a growing number of vigorous voices, the playwright David Hare among them – all of them show that there is a sensitivity in the United States and in England to the importance of an intellectual rally to affirm human and political dignity. After all these years, in a way ever since Chile in 1973, I have become more and more engaged in political matters. I have not written plays for some considerable time. In the light of this state of affairs, I can't. Having written *One for the Road* in 1984 and *Mountain Language* this year, I have not written anything else.'

In 1986 the Peruvian novelist Mario Vargas Llosa said that he was against all dictators, whether they were Stroessner, Pinochet, or Fidel Castro. He accused Gabriel García Márquez of being against Stroessner and Pinochet but for Castro. He also accused the German writer Günter Grass of supporting revolutions in Latin America that Grass would not want to happen on his own soil. The accusation is that European intellectuals are sympathetic to revolutions or reforms abroad which they would never want to support at home.

'Vargas Llosa is a celebrated figure and is much respected throughout the world. But I don't know how you can make a comparison between Western Europe and Latin America. They are totally different states of affairs, different societies. As I understand it, more than ninety per cent of the populations of Guatemala, El Salvador, and Honduras – not to mention anywhere else – for years have lived in a system of slavery. The profits have been rich for the United States and for the hierarchy of the country. In Nicaragua, I had a long conversation with President Ortega. One image of the past which he impressed upon me was that of certain houses, mansions – which are kept as museums – that contain a series of large boxes just a little bit bigger than coffins. Under Somoza, the peasants lived in these boxes. They did not simply sleep there. It was the only place they had a right to be. That is slavery. So a revolution which overcomes that and changes that state of affairs, but which also enters into a legal, above-board, democratic election (in 1984) in which over ninety per cent of the country voted, and sixty-seven per cent voted with the Sandinistas, is therefore a democratic society. The Sandinistas formed a democratically elected government and originally made a popular revolution by overthrowing an appalling dictatorship. Why doesn't Vargas Llosa get behind Nicaragua and support it?'

I think that Vargas Llosa's aspiration for Latin America is for European-style democracy where parties pit themselves against one another without guns and form a multi-party assembly called a parliament.

'That does not address the central reality of the region, which is that the United States is not interested in allowing any kind of democracy. Has Vargas Llosa addressed himself to the fact that US interests keep systems going which can hardly be called democracies? They are all dictatorships of one kind or another.'

In a book published in 1988, *The Culture of Terrorism*, Noam Chomsky said that ruling groups in the United States are dedicated to the use of force. Their leaning towards lawlessness is masked by an ideological system which prevents the population at home from seeing the clandestine action applied abroad.

'US foreign policy could be best defined as follows: kiss my arse or I'll kick your head in. It is as simple and crude as that. It can hardly be said to be a complicated foreign policy. What is interesting about it is that it is so incredibly successful. It possesses structures of disinformation, use of rhetoric, and distortion of language which are very persuasive but are actually a pack of lies. It is very successful propaganda. They have the money, they have the technology, they have all the means to get away with it, and they do. I find the ignorance in Britain and certainly the United States really quite deep. It is not only the Republican Party and the present administration in the US that are responsible for this state of affairs. I see the Democrats as differing only by degrees. While they say they do not believe they should send more military aid to the Contras, they still have an innate and deeply imbedded assumption that they are talking about a Marxist-Leninist totalitarian dictatorship – gangsters, thugs, instructed from Moscow, with the Kremlin behind it all.'

One political bolt hole, but also a political truism, is that many criticize the US but the US receives refugees by the thousands. If the US has so many faults, how come so many foreigners want to live there?

'The bulk of refugees from Central America are Salvadoreans who are trying to get away from being killed. Many of them are turned back by the US; a minority are let in. There are a number from Guatemala, and there was a good film about them, *El Norte*, which showed how difficult it is to get across the border. It seems to me that there is a discrepancy here. There was an amnesty of illegal immigrants last year and that was very good, but it should not be confused with the problem of the Central American refugees. I don't think anybody is saying that the whole of the US is bad. That is the way they used to talk about the Soviet Union. There is much that is admirable in the US. But I'm talking about its foreign policy. President Reagan declared a while ago something like, "We know that the Sandinistas are very deep into drug dealing." This was front-page news in the United States. A few days later you could have spied, if you looked at the back page, a couple of paragraphs saying that the assertion that the Sandinistas were in high-level drug dealing was unsupported. The president lied, blatantly, nakedly, unashamedly and was supported by the media. The drug dealing, as is now known from every angle and authority, was done by the CIA, who gave the money from drugs to the Contras. There is a book about it, *Out of Control*, by Leslie Cockburn, which has not been denied. The Sandinistas are trying to establish a decent society in an extremely poor country which, for over forty years, suffered a dictatorship supported by the US. Last November, I went to a US university to give a reading and then had a few questions from an academic audience of about 500 people. I offered one or two propositions about reality and masquerade in relation to their country's responsibilities. The bulk of the audience was resentful, uncomfortable, and would have preferred not to hear what I had to say. It was a body which actually was frightened of the truth and preferred to remain in ignorance.'

The 1960s and 1970s saw the North Americans challenging not only their own government but their own establishment and they are now full of mea culpas and regrets that Vietnam heroes have been neglected while noisy students were encouraged. We have moved into an unliberal (not anti-liberal) decade.

'Yes, fear of being seen as soft on Communism, and so on. There is a fear that is demonstrated not only in the US but in Britain and

Europe too. The idea of something called Communism, which is going to bite. The term has become institutionally pejorative; it is not descriptive, just foul language.'

The basic problem seems to lie in the inability of the US to let a small country be and get on with its own business because of the fear of 'Reds' – the 'Commies' in the backyard.

'That is a myth cultivated by the US administration. The actual truth is that it is about power and money.'

In Nicaragua a Sandinista commander once described the national sport as writing poetry – which may be an extreme way of showing social responsibility.

'I spent nine intense days in Nicaragua. I came away with a number of very distinct and quite vivid impressions. One of them was the realization that the country embodied the most remarkable, if not unique, synthesis of art, Christianity, and politics. You couldn't put a dividing line between any of those areas. I don't think there can be any other government on earth in which you have three priests, a well-known novelist, and a leading poet or in which there is such respect for other people's individuality and dignity. The literacy campaign was one of the extraordinary developments of the Sandinistas, along with health, the agrarian reform, and so on. These remarkable achievements have been stunted by the disgrace that is the American action. It is part of our disgrace – I mean ours as part of the West – of what we call democracy.'

General Vernon Walters, the US ambassador to the UN, who recently attended the UN Human Rights Subcommittee meeting in Geneva, admonished a business audience at the World Economic Forum, in Davos, Switzerland, in January. He said that the US sees itself as a bulwark against continental Communist penetration, which will use Central America as its landing stage.

'Just before I went to Nicaragua, I saw General Vernon Walters on British television. He said that the US would continue to support the Contras, as long as it is within the law, against a Marxist-Leninist totalitarian dictatorship. Since that remark was not corrected, people assume that description is true. We are educated by the media and the politicians to believe such a statement. When democracy in Nicaragua is referred to by the US, it refers to the previous regime. The Americans neglect to remind us that the previous regime was a vicious dictatorship supported by the US. In Nicaragua the peasants have a share in the country. The US perceives this as a threat because the sharing offers a concept of human decency, equality, and peace. The US finds this intolerable simply because it is not peace on US terms. What is happening to Nicaragua, a country in peril, is that it is being brutally attacked by the most powerful nation on earth. It is true that the US is getting other people to do its dirty tricks, but economically there are no holds barred; the economic and financial blockade of Nicaragua is quite devastating. This seems to me to be a classic expression of a depraved moral position, which is ignored by a substantial body of the world. The reason for our willed ignorance is that we already have our own brute; we have been told for years by our leaders that the brute is Russia. The Soviet Union encapsulated and contained all that was evil on earth. It is essential that Western Europe should act responsibly. It seems to me that in Nicaragua there is a serious attempt to establish a decent, civilized society, with a leadership of men of intelligence, culture, and ideas. It is in peril because it is independent.

'Hundreds of priests have been killed in Central America over the last few years in Guatemala and in El Salvador. But no priest has been killed in Nicaragua. The trouble is that such events in countries like Guatemala and El Salvador are more or less ignored. I'd like to emphasize that. But whenever the Sandinistas frown on a priest, because they think he is going too far in his support of the Contras, who are killing women and children, that is front-page news. I noticed in Managua that when at a public meeting some members of the Sandinista security services harried or hassled one or two people, the headline abroad was, "Sandinistas act brutally". So the presentation of facts is distorted, consistently unbalanced, and it is disgusting because it is lie upon lie upon lie. How can one correct all these lies? I don't know, but one can't stop trying.'

1988 & 1990

COMING UP FOR AIR

You would not want to go to Mexico City for the air. At 7,000 feet it is rare; exhaust fumes fill the space left by the lack of oxygen. The newspaper *Excelsior* has said that breathing in Mexico is like smoking two packets a day. Two million cars and sixteen million people in the capital compete for every gasp of breath.

Writers from all over Latin America used to go to Mexico City in droves. Sometimes they sought political asylum, but more often they went to make money from film scripts and writing for the theatre. Mexico used to produce films and theatre scripts at a rate that compared only with the radio soap-opera scripts that Cuba exported before the revolution (Havana sold them in South America by the kilo). Since the devaluation of the peso in Mexico in 1982, there has not been so much money to be made by writers; and devaluations everywhere else in Latin America have meant that royalties come in depreciated currency rather than in dollars. Yet writers still look prosperous in Mexico. Escapism is a very good market, José María Fernández Unsaín, the president of the Society of Writers of Mexico, told me.

'September is not a good month for the theatre, because school starts, and parents have to buy school gear,' he said. 'But at other times the theatres are always full.'

Protected by laws intended to gain prestige for the government, which likes to be seen as a promoter of culture and is also keen to discourage criticism, writers have thrived economically.

Mexico's thirty-two commercial theatres – including the state-owned Palace of Fine Arts, built in 1934, which has since sunk fifteen feet into the spongy undersoil – and ten experimental theatres showed little effect of the crisis. Every theatre and cinema was packed, with a long queue outside. There are so many people in Mexico City that there is always more public than can fit into any playhouse – fabulous balm for the vanity of producers and actors. That is how scriptwriters and playwrights are still in the money.

159

But how do the poor live? It is embarrassing to ask. My Latin American colleagues seem to be too busy making money to know.

How do the poor live?

They do odd jobs. Women with babies beg or sell dolls to tourists. Small boys – often barefoot, wearing ragged trousers and jumpers, hands filthy, and hair cropped by blunt shears in the manner of all small boys who seem to populate the pavements of every capital in the Third World – wipe car windscreens for a couple of pesos, or beg, or sell flowers. At night they perform as fire eaters, filling their mouths with alcohol and blowing it out over a lit candle at traffic lights. They have a better chance of collecting five pesos at this because there is the threat of frying a motorist in his seat. But their lips are raw, their throats parched, and within a year they have no voices. To make up for the loss of employment, street crime is on the rise. Bank robberies are two a week and only make headlines in the evening papers. By the next morning hold-up stories are used as fillers among the classified advertisements.

The poor, called *milusos* (a thousand uses), keep stalls of local crafts or food like *tacos*, pasties, and fried tripe. Or they clandestinely offer *caguama* eggs, the sale of which is banned because the tortoise that lays them is a protected species.

The eggs are sold as an aphrodisiac, with strong chili, known as 'buffalo sauce'. It made me snort puffs of fire all the way home. I cannot report on the virility, owing to the diarrhoea.

As a guest of the Mexican president on the occasion of his first state of the union message and cosseted and cared for by presidential order, it would be in bad taste for me to find too much amiss. In any case, the president told me that he was trying to pay the foreign debt, improve urban rubbish disposal, expand the drains, and purge the police force of its congenital corruption. The last should prove difficult. Bribery is, after all, what makes the system work. That is a thought to bear in mind when a policeman stops a motorist for a traffic offence. The policeman needs a bribe more than the fine. He has to share the bribe with his sergeant, who each week reports to his chief on how much he has collected in pay-offs. The chief decides whether the policeman and sergeant must be punished for not collecting enough. If so, they are made to pound the beat. Otherwise, they can be rewarded for good takings and promoted to mobile patrol, which affords the chance of hot pursuit and therefore better opportunities for catching the prey. The chief will not share his takings with the inspector, who operates at a higher level. Here the chief must report on the kind of crime and its severity. The inspector will convey this to the area commissioner – and thence to the district commissioner – who will decide the price for overlooking the newly-detected acts of illegality. That is the system.

The system, like all systems, is in the end best represented by humour. Two Mexicans meet in the street, the first being the worse for a beating. The second asks what has happened. The first asks if he should tell the good news or the bad news first. The second asks for the bad. 'I was mugged.' Poor man, and what is the good news? 'The police did not come.'

The grand old men of Mexican letters were not available for interviews. Juan Rulfo, aged sixty-five, had gone to Houston, Texas – where middle-class Mexicans went shopping before devaluation – for an eye operation. Carlos Fuentes, aged fifty-four, lives much of the time in the United States at one of the better universities. Octavio Paz, aged sixty-nine, convalescing from a severe kidney ailment, phones the office of his monthly magazine *Vuelta* to make sure that the telephones are answered and to pick up messages which he does not answer. You get like that when Jorge Luis Borges calls you a great poet.

Luis Spota, rapidly gaining in popularity as his novel *La plaza* – set in 1968 during the massacre of students in the Square of Three Cultures – becomes a bestseller, is available for interviews. He is quoted widely for his opinion of the current political situation and in his demand that the president keep to his commitment to carry out a kind of moral regeneration of Mexico.

After asking the way at several bars with signs that permit 'No entry to women, dogs, and men in uniform' and at building sites whose goods entrances are closed to the delivery of building materials with a notice to the effect that 'Materialists are forbidden to stop in the absolute' – presumably stopping is allowed post-Kantian idealists – the building of the Society of Writers of Mexico (founded in 1946) appeared at the end of José María Velasco Street, named after the nineteenth-century painter. It was not any old Society of Authors, at Drayton Gardens, or the Writers' Guild of Great Britain, in Edgware Road. This was a four-storey house, purpose-built in the 1970s, with a basement car park, ground-floor theatre, and specialist library (containing a collection of original scripts dating back to 1908), two floors of administration offices, and a fourth-floor restaurant operated by a former Argentine football player.

It was 4.00 p.m., and I was in time for lunch. Strange how lunchtimes vary: twelve noon in Paraguay, 1.30 p.m. in Buenos Aires, 3.00 p.m. in Madrid. It is rather like those words that vary from place to place. Durex is a sticky tape in Buenos Aires, a brand of shoes in Mexico, a condom in Britain.

The society's president, José María Fernández Unsaín, was in 1946 a poetry and theatre prizewinner who turned to the cinema to make money. And he did. He has written and sold 243 scripts and directed thirty-two films. His stage production of Tennessee Williams's *A Streetcar Named Desire* (starring his wife, Jacqueline Andere, a very popular actress) is playing to full houses. Fernández Unsaín thinks that the 2,750 members of the Writers' Society are well cared for. To assure their constant promotion, the society organizes annual competitions for film and stage scripts, with production guaranteed to the winners.

A critical economic situation will force the society to bring in pension contributions by members. Up to now, pensions – like life insurance, medical care, funeral expenses, and short-term subsidies (called a Solidarity Fund) for unemployed or destitute writers – are all given away by the Society from its rich coffers. These are filled with twenty per cent of all royalties collected on behalf of writers – and the society has a monopoly to do this. In the good times before devaluation, and while the hyperactive film industry was exporting all over the continent, the society's income at times reached a million pounds a year. The other eighty per cent goes to tax-exempt writers resident in Mexico and in royalties to (taxed) writers abroad. Playwrights in Mexico collect 0.6 per cent of box-office takings under a law passed in 1964, though full payment was not totally extracted until 1968. The Paris-based International Confederation of Authors and Composers' Societies has ranked Mexico's society among the three best in the world, the others being in France and West Germany. As you complete a tour of the building this information does not come as a surprise.

The only trouble for writers in Mexico City, really, is finding enough air to work in.

1983

CARLOS FUENTES: DEBT
AND DIPLOMACY

H e had arrived before me and was sipping champagne, reading a copy of the *International Herald-Tribune*. My then secretary, Biba McLellan, had chosen the Greenhouse Restaurant, in Hays Mews, W1, on the grounds that it is quietly elegant without being ostentatious and so would suit the taste of a former diplomat and best-selling novelist who, like many Latin Americans who have achieved fame and fortune, has become an authority in politics and an arbiter of good taste.

As I made my apologies, Carlos Fuentes smiled a pardon. I asked if he had heard the latest news from Mexico. A cargo plane carrying eighteen horses to a show-jumping event in Miami had crashed on rush-hour traffic just outside Mexico City. It had set cars ablaze, torn off restaurant fronts, and one wing had come to rest on four walls, making a roof where the roof had fallen in.

Fuentes put down his newspaper with a look of controlled exasperation. 'How can we write fiction in Latin America when this is the reality? This escapes fiction.'

He was about to leave England, bound first for Spain, then the United States to take up an academic post at Harvard. His year in the Simón Bolívar Chair of History at Cambridge University had just come to an end. He had enjoyed England and Cambridge, he had worked hard and was leaving in a good mood. The Spaniards, from the Madrid press to the royal family, awaited him anxiously. He was about to be awarded the 1987 Cervantes Prize, Spain's highest literary award.

Fuentes, the author of some ten or so novels, holds the highest profile of any living Mexican writer. Between him and the poet Octavio Paz, there has always been an elegant – what else could it be? – rivalry for the top position in Mexican letters. Paz, of course, represents the centre-right in the political spectrum, whereas Fuentes belongs to the centre-left, an inch farther to port than European liberalism.

Fuentes and Paz are part of a Latin American phenomenon which demands that the writer have an instant opinion about anything that happens in the world. Mexico is at once internationalist and cosmopolitan, provincial and backward. Rich intellectual curiosity mixes with a history of restriction and exploitation.

I first met Carlos Fuentes briefly on his arrival in Britain in September 1986. The English edition of *The Old Gringo* had just been published, and he addressed over one hundred people crowded into a small, stuffy room at the Institute of Contemporary Arts. After his talk, I asked him for an interview on matters other than literature. He agreed, and we met again in Cambridge on the second day of summer the following year.

That June day was grey, cold, and the rain came down with an English bloody-mindedness that made sure that every creature in the island was thoroughly soaked through. When I grumbled, Fuentes asked impatiently, 'What else can you expect from England?' He was alone in the house, his wife and children having gone out. But there was evidence of them everywhere – in her paintings in progress, in the children's school-books and bicycles.

Fuentes looked comfortable, and seemed at home. His normally starched appearance was relaxed. He wore elegant, expensive, casual clothes. Going into the kitchen, he made a pot of tea, then brought it in on a tray and fussed in a very domestic manner about making space for it. Among Latin Americans, the contrast between the public and private selves – as Borges tells us in one of his most famous pages – is marked and immediately noticeable. Latin Americans always keep the two separate. Fuentes is a very public man who openly enjoys a cosy family life.

At last, with tea in our cups, we sat down and began to talk.

Q. You have given a number of talks recently about writing and about your own books, but I'd prefer to talk to you now about political issues. You have, after all, studied law and served your country as a diplomat.

A. Yes, I studied law in Mexico and later on, in Geneva, I took up international law. That's when I was twenty-three and twenty-four. But at twenty-five I published my first book of stories, and that more or less settled my vocation.

Q. Did you become a diplomat by accident, then?

A.   No. I entered the diplomatic service so as to be able to work in Europe while I studied. I was a member of the Mexican Delegation to the International Labour Organization and after that I went into foreign affairs. That was for most of the 1940s. Once I began publishing I left the diplomatic corps, but I went back to it in 1975 when I became ambassador to France. I served three years and that was that. Of course, I was also the son of a diplomat, and so attended many schools and grew up in several countries. I was a near contemporary of the Chilean novelist José Donoso at the Grange School in Valparaiso. That was a British school. I had a further glimpse of British expatriate culture in Buenos Aires at the Belgrano Day School.

Q.   I heard a radio programme the other day in which the structure of the Mexican government was compared with that of the unofficial hierarchy set up by the people who make their living from the Mexico City refuse tips. The programme was asking whether the social structure of the tips imitated the structure of the official establishment or whether it was the other way round with the establishment imitating the elaborate structure of the tips. The analogy, it seems to me, reflects the denigratory view that Europeans tend to have of Latin America.

A.   Let me answer that point by point. In the first place, insofar as it is a view of Latin America it's not only denigratory but completely unjust as well as untrue. A similar analogy could be made for almost any country in the world. If you compared the numbers living in Manhattan penthouses with the numbers in the slums of Detroit or Atlanta you would be justified in speaking of the United States as a society of slum dwellers; the same goes for England if you compared the numbers living around Hyde Park with those in any black or Indian neighbourhood in any city of the north of England. It's a picture that could be presented of any nation under the sun, but it would be insulting and unjust. In the case of Mexico, it's simply untrue, because for all the injustice that still exists in Mexico, there is less injustice in the country than in other parts of the Third World. Mexico is a highly energetic, highly dynamic society. Right now Mexico's crisis arises from its extraordinary growth. Compare the country now to what it was in 1910 or 1920 or even at the end of the Cárdenas administration in 1940, and the change is colossal.

From a country dominated by a smallish bureaucracy and a land-owning class that sat on a vast peasantry, we have today a country that is thoroughly urban, a country with a growing middle class, a society where the military has no more power than is required by a democratic state. It is a solid, well-educated middle class, aware of its country's history, and it is the driving force behind what I see – in the face of this extremely rapid development – as a positive transformation. Mexico had a growth rate of somewhere between five and six per cent for twelve, fifteen, twenty years. That was an enormous rate. A more equitable distribution of wealth and at the same time the formation of a strong middle class has benefited half the country. But the middle class's capacity for consumption and production needs to be extended to the other half of the country. This underprivileged half must be incorporated into the process of development and given political and social institutions. I see in Mexico an enormous dynamism, an extraordinary creative capacity, despite the very serious problems that we Mexicans are the first to acknowledge. I talk about this in my novels all the time.

Q. Why does Europe compare social and political institutions in Latin America to life on a rubbish dump? Europeans made the same analogies with Africa.

A. I'm not sure. The example you gave was particularly hideous, but in the main I find European news coverage of Latin America to be balanced. There may be the occasional sort of excess you cite, but I don't know whether it is the rule. I think that *Le Monde* is very informative about Latin America, so is the *Guardian*, and the *Financial Times* even more so. I'm not trying to whitewash European news coverage of Latin America – there should be more of it – but I feel there is more news about Latin America in Europe than in the United States. The top American newspapers, like the *Washington Post*, the *New York Times*, and the *Los Angeles Times*, provide excellent world coverage, though not of Latin America. Europe gets little attention in the papers of Houston, Tucson, or Nebraska, as far as I'm aware. In ninety per cent of American papers you won't find a single column of foreign news. It's a country that does not care about the world, that isn't interested in the world, that doesn't understand the world. The irony of this is that the United States is not only our neighbour but it plays a major role in our destiny.

Q. The Latin American argues that certain European leftists support or side with revolutions in Latin America that they would never want for their own countries.

A. As I see it, a country's socio-historical change comes about in the cultural context of that country, not in the context of other countries. I recently went to see Peter Hall's Stratford production of some of Shakespeare's histories. It was titled *The War of the Roses* and chronicled in nine or ten hours that stormy period of English history when there were coups and counter-coups between warring houses and the kingdom was in a state of civil war. When asked what I made of it, I said it reminded me of the history of Central America. England has gone through periods of extraordinary historical upheaval. These stemmed from England's own reality.

I can think of no revolution in the western hemisphere bloodier or more brutal than the American Civil War. In terms of the size of the territory involved and of the population, there has not been another like it. The American War of Independence, too, was politically very violent and uncompromising. The Tories in the Carolinas were brought to ruin. Opponents of the war were executed; some 200,000 people in a population of twelve million were forced to emigrate. Some made for Canada in boats, like the Vietnamese boat people, and were drowned. Property was confiscated, there were firing squads, there was all the violence typical of an upheaval of this kind. And what was it all about? Siding or not siding with Washington and his boys. No, revolutions are neither importable nor exportable. They take place only when given the political, economic, social, and cultural factors that justify that revolution, and there is nothing in the world that can create acceptable false conditions. When Che Guevara went to Bolivia, the right conditions did not exist, and he failed. When it came to organizing guerrilla warfare against the Venezuelan government in the 1960s, the movement collapsed because the right conditions did not exist.

On the other hand, the revolutions in Mexico, Cuba, and Nicaragua – which are the only serious revolutions we have had in Latin America in this century – took place because conditions were ripe. Those revolutions would have taken place with or without outside aid. You couldn't say that the American revolution took place because the Bourbons in France decided it should, or that the

Solidarity movement in Poland exists because the CIA is financing Lech Walesa.

Q. There is a very European view of Mexico that stems from Malcolm Lowry's novel *Under the Volcano*. It is considered a masterpiece not only for its language but for its conception, its vision. How do you regard the novel?

A. A writer creates reality, he doesn't reflect it or reproduce it. There is reality, and added to it is the reality the writer creates, but his is a parallel reality, a new reality. Hence the vision of D. H. Lawrence, the vision of Graham Greene, and the vision of Malcolm Lowry are artistic visions that add a literary reality to the language in which they are written. They also add to Mexico's reality. Lowry's vision, given the extraordinary quality of his novel, enriches Mexican reality. It seems to me that this is the function of the art of writing. But no single novel says everything there is to say about a country.

Q. You are often asked your opinion of the present political climate in Latin America. But there is no common denominator in Latin American countries except for the problem of foreign debt.

A. That's what is most talked about, but it isn't the only unifying problem.

Q. However, at present it's as good as a political common denominator. So, in the light of the debts owed to Citycorp, Nat West, and Chase Manhattan, what future is there for such a debt-ridden continent?

A. Well, it's often said as a joke – a sick joke, perhaps – that companies go bust but countries don't. To begin with, we need some historical perspective. This is not the first time that countries have defaulted on a debt. The United States did not pay its debt to England in the last century, but they ended up paying it off by Roosevelt's lend-lease during World War II. At this moment

Latin America is paying a debt that very nearly amounts to a reparation – that's what I call it – greater than that paid by Germany after World War I. Ironically, it was this reparation that led to Nazism, yet the creditor nations showed more understanding and flexibility then than is now being shown to Latin America.

Previous *de facto* cancellation of debts show that basically we are dealing with a political problem that requires political solutions. What is lacking at present is a political will. We are witnessing what Henry Kissinger called a twice-yearly ritual, or minuet. A crisis is declared with a different country each time and all that's done is to put a plaster on the wounds of new loans, which themselves are going to have to be paid off. Latin America must resume its growth and pay its debt by economic development and not by one debt being piled on to another.

There is a whole range of solutions, some more practical than others, all the way from Fidel Castro's, which is not to pay, to Kissinger's, which is to create a kind of Marshall Plan for Latin America. Harold Lever, who was in Harold Wilson's cabinet, proposes a solution that I would back. It consists of giving the debtor nations a breathing space by temporarily suspending service payments on their debts. Even the United States has suffered repercussions from Latin America's debt. Senator Bill Bradley calculates that the debt has cost the United States a million jobs and fifteen billion dollars. This is the figure in the fall in US exports to Latin American countries during the last few years. At the same time, the United States has become the greatest debtor nation in the world. And it is a debt not connected with any increase in American productivity but rather with an increase in American consumption. It is inevitable, then, that this huge debt threatens bankruptcy not just for Latin America but for the entire international financial system. Right now the United States is adrift; it has neither a policy nor a firm view either of world economics or world politics, let alone Latin America. So I think we have to tighten up our belts and wait to deal with a future American government that is coherent and responsible.

Q. It seems to be the role of the Latin American writer to be a political observer. Whether the writer is Mario Vargas Llosa, Jorge Amado, Ernesto Sábato, or Carlos Fuentes he takes the role of moral guide.

A.   That's terrible!

Q.   Not at all. Latin Americans put a good deal of weight on what their writers say. Why is that?

A.   That's because of a simple regrettable fact, which is the weakness of civilian government in Latin America. When there are no political parties, parliaments, or trade unions – in other words, organized social forces – to act in a long-term articulate, and coherent way, writers are sought out to make statements about what might otherwise go unsaid. This happens in central Europe too – in what is wrongly called Eastern Europe – Hungary, Poland, Czechoslovakia. Civilian government there has always been weak. In Russia, the writer has had extraordinary power; the fact that the state has persecuted, stifled, or obliterated writers is evidence of this. In the United States or England or France, a writer's importance lies elsewhere, because those societies on the whole are free and their newspapers can speak out. To me, Latin America is in a sick situation. A writer when he speaks politically should do so only as a private citizen.

This brings me to another subject. You said that the debt is what unites Latin America politically. I think it does, but something else unites it too: the emergence of civilian government throughout Latin America for the first time in our history. For a period of three centuries we were governed by a colonial empire based on the orthodox ideas of the Spanish Counter-Reformation and by the three oldest institutions of Spanish America (I omit Brazil, which is a different case) – the imperial Spanish state, the Church, and the army. When the imperial state ended in 1821, the Church and the army – with their representative, the caudillo, a dictator more or less – remained to fill the extraordinary social vacuum. Our response was the government of a Juan Manuel de Rosas in Argentina, of an Antonio López de Santa Anna in Mexico. They tried to create viable national states, which is what Domingo Faustino Sarmiento and Bartolomé Mitre, in Argentina, and Benito Juárez, in Mexico, wanted. But today in addition to the viable national state, there is an attempt to build stronger civilian government. Such government wants to shape society, it wants to organize itself in its relations with the state, the army, and the Church. It wants to strengthen autonomous professional societies, special interests groups, intellectuals, etc. This is all quite new. We see it strong and clear in Mexico, especially since the 1986 earthquake; it was seen in the civilian government of Argentina at the time of the Easter army rebellion in 1987.

Q. The Church has undergone changes but the army hasn't.

A. In general it hasn't. Some have – the Mexican army for example, but at the cost of a revolution. In Latin America, the army has become an anachronism and nowhere as much as in Argentina. On one side you have the extraordinary development and reaffirmation of democratic society in Argentina, while on the other the army persists, completely blind to the terrible realities.

Q. The army has survived (except in Mexico, Cuba, and Nicaragua) as the best organized and most solid political party. For a long time in Argentina the army was the only political party, alongside the Church. Next to the Colombian, the Argentine Church was the most conservative church in Latin America. But all the same the Church has undergone deep splits. That is to say, beginning with Mexico and taking this century, the Church has continually adjusted to the facts, but you can't say the army has.

A. That's why the Church has lasted and is going to last longer than the army. The Church has been adapting itself for two thousand years, while these armies – above all the Argentine army – strike me as utterly deplorable. I can't understand how a country with the degree of intellectual sophistication and with the democratic society that Argentina has can put up with this sort of mammoth there in the middle of a china shop, this dinosaur that doesn't know it is dead. Break its bones, and it doesn't even know it. Deal it a blow, and it does odd things as it collapses. A bone falls off here or there and *wham!* it flattens people. I think the dinosaur has to be told, 'See here, either modernize – change into a Concorde instead of a dinosaur – or out you go.'

Q. One complaint of the military in Argentina is that the civilian government on assuming power – or on trying to assume power – has given the army neither a role nor a programme. Since 1930, and with few interruptions, the role of the Argentine military had been predominantly political. But having accepted defeat at the hands of a civilian power, what is their function now? They have no budget, no external wars to fight, and they claim they won the internal war against the guerrilla organizations.

A.   President Alfonsín spoke of modernizing or at least of taking the army out of its 'pretorian messianism'. An army has to be modern, as those of Germany, France, and the United States are. They simply fulfil the function of all armies, which is not to delve into economics or politics – those belong to the sphere of civilian government – but to protect the country against real threats.

Q.   I had to leave the Argentine in 1976 because of my opposition to the generals. Before Alfonsín initiated the trials against the junta he made an attempt to balance matters by putting on trial the heads of guerrilla groups. Anyway, it was thought necessary to try Mario Eduardo Firmenich, the leader of the Montoneros, before the junta could be tried. As an Argentine, I know how I feel about his ilk; as a matter of fact, I am responsible for Firmenich's being sentenced to thirty years, since I was the only witness called by Alfonsín to testify against the accused. Because my generation was the one responsible for the Argentine guerrilla movement I can explain its misdemeanours, but I have no explanation for the rest of Latin America. How do you explain a phenomenon such as the Shining Path in Peru?

A.   To me it belongs to the world of aberration, and it is the first time I have noted any political aberrations in Latin America. This is a public aberration, a fact born of the mind and projected by the mind without any historic, social, or ideological basis. It's a faraway response in the Andes to Maoist doctrine, a movement launched by hanging dead dogs from lamp posts in Arequipa and putting them in sacks with Chinese inscriptions that say 'Death to the Revisionists', 'Death to the Chauvinists'. I can't see what any of this has to do with Peru. They're criminals.
  Because of the way they operate I don't think the Sendero Luminoso can claim any serious political intent. They will raid a village, killing everyone in sight – men, women, and children. It's as if Charles Manson were suddenly to organize a guerrilla band in the Rocky Mountains and pit himself against the cities of California.

Q. With regard to the phenomenon of urban guerrilla warfare from 1965 to 1975, it is often explained as the product of a society in transformation, of a generation's frustration. To you, is that a justification for what took place?

A. In 1968 there was an almost world-wide reaction against the society that was preparing for the next century. It was a moment when the young tried to set their own view of how the world should be against the view that was being laid down for them. This took place on the Berkeley campus, in Paris during that May, and in Mexico City in the summer of 1968, and right on down to the Montoneros and the Tupamaros in Argentina and Uruguay. It was part of a cultural revision of the civilization that the young were being offered. But because they were movements headed by young people they could not be revolutionary movements. The young are neither a revolutionary class nor a social class; they are a transitional stage in life. You have to see what happened to all these young rebels of 1968 to judge what political function they finally played.

In France, the movement of 1968 translated into two things: first, the reinforcement of the structure of higher education in France, because the anarchy introduced into French schools by the 'triumphs' of the young in 1968 permitted the ruling class to reaffirm its method of selecting the élite by means of the *grandes écoles*. On the other hand, what the young achieved was, as Malraux pointed out, a cultural fact, a revolutionary criticism of a civilization. Second, it was translated into political fact – the re-emergence of the Socialists as the leading French political party, bringing François Mitterand to power, purified of all the baggage of monetarism, which came later.

In Mexico, the events of 1968 seemed to culminate in the government's repression, when 500 young Mexicans died. This evidence that the Mexican government could offer no political response to a political challenge and did not know how to take account of what the middle-class young were thinking was a terrible failure. As a result of this failure, three successive governments have had to abstain carefully from all repression and provide an opening – a political, social, and intellectual channel – for the aspirations of the young of 1968, who make up the present government.

Each country came up with a different response. Some elements

173

in Argentina and Uruguay prevented a political solution like that of Mexico. The response of those governments to this violent challenge was to resort to violent repression, often to breaking the law themselves. If those who defied the state broke the law, the state should not have responded by breaking the law, for that risked plunging the state – as was to happen – into a grim spiral of violence and lawless acts.

In the past many Argentines supported the military on the grounds that civilian governments governed badly. But I get the clearest impression that nobody any longer really wants military rule and the army knows it. So maybe all the terrible sacrifices and frightful crimes will prove to have had historical significance if they have contributed to constitutional continuity in Argentina. The country has not had a peaceful transfer of power since 1928, until Alfonsín came to power in 1983. In Mexico we have had nine constitutional changes of government between Lázaro Cárdenas and Miguel de la Madrid. The constitutional structure in Argentina was violated for half a century. This created a terrible vacuum. I think all those who took part in urban guerrilla warfare now realize that democracy is the only way for the countries of the River Plate.

Q.   What solution do you see for Chile?

A.   I am not a provider of solutions for any Latin American country. I wish I had solutions for my own life. I have the greatest affection for Chile. I spent my childhood and early school years there, so I feel a close bond with the country. What has happened to Chile distresses me greatly. Of all the Latin American countries, Chile has had the greatest experience of democracy. Chile was once wealthy. It has had a middle class since the nineteenth century, as well as a whole series of democratic freedoms that also date from the last century – a free press, free trade unions, a tradition of political parties – and the whole thing ends up in a dictatorship like Pinochet's. It boggles the mind.

Still, my optimism is greater than my pessimism because I think I know Chile. I don't think one Pinochet or even ten Pinochets can cancel Chile's democratic experience. I see Chile's problem as more social than political. This problem consists in working out how the social forces can organize themselves to transcend Pinochetism and the problems of political parties and sectarian organizations. In the long run it's the unions, the workers' movements, the social and economic realities that are going to create a new model and a solution. Chile will recover its experience of the past and wake up out of the nightmare of this Pinochet era.

Q.   Brazilian writers, even the great ones like Jorge Amado or Mario de Andrade, have had large enough audiences at home not to have found it necessary to go out into the world. They seem to be self-sufficient. This is a quite an anomaly within Latin America.

A.   Such artificial barriers have to be broken down. After all, the only really great nineteenth-century Latin American novelist was the Brazilian Machado de Assis. He is the greatest Latin American novelist, because he's the only one really in touch with the great tradition of the European novel. Machado read Diderot and Sterne and was able to renew the lesson of Cervantes's *Don Quixote*. In Spanish America the two great books of the nineteenth century are not novels – or, one could say, the two best novels are Argentine. One is a poem, José Hernández's *Martín Fierro*, and the other is a sociological study, Sarmiento's *Facundo*. After Machado de Assis, the leading figure of Latin American literature, there is a very rich Brazilian literature. I recently read *The Republic of Dreams*, a masterly novel by Nélida Piñón, and novels by Rubén Fonseca, Marcio Souza, and Clarice Lispector. There is a whole constellation of first-class writers in Brazil about whom we should know much more than we do.

A.   We have not mentioned Latin American relations with the United States.

A.   I think that will round off our conversation. One of the great tasks we are faced with in Latin American politics now and well into the next century is the restructuring of our relations with the United States. At present, these relations have been almost destroyed, mainly by the United States's continuing violation of the laws and treaties governing those relations. The Reagan government set itself above the law and existing treaties on the grounds of practical considerations that are in fact self-defeating. If the US policy was to unseat Fidel Castro, all they have done has been to reaffirm him in power. If their policy was to unseat the Sandinistas, all they have done is to reinforce the power of the Sandinistas. We are going to open new fronts in the hemisphere and to work out diplomatic and political solutions that will cost the United States dear from now until the end of the century. One way of doing this is by developing relations with the European Community and with the nations of the Pacific. The twenty-first century will see a new structuring of international relations, which will be as much multilateral as bilateral. The Latin American countries will have a role to play in this, and we can't play it alone. We will have to play it in the form of a Latin American alliance. We will have to be in touch with other centres of power. To me, the two most natural are Europe and the Far East.

Q. To Latin America, Japan and China may as well be the moon.

A. One of the things I said in a speech I gave in Buenos Aires at the National Institute of Industrial Technology is that I felt that Argentina and Mexico both had important roles to play. Because of its wide experience of immigration – greater than that of any other Latin American country – Argentina will take the lead in relations with Europe. And Mexico – because we face the Pacific on one side and have had relations with Japan and China since the sixteenth century – will lead Latin American participation in the Pacific, the area with the greatest trade and technological interchange in the world today.

Q. The problem is that Europe, the culture closest to Latin America, is closing itself off. Europe is moving politically to the right. Only two of the twelve Common Market countries, Spain and Italy, have moved closer to Latin America. At the foreign ministers' meeting in San José, in 1985, a lot was offered but very little delivered.

A. Europeans are going to have to recognize that there are other Europeans – Poles, Hungarians, Czechs – who are out there hoping for the possibility of a very important rapprochement with regard to the future of all Europe. There are too many challenges for Europe just to turn in on itself. I think Europe is practical and is going to have to learn to operate in terms of international economies and not lose opportunities. I don't think Europe will lose out. It has too wide a variety of peoples and politics.

Q.   Within the western hemisphere, the revolutions in Cuba and Nicaragua have been bolstered by the blunders of United States foreign policy and by the moral support of ordinary citizens all over Latin America. What role do you see these two countries playing in Latin America? Or are they too busy consolidating their revolutions and internal affairs to play any role?

A.   In the case of Nicaragua, the number one priority is obviously to consolidate the country and create the basic institutions that Nicaragua never had before. This has to start with an assertion of Nicaragua's independence *vis-à-vis* the United States. Beyond that it is hard to prognosticate, because Nicaragua is under constant threat from the United States and from internal warring factions. I think the country will consolidate eventually. After that the problem must shift to one that concerns the future of all Central America. The solution may be neutrality and demilitarization. Since the viability of these countries is very fragile, what better way to ensure this viability than by these means? I think that the Peace Commission for Central America – peace in the area – is the first step. But in a certain sense, compared with the problems of debt and democracy that we have been discussing, the question of Central America is somewhat spurious. It is what happens in the three great countries – Brazil, Argentina, and Mexico – that matters most. They represent eighty per cent of the population, economic resources, and land area of Latin America. In this sense, Central America is hardly central. I'm going to resist speaking as a Mexican imperialist by saying that the best thing that could happen to Central America would be for it to become part of Mexico. It is a temptation to say it, but I'm not going to. It's a joke.

A.   A director of the Bank of Canada who spent a number of years in Argentina is of the opinion that within four or five years the three great countries of Latin America will have found solutions to their civil versus military problems and to the problem of their debt. The Canadians are therefore recommending to their clients that they look ahead to a Latin American society that will achieve stability and that will provide great opportunities and expanding markets.

A.   With that we come back again to what we were saying at the

177

beginning and can close the circle of our interview. The present crisis in Latin America is one of excessive growth.

1987

Postscript: In June 1988, Octavio Paz's monthly magazine *Vuelta* published an article by the Mexican historian Enrique Krauze that was strongly critical of Carlos Fuentes. The piece was translated for the neo-Conservative American weekly *New Republic*, whose cover depicted Fuentes with a Pancho Villa-type moustache, under the headline, 'The Guerrillas' Dandy: The Life and Good Times of Carlos Fuentes'. In essence, the article does not deny the novelist's talent but criticizes the combination of his financial success and his support for the Sandinista leaders in Nicaragua. It is a not unusual line for the right: socialists should not be rich. Krauze concludes that so long as Fuentes is both rich and outspoken in his support of a left-wing government in Nicaragua he is not to be taken seriously. In October 1990, Octavio Paz was awarded the Nobel Prize for Literature.

MARGO GLANTZ:
STETL IN COYOACÁN

W e met at the start of her two-year posting as cultural attaché at the Mexican embassy in London during the presidency of Miguel de la Madrid Hurtado. Such encounters promote little conversation that is not an excess of advice on house moving and property rentals – all of it quite useless. In the weeks and months that followed, on her round of diplomatic receptions and cultural exchange conferences – to which I was frequently invited – Margo Glantz and I became better acquainted. It soon becomes clear that Mexicans put human contact first and everything else second.

Margo Glantz's professional record is magnificent. Born in 1930, she has a distinguished teaching career at the Universidad Autónoma de México (UNAM), where she gives courses on nineteenth- and twentieth-century Mexican literature and on the chronicles of the Spanish conquest. She had travelled widely, in part due to a former marriage to a diplomat. She has some sixteen or so published books to her credit, and now here she was trying her hand at diplomacy herself.

Beyond the formality of academe and the courtesies of diplomatic life was a rich personality that burst out in instalments at each subsequent meeting. Her concerns, interests, and curiosity – which she describes as obsessions – emerged in our conversations. At some point, over lunch one day at a pasta restaurant in Haymarket, we agreed that, really, we should stop gossiping about the dozens of friends we had in common, a natural enough phenomenon between Latin Americans, and try to put a finger on what made the literature of Latin America tick. She visited me at work, and the debate about how to start an interview began. A mutual interest was expatriation and exile, and how they affect the individual, the creative mind. The recorder whirred away, but however much we got down on tape we were always aware of how far short we were of a deeper exploration. Then her posting was over. It seemed sudden, although we had known for months that it had to end. We never felt that enough conversation had been taped.

On one of her return visits to London, the scene of our talks moved to my house, where we sat in the garden in the beautiful summer of 1989 and spoke of the deep-rooted economic problems of Mexico and all of Latin America. The discussion had the intensity of a personal drama, as if the solution to a whole continent's foreign debt could come out of our own pockets. We tried to place literature in the context of the political and economic struggle of the entire land mass from the California border to Tierra del Fuego.

When Margo Glantz left London to return to Mexico, we agreed to write. The many facets of exile, the history of our respective families and their assimilation from Europe into Latin America would be the subject of our letters. My first to her was from Muscat, Oman, where work had taken me. The second, if memory serves me, was from Bangkok. Her replies ran from the telegraphic text of a picture postcard to several sheets of domestic crisis on the difficulties of settling down in a new home in a familiar environment and the writer's block that moving house caused.

A belated transcription of the tapes revealed hours of intense conversation, and the listening and reading brought out a well-known yet totally new character. We never did get around to that epistolary study of exile.

Q. Let's begin with a simple question. What is the state of health of Mexican writing today?

A. Mexico has recently been a hive of literary activity. On a visit home in February and March, I found that the number of new titles being published – books by Mexican authors – was vast. Considering the crisis in publishing, the country's general economic crisis, and the hardship readers face when they buy books whose prices have skyrocketed, this is impressive. So were the numbers who attend book launches. I went to a few myself – two books by Carlos Monsiváis and one by Elena Poniatowska.

People were still talking about the books that had won the Villaurrutia Prize, Mexico's premier literary award. The publication of poetry has been considerable too. There can be few countries in the world where so many poets and books of poetry make their way into print. I feel quite optimistic about Mexican writing. Of course, all this activity concerns writers completely unknown outside the country. But with regard to its literary output, the excellence of its authors, and the printing of books, Mexico – I can safely say – is one of the most vital countries on earth. As for those writers known abroad, of course Octavio Paz and Carlos Fuentes top the bill. Not long ago an article unfavourable to Fuentes came out in Paz's magazine *Vuelta*. It was written by Enrique Krauze, an intelligent historian and a good polemicist. He claims that Fuentes's work is a bit outmoded.

Q.   Yes, but is this not merely a case of local princes having a tiff? Remember the clashes between Mario Vargas Llosa and Günter Grass, and before that Vargas Llosa and García Márquez. Perhaps Paz and Fuentes were just sparring to elicit enthusiasm. To your mind, between the two – despite the difficulty of comparing the work of a novelist to that of a poet and essayist – who is the more praiseworthy?

A.   Juan Rulfo.

Q.   You are evading my question.

A.   It may be that some of Fuentes's books have dated; but others are still as good as ever – the short novel *Aura*; several excellent stories; the novel *Distant Relations*; large parts of *Terra Nostra*; some of his novel *Cumpleaños*, which has not appeared in English. *The Death of Artemio Cruz* is a masterpiece of our literature. Perhaps Fuentes should be a bit more selective, publish less, but he is verbose, baroque, and it seems in keeping that he should go on publishing with such superabundance. But take *The Old Gringo*. It was praised in the United States and in Britain; to me, however, it was far from successful. The same with *The Hydra Head*, a thriller, which is written with great skill; I was not much taken with *Christopher Unborn* either. Obviously, as I just said, a writer so prolific and baroque is bound to produce some less enduring work.

Paz, as a poet and essayist, is one of the greatest writers of contemporary literature, and many of his essays are masterpieces: *The Labyrinth of Solitude*; *Sor Juana: or the Traps of Faith*; *The Monkey Grammarian*; and *El ogro filantrópico*. The essays in the last, unfortunately, have been divided up among several different books in English. For the breadth of his work and brilliance of his imagery Paz is one of the greatest poets in the world. *Libertad bajo palabra* and *Eagle or Sun?* are extraordinary. A three-volume collection of his essays on Mexico has just been published – *El peregrino en su patria*. Significantly, the title comes from a line by Lope de Vega. These are Paz's views of Mexican literature, politics, and art. Of course, he too repeats himself and sometimes publishes more than he should; his phobias are virulent and obsessive, and he has blind spots. You can disagree with him, but you have to acknowledge his greatness.

Q. And Rulfo?

A. Well, Rulfo wrote a single novel and a book of stories, but without any doubt he is one of the greatest writers of our time. The fact that he left only two books is of no consequence whatsoever.

Q. How do you rate Mexican writing with that of the rest of Latin America?

A. In Mexico, as in the rest of Latin America, there is a magnificent literary output. Unhappily, the writing of one country does not always make its way into other countries. The balkanization of Latin America is a fact, and the lack of communication between countries is frightful. Political problems, foreign debts, terrorism, and dictatorships are all obstacles to a greater knowledge of the literature of our different countries. It is always good for Latin American books to get published in Spain, for then they stand a chance of getting to that great marketplace of European books, the Frankfurt Book Fair, where often, unfortunately, they are subject to the laws of the supermarket – that is, the cheapest sells best.

Earlier in the century, it was a lot easier to know what was going on, because the great reviews published writers from all over the Americas as well as translations of European writers. These reviews had a circulation throughout the continent. The *Revista Moderna*, for example, which was published in Mexico by José Juan Tablada, printed the work not only of a Mexican poet like Amado Nervo but of the Uruguayan Julio Herrera y Reissig, the Cuban Julián del Casal, and the Nicaraguan Rubén Darío. We no longer have a literary magazine that brings together the writing of all Latin America – *Vuelta*, in Mexico, and *Eco*, in Colombia, perhaps, and for a time in Paris during the boom in the 1960s there was

Emir Rodríguez Monegal's *Mundo Nuevo*. In other days writers could travel more, take part in congresses, exchange their books; postage was cheaper then, and the cost of books less, especially the cost of paper and the photographic materials essential for book production. We had greater possibilities of access to the great writers of Latin America. While Franco ruled in Spain, Mexico and Argentina were the two centres of book publishing in the Spanish-speaking world. Now Argentina hardly publishes anything, but the threat of international best sellers and economic crisis hang over Mexico. Anyway, in Mexico our best work may very well be in poetry.

Q.   Has this always been the case or is it something recent?

A.   Well, we have Sor Juana Inés de la Cruz, who goes back to the seventeenth century and is as important a figure in Spanish literature as Góngora and Quevedo. At the end of the nineteenth and the beginning of this century, we had poets like Manuel José Othón, Salvador Díaz Mirón, Tablada, Ramón López Velarde, and so forth. Then there was the group that includes José Gorostiza, Xavier Villaurrutia, Salvador Novo, Gilberto Owen, Jorge Cuesta, and so on.

Q.   Where do you rank Brazilian writing in the spectrum of Latin American literature?

A.   I may be speaking in hyperbole, but at a time when we all think that the Third World is in a bad state – which is really quite obvious – I find that there is a vitality, an originality, a strength in Latin American writing that is often lacking in the Europeans. A broad comparison between what is written in England with what is written in Latin America is instructive. Brazil, a vast, extraordinary, grotesque, incomparable country, has a colossal strength. There I go into hyperbole again. There is a particular phenomenon at work in Brazil. It is the country which best combines the popular and the cultivated, and there are figures like Vinicius de Moraes and Chico Buarque de Holanda, very good poets who are – or were – bossa nova singers. We are fairly well acquainted with Brazil in Mexico owing to the wealth of translations published in our literary supplements. All the Brazilian classics – João Guimarães

Rosa, Joaquim Maria Machado de Assis, Euclides da Cunha – have been translated and published in Mexico. We have courses in Brazilian literature and we have translators of it. The Brazilian ambassador to Mexico, Guilhermo Melchior, who had previously worked in cultural affairs at the Brazilian embassy in London, has taken great pains to publicize his country's literature in Mexico.

Q. Here in London one sees little Latin American literature published, and that little presents a limited view.

A. If we in Latin America have difficulty getting access to our different authors, in Europe the problem is bound to be worse. There are too many barriers, from those of language down to historical restrictions inherited from colonial rulers. Often even the most intelligent and most liberal writers fall into prejudices and stereotypes. It is not easy to belong to a neo-colonial culture and not partake of some of these stereotypes. The newspapers in Britain, France, and Germany are full of them.

Q. What about the academic community? I find – especially among the North Americans – that those who teach Latin American literature and write about it understand little of Latin American history or politics and deal with the literature divorced from everything else. Then too their first-hand knowledge may be limited to a single country, this may even be only a Caribbean island, which they occasionally visit during their summer holidays. Maybe I am unfair, but I don't find that they begin to see the continent as a whole.

A. Of course, it is impossible to be a specialist in all Latin America. But critics and teachers like Jean Franco, Gerald Martin, William Rowe, John King, Jason Wilson, Steven Boldy, and exiled Spaniards in London such as Nissa Torrents and Juan Antonio Masoliver are very important because they appreciate and publicize our literature. In general, however, it is hard for anyone to be up to date about the enormous quantity of writing that the continent is producing. North American and European critics come dangerously close to showing colonialist attitudes. I don't think we are accepted as critics, and our own views of Latin American literature are often dismissed. It may be presumptuous of me to say so, but the very fact of our being Latin Americans makes us better read than many other people. The Italians translate most of our work, but France and England have only recently begun to translate us. Latin America has to break into the Common Market if it wants its literature to be known in Europe. This would be a good way of exporting quality manufactured products that would represent us better than oil or coffee or cocoa beans. It would be enriching to exchange teachers. If a teacher from Britain visits Latin American countries, reads our literature, and understands various phenomena in the places where they are taking place, and, conversely, if Latin American writers and critics could teach in European universities, some sort of balance would be established. Perhaps this would also increase the translations, which right now is a lopsided affair. As I just said, we in the Third World countries tend to translate everything that comes from the developed world, and we often know better than Europeans what is being written by their authors. It would not be a bad idea if the reverse could take place. The generalizations and hasty judgements about Latin America that one comes across in the press in Europe are galling.

Q.   I have noted that too. Joan Didion went to El Salvador for two weeks and wrote a book. Salman Rushdie did the same in Nicaragua in 1987, when he published *The Jaguar Smile*.

A.   You're right, it's absurd. I know neither book well, but I have read some of Rushdie's. At the embassy I am constantly telephoned by people going out to make documentaries in Mexico. I'm obviously considered some sort of Latin American *Encyclopedia Britannica*. What train runs to such-and-such place? What time does it arrive? What are the habits of the male tarantula? Why do we kill them? What are Mexico's political problems? They know next to nothing, yet try to palm themselves off as serious, painstaking people. They go to Mexico and return with something that is taken as gospel here when I find it the shoddiest sort of improvisation.

Meanwhile, economic breakdown, the campaign against drugs, the foreign debt, the dictatorships, and other such things devalue us. In Europe, the Common Market, consumerism, and speculation make Europeans more and more insensitive to the problems of other countries. It seems that they take notice of us only when we have earthquakes or floods or droughts or when a president is assassinated and a US ambassador happened to be flying in the same plane. Then we appear in the news and are on the receiving end of charity that collects millions of dollars to help us buy roofing materials and tents from our 'benefactors', who ignore the fact that droughts and floods may be the consequence of the brutal and systematic destruction of the environment by the colonizing countries. But if Latin Americans travelled to Europe more, perhaps public opinion would begin to change. That is the strength of people like Fuentes or Paz, who have caught the attention of outsiders. I only hope they are not the only Mexicans who are listened to.

Q. Latin American women have been producing good writing for many years, yet until recently there was little evidence of a continent-wide feminist identity. When did that begin to arise?

A. At the beginning of the 1970s, I think, or perhaps a bit before that. For my part, I am a feminist because I am a woman. The whole debate about feminism appears to have stagnated somewhat, and it's time it was reviewed. This is my impression after having read some of the many volumes of interviews with women writers. I participated in one of these not long ago, and there I believe I show that my feminism has its roots in a number of very personal and literary obsessions.

My reading of Spanish theatre, Calderón de la Barca in particular, together with a long-standing compulsion about hair, come together in my book *De la amorosa inclinación a enredarse en cabellos* – On the Amorous (or as I vary it in the book, Erotic) Taste for Entwining Oneself in Hair. In a study of Calderón, I found in thirteen or fourteen of his plays a continuous, repeated obsession with hair. All this may stem from my own long-time dissatisfaction with the way I wore my hair. After all, one of the things that women most associate with their bodies and their sexuality is their hair. But I am also interested in the hirsute beast King Kong, the actual source of my fixation. I began to study anthropological and mythological sources about hair in a number of different cultures. Then I began looking for hair in literary connections. Of course there is the German fairy tale 'Rapunzel'. There is the fact of the severe repression associated with the hiding of one's hair – take nuns, for example; and there is that extreme display of love which is keeping a lock of hair. I even see a very feminine way of ordering the world in the traditional tasks of spinning, weaving, and embroidering. Nuns shut away in convents, women shut up in rooms, weaving life with their fingers. One of the ways that women have related to the world has been, and is, through weaving, embroidery, and cookery; in the kitchen a woman could invent a range of exquisite combinations with which to regale a father, a bishop, or whatever man.

Again, I am interested in the personality of Scheherazade, and through the *Arabian Nights* I have worked out a whole theory of sex and the feminine text. The translation of the *Arabian Nights* into French unleashed a whole genre of libertine literature that was very important in the eighteenth century.

I shall soon be working on a new book, which will succeed *The Family Tree*, and it will be about my mother. My three sisters and I had an exceptional home life. My father was a fascinating but a very self-absorbed person. Yet my mother was so devoted to him that she was sometimes troubled by the fact that she had to bother about us and not be with my father. She was the classic housewife, the far more down to earth of the two, and the real head of the family, the breadwinner. My father was a bohemian and a poet. But she saw no difference between his work and hers. He did what he did for her. At the same time, he could not have been what he was without her. Nor could she have been what she is without him.

A Mexican friend once told me he could not understand how, being the three worst possible things in the world – Jewish, Mexican, and a woman – I ever managed to survive.

Q.   You have a long list of books to your credit – some sixteen or so, if my count is correct. This does not include your translations of two books by Georges Bataille. You have also adapted a number of novels for radio and television.

A.   Yes, and I began to write relatively late – when I was thirty-two or thirty-three. I had always wanted to study literature, and from the time I was a young girl I kept a diary.

Q.   Your titles are intriguing. *Two Hundred Blue Whales . . . and Four Horses* and *The Thousand and One Calories, a Dietetic Novel*, which, of course, is not a novel at all. Your books seem to be miscellanies or collections of short articles and essays, sometimes around a central idea. You combine your reading with an insatiable interest in curiosities, the erotic, cookery, fashion, and so forth.

A.   My books often begin as fragments, published as instalments in the newspaper *Unomásuno*, to which I contributed a column. Writing is important to me as a way of redeeming myself, as a form of self-reconstruction. As for *Two Hundred Blue Whales* ... , well, as animals whales always fascinated me. They are fat, they give milk, they have breasts, and they take a long time to give birth. They suckle their young, they make gentle love, and at some point they commit suicide when they can no longer stand the world. They are also persecuted. *Moby Dick* was the great epic of their destruction. Writing about them was my way of relating to a world of adventure that I was unable to live except from the margins of a book.

Q.   I notice several parallels between you and Jorge Luis Borges. You once said, 'My relation to the world has been through books.' In his autobiography, which was written in English, Borges said, 'I have always come to things after coming to books.' He too was an omnivorous reader in his childhood. And his books too were collections of short pieces he had published in newspapers and reviews.

A.   Like him, when I was young, I was also extremely shy. Reading to me was a form of protection. My family owned a shoe shop, and we lived upstairs. In the afternoons, when the shop closed for the long siesta period, I stayed there with my nose in a book. I read everything – some twenty different novels by Jules Verne; Greek mythology; books of polar discovery and Himalayan expeditions; at thirteen I even read some pornographic novels my father had lying about; I read Fenimore Cooper, Dos Passos, Steinbeck, Upton Sinclair, Sinclair Lewis, and Faulkner's *Wild Palms*, translated by Borges, but I did not know who Borges was then. Years later I discovered him. There was a time when I couldn't write without a book by Borges at my side. He helped me a great deal with the Spanish language – as he has many others. He taught me to synthesize, to handle certain turns and expressions, to avoid a stream of useless introductory sentences, to avoid the word 'that' whenever possible. The way Borges used adjectives fascinated me, and above all his ability to concentrate in a brief space a vast amount of thought. His erudition and encyclopedic knowledge have been important to me too.

How I hated it in the shoe shop when I had to wait on a customer. I didn't like having my reading interrupted. Years later, after I was married, I went to live in France, where I learned the language and read French literature systematically – Stendhal, Proust, Flaubert.

Q. Your book *Las genealogías*, which Serpent's Tail is publishing in translation as *The Family Tree*, is about your family and mostly your father. I loved this passage in it, in which he is so offhand about his acquaintance with some of the great figures of Mexican literature:

'Did you know González Martínez?'
My father had known the poet well, and González Martínez had even written a foreword, which never got published, to one of my father's books of poems.
'I had it in a drawer somewhere, but I can't find it now. I knew his son too, González Rojo, a fine poet who died young, and I know the grandson. I used to see a lot of Mariano Azuela. He was a doctor when I knew him.'
'How did you know him?'
'I knew him because he gave me his book.'
'But that explains nothing. Who introduced you to him?'
'I don't remember. I just met him, that's all. I used to visit him at his house in Santa María. Everybody looked at me out of curiosity – a Jewish poet, what a strange thing! He gave me a signed copy of his novel *The Underdogs*. Mrs Tfass has the book now. I lent it to her; you must ask her for it back.'
'What was Azuela's house like?'
'You mean how did he live? How do you say *kleine bürger*? Typically lower middle class. Like any family, he had a lot of books, a piano, and he was one of Mexico's best writers. I knew a lot of writers; at that time, I wanted to get to know them all. But don't ask me where I met them.'

What else can you tell us about your father?

A. My parents arrived in Mexico, married, in 1925. They were from one of those small Jewish villages in the Ukraine, where he had been born in 1902. It was a ghetto, really, a village the tsar had granted the Jews. In the years of great hardship between 1905 and 1918 these places filled up with Jewish refugees from the cities. Anyone belonging to a clandestine movement headed to the countryside. Many of the revolutionaries were Jews. Other members of my parents' families had long since emigrated to the

United States and some to Mexico. I have flocks of cousins in Philadelphia.

My father began his life in Mexico selling bread door to door, carrying a basket on his head. It was the first rye bread in Mexico. The bakery belonged to an uncle of his who had come from Poland three years before. That was the first of some thirty-five businesses that my father was involved in. Early on, he also studied dentistry, but it bored him and he gave it up. My parents spoke Yiddish and Russian between themselves and Spanish to us, so we children never learned Yiddish. The only thing that interested my father was writing poetry. He wrote in Yiddish. He published a good deal in Yiddish newspapers both in Mexico and New York. He even founded a Yiddish magazine with two other poets.

But as far as making money, he never quite managed to get things together. Quite frankly, he was not a good businessman, and we never had much money. We were always moving from one part of the city to another. Every once in a while a business of his would go down the drain, and we moved house. We had a cardboard box business, a comb business, a steel business. Twice in my childhood, for long periods, we had shoe shops. That was from 1935 to 1937 and again from 1941 to 1947.

At the same time, my father knew everybody – painters like David Alfaro Siqueiros and Diego Rivera, and all the poets and writers. He looked something like Trotsky, and I remember walking down the street with him and people pointing and saying 'There goes Trotsky with his daughter.' It embarrassed me terribly. Once my father was nearly lynched by a mob of Fascists, and Siqueiros's brother helped save him. At the end of the war my father got a job with a world-wide Jewish organization to raise funds for survivors to emigrate to Israel. He was well paid and things improved for us. My mother had the idea of opening a restaurant. My father was something of a spendthrift, but she ran the restaurant and they had it for twenty-two years – until 1976.

In the early 1960s, my father turned to sculpture and painting. He came to these things late in life because he had to find some new way of communicating. Yiddish as a language was nearly dead; with the founding of Israel, Hebrew had begun to take over. My father's command of Yiddish was impressive; he spoke Spanish well and was familiar with Spanish and Latin American literature. He even wrote poetry in Spanish, but it wasn't as good as his Yiddish poetry. That was when he turned to art. He had several shows in national museums, and after he died there was an important retrospective of his work at the Fine Arts Museum.

He was a true bohemian. It is because of this that I did not receive a very Jewish education. It was also because of him that I am a writer.

Q. And the new book about your mother?

A. In the book about my mother I want to try to pin down as precisely as I can the exile's lack of identity and the impact this can have on a family. I am interested in what exile meant to my mother – the fact of having left her country and her family for ever, the fact of the violent changes in the Soviet Union, where many of her family died in the war. She is the last of her generation still alive, and when I was in Mexico a few months ago I taped a number of conversations with her. I also want to compare the different childhood memories of my three sisters and myself. Here we are, daughters of the same mother and father, and the four of us have very different ideas from our mother.

1988

GUILLERMO CABRERA INFANTE: LA HABANA, LONDON SW7

The 1980s have mellowed him. His manner seems less aggressive now. A few years back he gave the impression of being about to chew any visitor's head off. London has been his home for most of the twenty-five years of his exile since 1965, when, angered by Fidel Castro's increasingly autocratic rule, he left the Cuban diplomatic service. Guillermo Cabrera Infante was born into the family of one of the founders of Cuba's Communist Party. The revolution went sour on him. He realizes, however, that his political past as a member of Castro's government – he was the cultural attaché in Brussels – will always be with him no matter how hard he tries to turn his back on it. He once described himself as 'a whore who gets married and now tries to be a respectable lady'.

When he became a British subject, with Sir Keith (later Lord) Joseph as his witness, Cabrera asked the Home Office clerk whether he could swear his new allegiance on the complete works of William Shakespeare rather than on the Bible. This, he thought, would be more in tune with the spiritual state of England.

The flat in Gloucester Road, SW7, has become his tropical island. Huge indoor plants, protected from the cold damp of London, thrive and reach to the ceiling, cutting out northern Europe from his view. This is his base, and from here he travels on writing assignments to Spain or to seminars at universities in the United States. Cabrera has adopted the stance of the well-known author, or international literary personality, which requires a particular style of dress and manner of speech. Latin Americans are good at this; they arrive at such postures without really trying. Thus, Octavio Paz walks in the role of the 'great writer', Carlos Fuentes's hands move in the fashion of the statesman, and Mario Vargas Llosa speaks as the passionate crusader. Guillermo Cabrera Infante sucks on his pipe and looks out over his granny glasses with mild detachment.

To me he has always been an object of admiration whether in

his good times or bad. My awe is provoked not just by the out-rageous richness of his prose – erotic, exuberant, and linguistically adventurous – but also by his ability to cut through the personal ups and downs to write what he wants, to preserve ideas and views in defiance of changing fashion. He bravely recovered from illness – with an enormous dose of love and care from his wife and a handful of friends – in a way that invites praise and warm respect.

My first visit to his flat was for the purpose of interviewing him. It was the summer of 1981, and I had begun a series of articles on the lives of Third World literary exiles for publication in the *Guardian*. The Cabrera piece never saw print, because the section editor on duty at the time would not countenance squandering space on a counter-revolutionary. Of course, English journalists in those days knew all about revolutions. Since then, even at the *Guardian*, things have changed, and counter-revolutionary or no the English have come to realize what a good writer Cabrera Infante is. I apologized to him, but we agreed that the text was a good one. In a letter, he said, 'I hope you will be able to use it some time, because it is worth more than an article in the *Guardian*.'

On that occasion, in 1981, he looked smart in a light-coloured suit and open collar with a carefully knotted cravat. This first impression of him, if his spectacular novel *Three Trapped Tigers* can be omitted as the real first impression, was bad. Cabrera was impatient and vain in a way that was almost oppressive in the confines of his small study. His opening remark concerned the Mexican novelist Carlos Fuentes. He asked me how in some article of mine I could have referred to Fuentes as being a more important writer than he. I thought that Fuentes was better known in English, I said, but my grovelling without apology was obviously unsatisfactory. Cabrera went on to size up other Latin Ameri-can writers. He thought little of Vargas Llosa then, though sub-sequently his appreciation of Mario has risen. With the excep-tion of Vargas Llosa's short story collection *The Cubs*, which Cabrera judged to be admirable, he found that the Peruvian had little to offer. Cabrera did say, however, that no one had yet noticed that Gabriel García Márquez had borrowed much from Mario.

When Cabrera and I touched on Julio Cortázar, who was still alive at the time and living in Paris, the Cuban was not only derogatory but mocking. In his view, political activism had ruined Cortázar; his writing was dated, especially *Hopscotch*, which was too contrived. Cabrera reluctantly agreed that the stories in *All Fires the Fire* were good. Cabrera Infante reinforced his mockery with an anecdote of Cortázar's to him, which the Argentine had related with great pride, to the effect that he had been granted an audience with Fidel Castro only after years of repeated trial and failure. Cortázar had said that during the meeting Fidel had put his hand on Julio's knee. 'I felt the vibes,' said Cortázar, 'that told me I was in the presence of a real revolutionary.'

There was no stopping the outpour of literary gossip. To Cabrera, the Argentine novelist Ernesto Sábato was not a good writer, although he agreed that *The Tunnel* was good. But he had also enjoyed *Abaddón el exterminador* (Abaddon the Destroyer), which reflected Sabato's fears about the wave of terror that was sweeping Argentina. In light of the bloodbath in the Argentine during the late 1970s, we reflected that perhaps more people should have heeded Sábato's message.

Cabrera Infante had a severe nervous breakdown in 1972. He had become almost catatonic, he said. It was not until six years later that he fully recovered. He had few friends in London then and entertained little. Dinner engagements he found he could manage only if they were restricted to a foursome, otherwise he was unable to concentrate on a conversation that involved any greater number.

We parted after working through a long and thorough questionnaire, the answers to which he wrote out in a lively style. In a copy of his recent novel *La Habana para un infante difunto*, later translated as *Infante's Inferno* (1984), he inscribed a message of friendship and described the book as 'a clean memoir from a dirty mind'.

Q. Tell us something about your early life.

A. What is there to say other than the basic details? I was born in Gibara, Oriente Province, exactly fifty kilometres from where General Fulgencio Batista, twice dictator of Cuba and once president-elect, was born, in Banes, and from where Fidel Castro, commander-in-chief, prime minister, and now president-never-elected, was born in Birán. I was born on 22 April 1929 and was taken by my parents to Havana in 1941. My parents were founders of the Cuban Communist Party. I left Cuba as a diplomat, posted to Belgium in 1962. My exile began in 1965.

I have two daughters from a first marriage. One of them is British; the other has remained Cuban. I am now married to an actress, Miriam Gómez, who is also British. I have been a British subject since 1979.

Q.   Why are you living in England?

A.   As with everything in life, by accident – sometimes vengeful, sometimes just, always a joker. This is but another joke by Miss Fortune. I have no other explanation, really, except that that accident had some help from Cuban counter-intelligence, which forced me to leave Cuba, and General Franco's police, who forced me out of Spain, where I lived, in Madrid, at the beginning of my exile for less than a year in 1965 and 1966.

I have been living in England since October 1966. I have travelled so much that I can't begin to list my exits and returns. The first time I left was as a guest of the Festival of Experimental Film at Knokke-le-Zoute, in Belgium, in 1967. My most memorable journeys out of England, however, were to Hollywood, in 1970, to supervise locations for *Vanishing Point*, for which I wrote the script, and a tour of Mexico, Colombia, and Venezuela, in 1980, to promote my novel *La Habana para un infante difunto*, followed by a six-month visit to the University of West Virginia as guest professor and writer-in-residence. I spent two months on holiday in New York, a city that has always fascinated me.

Q.   What did you publish in Cuba before you left?

A.   Only my two first books, *Así en la paz como en la guerra* (1960), a story collection, and *Un oficio del siglo XX* (1963), a collection of film criticism. I think of the latter, really, as my first book. That was all. Now not only are my books not published in Cuba but their entry into the country is forbidden. Even the copies sent to my father by my publishers in Barcelona have been secretly confiscated.

Q. What have you published since leaving Cuba?

A. My first novel, *Tres tristes tigres*, published in 1964, which, after serious troubles with Spanish censorship, won the prestigious 1967 Biblioteca Breve Prize – the one that made Vargas Llosa's name famous. The book has since been translated into English – as *Three Trapped Tigers* (1971) – French, Italian, Portuguese, Brazilian, and German, and in 1971 it was awarded the Prix du Meilleur Livre Étranger, in France. Seix Barral subsequently reissued my two Cuban books, which had been unavailable abroad, and has gone on to publish all the rest of my work. That would include: *Vista del amanecer en el trópico* (1974), an overview, in vignettes, of violence all through the history of Cuba [*View of Dawn in the Tropics* (1978), revised London edition, 1988]; *O* (1975), a collection of articles and essays written in London*; *Exorcismos de esti(l)o* (1976), games with style and writing, which was written in Brussels; *Arcadia todas las noches* (1978), lectures on five US film directors, Welles, Hitchcock, Howard Hawks, John Huston, and Vincente Minnelli; and *La Habana para un infante difunto* (1979), my second novel. The lectures had been given in Havana, in the summer of 1962, but could not be published in Cuba, because by then I had already begun to be a persona non grata. The novel, my longest book, has also had the widest sales of all my work – to date, over 100,000 copies in Spanish alone.

Q. How settled are you in the United Kingdom? Has exile produced a feeling of being displaced?

A. If a single journey can be a displacement, how can we help but feel displaced by that journey which may prove definitive, which is exile? I live quite well, not in England but in London, and hardly know any other part of the country. I have never been to Scotland, Wales, or Cornwall, and of course have never set foot in Northern Ireland or the other Ireland. Still, I live comfortably

---

* This title, explains the author, may be read as either the letter 'O' or a zero. Similarly, the reader of Cabrera Infante's forthcoming collection of political essays, *Mea Cuba*, will decide for himself whether the title means 'my Cuba' or 'Cuba pisses', as well as the obvious play on mea culpa.

in Kensington, working in the study at the back of my flat, from which I look out over a landscape of bricks, columns, and arches, which no doubt owe their design to some English Piranesi. But in London I have discovered a number of truths that give the lie to such notions as that the English have a sense of humour; that London fogs existed only in Dickens's novels; that the English have five o'clock tea at five; that all the English speak English; and that English women, though blonde, beautiful, and blue-eyed, are absolute pushovers.

Q. How long does the feeling of exile last? Does it ever vanish from the writer's behaviour or from his or her writing?

A. There is no such thing as a sense of exile. There is the reality of exile. My exile is not ex-isle; I still live on an island. I have always enjoyed symmetries; evil is asymmetrical. So, I was born on a tropical island on one side of the Atlantic and I now live on a northern island on the other. Somehow, England is a mirror image of Cuba; English is Spanish spoken back to front; blondes are the positive (or negative) of blacks. I have no idea where exile ends or begins. In any case, my exile did not begin with my exile. Even in Cuba I felt a desire, a glimmer, an ultimate need to go into exile. When will my exile end? When I stop feeling like a Cuban abroad. That would not necessarily end with a return to Cuba, which, in point of fact, I contemplate in the same way an escaped convict looks forward to a return to prison. This time prison is called Devil's Island.

Q. What relations have you kept up with writers and intellectuals in Cuba?

A. I have no other link with Cuba than with my father and my uncle. Even if I wanted, it could be no other way.

Q. And with your fellow exiles and expatriates?

A. I continue as before to see whom I want, but not necessarily wanting whom I see. There are a number of Cuban writers in exile on three continents with whom I keep up a correspondence. Some of these writers, such as Lydia Cabrera, who is eighty-two, or Severo Sarduy, or Reinaldo Arenas, who is thirty-six, are a gift. It is pure pleasure to write to them, receive letters from them, speak to them on the telephone, and sometimes see them. With others I just go through the ritual. I am pleased to learn that there are now more Cuban writers of consequence in exile than five or ten years ago. Two was a crowd before, now three's company.

Q.   What about contacts with British or European writers?

A.   Getting to know people has always been difficult for me. The friends I had in Cuba go back to my childhood or high-school days. I didn't even make many friends at journalism school. I get on better with women than with men, who are ugly versions of women. Writers tend to be as vain as women, but without their beauty. To me, relationships are more aesthetical than ethical, and I am less interested in what my neighbour thinks than in his appearance or dress. I have writer friends in Spain, the United States, Mexico, South America, and even Cuba. I know few English writers personally. Only through their work do I know a few. But, as the Holy Scriptures say, by their fruits ye shall know them. What I find more interesting is the English attitude to writers, which is one of contempt. As a foreign resident, whenever I moved I had to report to the police. On one occasion I went to the police station and was asked my name, which they of course wrote out wrongly in spite of how easy it is even after I had spelled it for them. Finally, the officer asked my occupation and I said straightforwardly, 'Writer'. When I looked at my certificate of registration I saw that he had written 'Unemployed'. I wonder, was it experience on his part or prognostication? England, or rather, London, is a vast stage, the territory of actors, and my only interest in actors is as a spectator. By the same token, actors are only friends (or enemies) of other actors.

Q.   How do you feel about the England you live in and about recent social upheavals that are marks of discontent and imbalance? What thoughts have you about working in a metropolis increasingly concerned with nuclear devastation?

A. Like those women who grow old but no less beautiful, what is attractive about England has not diminished over the years. Economic unrest and social disturbances do not surprise me. On the contrary, given the circumstances I think they have been quite limited. This is owing to that absolute imperturbability which is part and parcel of the English character. It was not really stoicism that made England an anti-Nazi bastion but a phlegm that went from the appeasement of Hitler in the face of war to an impassiveness in the face of his hysterical attacks. It is undeniable that at the time, compared to France, England looked heroic. But the real heroism lay elsewhere. In Poland, for example, and in the Russian people, trapped between Hitler and Stalin. I wonder if English phlegm is not a sign of old age. The way in which the Irish problem and the latest racial street violence are looked upon shows that very few people in England know anything about religious or racial relations. These are new problems, some people explain or try to explain. Conflict with the Catholics is old hat in England, as any schoolboy or scholar knows. As resident imperialist, England was long enough in India, in the Arab countries, and all over Africa to know something about what it now tries to ignore. The many explanations for street riots in Liverpool and Brixton are so absurd as to be comic, not economic. They go from J. Edgar Hoover to Karl Marx. From there to Groucho is only a short step.

I am not at all bothered by the nuclear threat nor by any armed danger that is presented as a political solution. For forty-four years we have been kept frightened about the atomic bomb by people who a year earlier would not have been opposed to dropping one not on Hiroshima or Nagasaki but on Tokyo itself. Everybody knows that British bombers caused greater destruction and death in Dresden than the atom bomb in Nagasaki. Be that as it may, the Japanese were not exactly gentlemen in that war, which they themselves unleashed. I can't find it in me to worry about a nuclear death, which I imagine must be a death like any other. A heart attack or a bullet in the head do not seem very different. Obviously any sensible person would prefer an atomic bomb, swift and efficient, to a death in instalments from cancer. I am confident that we shall all get less of the former than, regrettably, the latter. As for the race question, I think that is best answered by Mark Twain, who, when asked about the problem, said, 'Don't talk to me about whites or blacks. Talk about men. There can be nothing worse.' I agree. The only new thing to add is that we now have more men than in Mark Twain's day.

Q.   Writing by exiles is usually marked by political overtones – not always politics with a clear ideological content but political in the sense that distance sharpens criticism, as it does perspective, though it may not always lead to realistic conclusions. To me, political overtone is as much the driving force of the literature of exile and it is often the cause of its deterioration and banality. How do you see this?

A.   Separation has the same effect. Just going to the corner to buy a newspaper may change not only writing but life itself, as Hawthorne shows in 'Wakefield'. Exile is a separation in space. A separation in time would be the same, like the passage of days and years. Writers always speak of the past, even those writers of the present, who are the journalists, and the more up to date they are ('An incident took place today in Addis Ababa') the farther away they are from the event. Journalism at most covers news but always aspires to the condition of history. Even science fiction is no more than a projection of the past into the future, like a time ship.

Of course exile leaves political marks, but the very act of going into exile is political. It does not matter from what country or regime. But an election also leaves political marks. Who I vote for is as important as where I am going. The exile is a citizen who has lost the right to vote in his own country but has won a trip. I have always been politically minded. Not in the sense of elections but by election. I was born of Communist parents, I grew up in a Communist home. My first job, as a translator oddly enough, was on the Communist newspaper for which my father wrote. I was mixed up with young Communists who, due to political pressure, became Trotskyites and, later, revolutionaries. I was deeply involved in the anti-Batista group beginning in 1952, when Batista staged his last coup. I was with the revolutionary forces in January 1959. I edited the newspaper *Revolución*, the official paper at the time, and was founder of *Lunes*, which was more than a literary supplement of *Revolución* in that it combined, or tried to combine, ideology with literature. (The *TLS*, for example, is so engrossed in itself that it would never have understood *Lunes*, and I am not talking about the barrier of language.) For me the failure of *Lunes* was a sign of the failure of the revolution as government and as a source of ideology. That was one of the causes of my exile. After such a rich life, how could I not be politically minded in my exile? However, I have always tried not to let my style be political, even if my exile is. I would never say '*L'exile c'est moi.*'

Q.   What is the telling mark of the writing of exiles? Can it claim to belong to the country of the author's origin or is it something part way between that country and the exile's new country? Does this writing lose identity when it takes on new turns of language and sheds the cautiousness which social mores and political customs imposed on the writer in his home country?

A.   There are as many kinds of exile writing as there are exiles. What is the difference between the exile of Joseph Conrad and Henry James, absolute contemporaries, residents of the same country, and in the end subjects of the same king? What are the similarities between Vladimir Nabokov and Jerzy Kosinsky? Or between Nabokov and Alexander Solzhenitsyn? Henry James lived among his caste, Conrad in the countries he invented after having paid them brief visits. Nabokov invented a continent. Kosinski, more modestly, or with less talent, created a character. All these writers have a central obsession in common – they write, as even James did, in a language which must have been strange to them but which became quite intimate. In Solzhenitsyn's case, he spends his banishment in Iowa – or wherever it is he has installed himself in that American concentration camp which he has fabricated. As for myself, I can say that I am the only English writer who writes in Spanish. In fact, I came to England to learn Spanish. Before that – I must not forget it – I only knew Cuban. I used to worry about infiltration, as if by enemy agents, of English words into my Spanish. Now I have to be careful of guerrilla incursions into my English. I am imperfectly bilingual.

Q.   If the intellectual's mission is to get to the root of issues, social crises, and political incidents, this must be something of a rebellious mission, a subversive undertaking. But does the exiled writer not run the risk of subverting no more than literature? Is it the exile's task to raise partisan banners or to try to write intending to 'cure the poisoned hearts', as Albert Camus said?

A.   I don't think the intellectual has a mission. Missionaries have missions. In any case, I cannot talk about the intellectual, because I am not one. What better task than to subvert no more than literature? Other human activities are relatively submissive – politics, for example. I have not known any political leader (and in Cuba there were quite a few) who was not interested in subverting order only to install a new order of his own. I think this is the general rule everywhere. Margaret Thatcher and Anthony Wedgwood Benn want the same thing – power. To get it, one has gone as far as to change her accent, the other to change his name.

Subverting literature was the supreme goal of artists like Flaubert, Joyce, and Gertrude Stein. Flaubert wanted to *écraser l'infâme*, which was not – as in Voltaire's time – Christianity but philistinism, what Flaubert called the good bourgeois. This has been the prime aim of art right up to the surrealists. Since then, and coinciding with the aims of the Russians, art and literature became more and more a medium – or a product – and even Picasso, once so subversive, began to manufacture and sell it. Literature has been a political medium, an aesthetic *corsi recorsi*, throughout the West and a tool of the state in Communist countries. Some people claim they know nothing worse than these two options. But I do. Between censorship and self-censorship I am in no doubt which is worse. At the same time, I have always felt rebellious. In the early days of the revolution I felt I was a rebel not a revolutionary. Later I found out that the Cuban revolution was a cause without rebels. Naturally I prefer to be a rebel with causalgia.

Q.   Does not antagonistic writing from abroad have the same adverse effect (as well as being rejected by those at home) as the intellectuals who stay behind to whisper in generals' ears and write speeches for dictators?

A.   I really can't say. I have never whispered in a general's ears. Not even a few sweet nothings to General Raúl Castro. Commander-in-Chief Fidel Castro is too tall for me to reach his left ear. But I do not think that the writing of exiles necessarily has a bad effect on the government or system which gives rise to such writing. You have only to look at the Russian reception to Solzhenitsyn's books about the Gulag archipelago. I have never written that kind of book – among other reasons, because I have not had Solzhenitsyn's experience. If I were to talk about prison in Cuba I would have to do so as a piece of fiction, in the manner, say, of Kafka's 'Penal Colony'. I have no idea what effect Kafka's work has on Czech exiles. Naturally subversive writing can only be done from the inside. The subversive writing I knew and did under Batista was seen by those who mattered. After all, subversion, like pugilism, is a boxing match practised between three or four. The rest watch the bulls from the sidelines. (There's nothing like a well-mixed but not stirred metaphor in the morning. It's like W. C. Fields's instructions for breakfast: 'Please don't sloe the gin – I mean, don't bruise the eggs.') Under Castro, nevertheless, practitioners of the art of the pamphlet ('If you write a tract, you must retract.') have three almost Joycean options – cunning, silence, exile. Or else.

Q. What language do you write in? How difficult is it to get across to the English-speaking reader your stories and your country's customs?

A. My relationship with English is a love affair that started when I was twelve. I fell in love with the language at first hearing. It has been a one-sided love mismatch ever since. I still love her. Never mind the rejections. Like Van Gogh for painting, I have an ear for languages. I mean for language. One language only – English. When you read this you'll know why she always rejects me. I began writing English when I needed to earn a living as a screenwriter. As you know, English is the language of the movies. But perhaps you don't know that writing a screenplay is not writing really. Or it is like writing a letter to your producer and your director. Most producers are actually dumb, and directors simply cannot read. (Some cannot even direct traffic, as they say. But that's another story.) So I found myself writing this literary language for illiterate dumb-bells. Therefore I suffered, but it was English that suffered most. Then I had the opportunity to rewrite my first novel, *Three Trapped Tigers*, into something very close to English, which is American. Later I wrote a screenplay based on *Under the Volcano* for a very literate and intelligent director, Joseph Losey. But the metaphysics of madness intruded on my happiness, and I spent many years in limbo, which is living on the borders of hell. Now I am back in the world of the word. I've recently written a long, long article on Cuba – literature under Castro – and how this quarter of a century of Castroite culture really is the Renaissance that never was. I don't know how much of it got through to the English-language reader. I don't even know how much of it got through the English-language barrier! A pilot can easily tell when he crashes the sound barrier. But in a language there's no sonic boom to let you know. You are always gate-crashing and begging that trespassers shall not be prosecuted, as the sign says.

Q. Having been born in Argentina, where I lived until 1976, and with most of my books published in Spanish, my examples and experiences are mostly drawn from that country. One of the anecdotes of literary exile – in fact of any exile – that I find most quotable is that of a novelist and naturalist, not a political man, but a very gentle human being, William Henry Hudson, who was born in the Argentine in 1841 and left South America in 1874, disgusted by the perversity of people who could not understand the beauty of nature and the need to protect it. He thought he could find the freedom and satisfaction he needed in England, where he lived until his death forty-eight years later. Yet all the time he lived in England, he yearned for the country he had left, aware, nonetheless, that he would never have been able to study, write, or publish in Argentina as he did in the England he had come to and wished to leave. Would you say that this state of spiritual displacement is common to the exiled expatriate writer?

A. It's a pity that you should mention William Henry Hudson – or Guillermo Enrique Hudson, as he is known in the Spanish-speaking world – so late in the day, when our interview is almost over. Otherwise this exchange could have been more pleasant for the two of us. This British writer born in Argentina (just like Old Man Borges, though the latter has spent a lifetime trying to write in Spanish without achieving it) has been for a long time one of my favourite Argentine authors. The first book of his that I read, *Far Away and Long Ago*, I read in Spanish. I still remember those too short hours of pleasure of long ago and far away. I particularly remember the exotic delights of his prose and his Argentine stories – the almost derelict farmhouse, so solitary, the company of animals and birds, and life with his American family, contrary people who having the prairie so near chose to settle instead on the distant pampas.

It was while living in London (when I read *Far Away and Long Ago*, a title I treasure, this now so familiar city was a place more exotic to me than the vast pampas, another metaphor for the sea), in Earls Court, many years and many miles later, that I read *The Purple Land* in English, written in that beautiful prose style praised by James and Conrad and Borges. I thought then of writing a screenplay based on this book. Unfortunately, copyright problems dissuaded me from doing so. Nevertheless, I read as many of Hudson's books as I could. I was as poor then as Hudson was all his life but I managed to read his books as he had managed to write them. There are wonderful things here and there in all his work. The kind of writing that an exile from America, an exile from almost anywhere – any exile – can truly appreciate.

I remember one particular moment, just a crack in the door of memory, a fleeting instant in one of his books. The writer, Hudson himself, is going down a street when he hears a bird singing somewhere, though there are no trees to be seen. The singing, however, is familiar and yet strange. I don't remember the name of the bird this naturalist from La Plata had just discovered in London. I don't remember the name of the Chelsea street where this happened. I don't even remember which book it was. All I recall (and what recollection!) is that Hudson stops in his tracks, crosses the street resolutely, and knocks on a nearby door. He asks the woman who comes to the door if the singing bird is hers? The lady says yes. Is it by any chance a bird from Argentina? The lady says yes again. She brought it with her all the way from Buenos Aires, where she lived. Suddenly Hudson (and the reader) realizes that this bird does not come from Argentina. It comes from his own childhood, in a dream, flying out of the past. That bird of Hudson's comes from memory and of course, as I now remember, it's more usual name is nostalgia. That bird – from Hudson's pampas, from my savannahs, from the prairies, from the plains, from the steppes, from the desert, can be heard by every exile. It's the emperor's nightingale that has finally come back.

1981

Epilogue
HOMAGE TO SÁBATO

A n interview with Ernesto Sábato is missing from this book. Though accidental, it is a serious omission. If there was any one man among Latin American writers who fought the despots of the 1970s it was Sábato. When many had to flee, he stayed at home in Argentina and defied death threats against him and his family from both military thugs whose masters equated terror with good government and from emissaries of the deranged guerrilla groups who equated terror with liberation. Born in 1911 and trained as a physicist, Sábato abandoned science for writing in 1945. He is (or was – he gave up writing several years ago, in part due to oncoming blindness, and now devotes himself to painting) a prolific essayist and the author of just three novels, *The Tunnel*, *On Heroes and Tombs*, and *Abaddón el exterminador*.

Sábato's books paraphrased Argentina – especially, for me, the long section entitled 'Report on the Blind' from his second novel and the compilation of the frightening *Nunca Más (Never Again)*, which he was responsible for and which reported on the murders of thousands of people by the military government of Argentina whose power ran from 1976 to 1983. Through those dark days, Sábato was the moral conscience of decent Argentines. In a page that perfectly sums up his vision and his spirit, he has written of that time that:

> During the years preceding the military coup in 1976 acts of terror-
> ism were committed that no civilized nation can condone. Invoking
> these deeds, Argentina's military dictatorship unleashed an even
> worse terrorism – worse because it was carried out with the colossal
> might and total impunity that only an absolute state can sanction.
> This new terrorism initiated a witch-hunt in which not only the
> original terrorists but also thousands and thousands of innocent
> people suffered. The writings of some of these victims have been
> collected and, whatever the literary merits of their work, there shine

through much of it the high ideals of the authors, their devotion to their families and the land of their birth, and their sometimes evangelical appreciation of the plight of the helpless and forgotten. It is a sinister irony that the extermination of thousands of human beings of such calibre should have been perpetrated in the name of God, country, and family. There is cause for bitter reflection on the fate of these young Argentines who formed part of their country's best younger generation and whose only crime was to dream of a more humane world. A great number of those who disappeared were barely adolescents, and yet they were barbarically torn from their homes and dragged off to dens of torture, rape, and death.

The state's terrorism also involved a further scheme of diabolical destruction, torturing the families of those who disappeared with hideous uncertainty over the fate of their sons and daughters who had been swallowed up in that dark, bottomless pit. Day after day in their tormented imaginations fathers and mothers buried and resuscitated their loved ones without ever finding out the truth. Year after year these parents were subjected to the direst speculations concerning the martyrdom of their kidnapped children, not knowing how or where they had suffered or – if they were no longer alive – when their sufferings had ended. We may never learn how many mothers and fathers died or let themselves die, or how many went mad, as a result of their anguish and grief. But we have one example of the highest humanitarianism – that enemy of all forms of violence and tyranny – one symbol in the person of Alfredo Galletti, a man whose life was governed by idealism, in which spirit he educated his daughter. The last years of his life had one aim – that of finding out the truth about her fate and seeking justice. But his confrontation with such a nightmare, made up of the cruelty of some and indifference of others, in the end crushed his admirable spirit. In an act which he intended as a denunciation, as a gesture of protest, he took his own life.

The immeasurable tragedy which Argentina lived through in these contemptible years will never be forgotten by those with even a grain of compassion in their hearts. And the guilty – whatever the casuistry by which they escape the punishment of the courts – will have to sustain the moral condemnation not only of those who survived the horror but also of the conscience of the whole world.

How was Ernesto Sábato left out of this book? Very simply – by accident. He and I enjoyed a long and friendly acquaintance that dates back to the early 1970s. A photograph in 1973 shows us at a gathering to launch a collection of his essays, a party which doubled as a small tribute to the Chilean ambassador in Buenos Aires in recognition of his outspoken criticism (and sudden dismissal) after General Augusto Pinochet seized Chile by blood and fire.

Sábato did not leave the Argentine when the military took over the country in 1976. I did. I left with my wife and children and took up residence in London. Sábato and I kept up a correspondence in the years that followed. Sometimes the letters were telegraphic, other times they discussed personal, political, and literary matters at greater length. The correspondence became even more frequent as I tried to find a London publisher for the translation of *On Heroes and Tombs*, which had been published in the United States in 1981. I failed, and Britain did not get Sábato until Jonathan Cape published the novel in February 1990.

When I returned to Argentina in 1982 to cover the Malvinas/ Falkland war for the *Guardian*, we arranged to meet. Three months later we had had to cancel several proposed encounters. By then the war was over. The night before the day we were about to have tea and talk together, I was beaten up in the street not by robbers but by members of the security forces with long memories. After a quick medical check I flew out of Buenos Aires in pain, hurry, and embarrassment – for the second time in my life. On 29 June 1982, Sábato wrote in a letter to *La Nación*:

> As an Argentine, I am ashamed to learn of the cowardly assault on the writer and journalist Andrew Graham-Yooll. And then we wonder why we have an abominable image abroad!

One year later, on my return to Argentina, we managed at last to get together, this time at his home in Santos Lugares. But such a reunion was no place for a formal interview. We went back to our correspondence and, at the end of 1983, Sábato was euphoric about the restoration of constitutional rule. President Raúl Alfonsín appointed Sábato to head the inquiry by the National Commission on Missing Persons, the *desaparecidos*. The result of that investigation, published in Buenos Aires in 1984 (and in London by Faber and Faber with *Index on Censorship* in 1986), was a harrowing record of Argentina's nightmare. Having unmasked the torturers and tormentors whom the military used in the name of national security, Sábato – with the rank of national hero – retired quietly to Santos Lugares, from where he painted, commented on political events, and received visitors.

That is why he was omitted from this book. That is why these last pages belong to him.

BOOK LIST

The principal works in English translation of the Latin American authors interviewed in this book

Claribel Alegría

Flowers from the Volcano, 1982
They Won't Take Me Alive, 1986
Luisa in Realityland, 1987
Woman of the River, 1989
Ashes of Izalco (with Darwin J. Flakoll), 1989
Family Album. Stories of Catholic Girlhood, 1990

Isabel Allende

The House of the Spirits, 1985
Of Love and Shadows, 1987
Eva Luna, 1988
The Stories of Eva Luna, 1990

Jorge Amado

The Violent Land, 1945
Gabriela, Clove and Cinnamon, 1962
Home is the Sailor, 1964
The Two Deaths of Quincas Wateryell, 1965
Shepherds of the Night, 1967
Doña Flor and Her Two Husbands, 1969
Tent of Miracles, 1971
Tereza Batista: Home from the Wars, 1975
Tieta, 1979
Jubiabá, 1984
Sea of Death, 1984

BOOK LIST

Pen-Sword, Camisole: A Fable to Kindle Hope, 1985
Showdown, 1988
Captains of the Sand, 1988

Mario Benedetti

The Truce, 1969

Jorge Luis Borges

Labyrinths, 1962
Ficciones, 1962
Other Inquisitions, 1964
Dreamtigers, 1964
A Personal Anthology, 1967
The Book of Imaginary Beings (with Margarita Guerrero), 1969
The Aleph and Other Stories 1933–1969, 1970
Selected Poems 1923–1967, 1972
A Universal History of Infamy, 1972
Doctor Brodie's Report, 1972
In Praise of Darkness, 1974
Chronicles of Bustos Domecq (with Adolfo Bioy-Casares), 1976
The Gold of the Tigers, 1977
The Book of Sand, 1977
Six Problems for don Isidro Parodi
(with Adolfo Bioy-Casares), 1981
Evaristo Carriego, 1984
Seven Nights, 1984
Atlas, 1985

Guillermo Cabrera Infante

Three Trapped Tigers, 1971
View of Dawn in the Tropics, 1978 & 1988
Infante's Inferno, 1984
Holy Smoke [written in English], 1985

Ariel Dorfman

Widows, 1983
The Empire's Old Clothes: What the Lone Ranger, Babar and Other Innocent Heroes do to Our Minds, 1983

211

How to Read Donald Duck: Imperialist Ideology in the Disney
Comic (with Armand Mattelart), 1984
The Last Song of Manuel Sendero, 1987
Last Waltz in Santiago and Other Poems of Exile
and Disappearance, 1988
Mascara [written in English], 1988
My House Is on Fire, 1990

Jorge Edwards

Persona Non Grata, 1976

Carlos Fuentes

Where the Air is Clear, 1960
The Death of Artemio Cruz, 1964
Aura, 1966
A Change of Skin, 1968
The Good Conscience, 1971
Terra Nostra, 1976
The Hydra Head, 1978
Burnt Water, 1980
Distant Relations, 1982
The Old Gringo, 1986
Myself With Others [written in English], 1988
Christopher Unborn, 1989
Constancia and Other Stories for Virgins, 1990

Gabriel García Márquez

No One Writes to the Colonel and Other Stories, 1968
One Hundred Years of Solitude, 1970
Leaf Storm and Other Stories, 1972
The Autumn of the Patriarch, 1976
Innocent Eréndira and Other Stories, 1978
In Evil Hour, 1980
Chronicle of a Death Foretold, 1982
Collected Stories, 1984
The Story of a Shipwrecked Sailor, 1986
Clandestine in Chile: Adventures of Miguel Littin, 1987

BOOK LIST

Love in the Time of Cholera, 1988
The General in His Labyrinth, 1990
Collected Novellas, 1990

Margo Glantz

The Family Tree, 1991

Daniel Moyano

The Devil's Trill, 1988

Augusto Roa Bastos

Son of Man, 1965
I the Supreme, 1986

Ernesto Sábato

The Outsider, 1950
On Heroes and Tombs, 1981
The Tunnel [new translation of *The Outsider*], 1988

Mario Vargas Llosa

The Time of the Hero, 1966
The Green House, 1968
Conversation in the Cathedral, 1975
Captain Pantoja and the Special Service, 1978
The Cubs and Other Stories, 1980
Aunt Julia and the Scriptwriter, 1982
The War of the End of the World, 1984
The Real Life of Alejandro Mayta, 1986
The Perpetual Orgy, 1986
Who Killed Palomino Molero? 1987
The Storyteller, 1990
Three Plays: The Young Lady from Tacna,
Kathie and the Hippopotamus,
La Chunga, 1990
In Praise of the Stepmother, 1990

INDEX

INDEX

INDEX

A NOTE ON THE AUTHOR AND EDITOR

ANDREW GRAHAM-YOOLL is the editor of *Index on Censorship*. Born and brought up in Argentina, he worked as a journalist and writer in Buenos Aires before circumstances compelled him to move to Europe with his family in 1976. He is the author of over a dozen books in English and Spanish. Of *A State of Fear* (1986), Graham Greene, writing in the *Observer*, said:

'I have never read any book that so conveys what it is like to live in a state of permanent fear, written by a journalist who endured the years of the Generals in Argentina.'

NORMAN THOMAS DI GIOVANNI is the translator of eleven books by Jorge Luis Borges, with whom he worked between 1967 and 1972. He has also translated other works by Argentine writers, such as Humberto Costantini and Adolfo Bioy-Casares, and is the editor of the anthology of Argentine short stories, *Celeste Goes Dancing* (1988).